国际课程经济核心词汇
Economics

唯寻国际教育 组编 ◎ 芮文珍 编著

机械工业出版社
CHINA MACHINE PRESS

本书精选国际教育经济学科的核心词汇，按照通用词汇和高频专业词汇两个部分进行讲解，涵盖 GCSE、A-Level 和 IB-MYP 等国际课程。本书第一部分通用词汇，涵盖近十年的考试真题中高频出现的词汇，采用字母顺序排列，单词配备词频、用法、例句、同义词和漫画等，以帮助学生熟练掌握并运用此部分词汇；第二部分高频专业词汇，是课程学习阶段的专业词汇，词汇编排与教材中的顺序保持一致，按照主题进行分类，配备 definition、定义、explanation、翻译、同义词和图片等，帮助学生准确理解学科专业词汇，并建立用英语学习的习惯。本书采用便携开本，并配有标准英音朗读音频，愿本书能够成为学生学习经济的好帮手。

图书在版编目（CIP）数据

国际课程经济核心词汇 / 芮文珍编著 . -- 北京：机械工业出版社，2020.7（2024.1 重印）
 ISBN 978-7-111-66098-9

Ⅰ . ①国… Ⅱ . ①芮… Ⅲ . ①经济—英语—词汇—教学参考资料 Ⅳ . ① F

中国版本图书馆 CIP 数据核字 (2020) 第 124318 号

机械工业出版社（北京市百万庄大街 22 号 邮政编码 100037）
策划编辑：孙铁军　　　　　　　责任编辑：孙铁军
责任印制：单爱军
保定市中画美凯印刷有限公司印刷

2024 年 1 月第 1 版第 4 次印刷
105mm×175mm・9.5 印张・1 插页・411 千字
标准书号：ISBN 978-7-111-66098-9
定价：45.00 元

凡购本书，如有缺页、倒页、脱页，由本社发行部调换

电话服务	网络服务
服务咨询热线：010-88361066	机 工 官 网：www.cmpbook.com
读者购书热线：010-68326294	机 工 官 博：weibo.com/cmp1952
010-88379203	金 书 网：www.golden-book.com
封面无防伪标均为盗版	教育服务网：www.cmpedu.com

唯寻国际教育丛书编委会

总 策 划 吴　昊　潘田翰
执行策划 蔡芷桐　李晟月
特约编辑 刘　桐　张　瑞
编　　委 芮文珍　陈　啸　袁　方
　　　　　　田晓捷　袁心莹　贾茹媛
　　　　　　陈博林　居佳星

推荐序
FOREWORD

2007年,我前往英国就读当地一所国际学校,开始学习A-Level课程,亲身经历了从高考体系到国际课程的转变。如果问我最大的挑战是什么,一定是使用英文来学习学术课程本身,因为不仅要适应用英文阅读、理解和回答问题,还要适应西方人不同的思维习惯和答题方式。我印象最深的就是经济这门课,每节课都有非常多的阅读,大量生词查找已经非常麻烦,定义和理论也是英文的,更别说用英文来学习英文时还会碰到意思不理解的困难了。现在回过头去翻我的经济课本还可以看到密密麻麻的批注——专业词汇量不足和词义的不理解让我在之后长达一年的学习中备受折磨。

这段学习经历也成为了我们作为国际课程亲身经历者想要制作一套专业词汇书的初衷。如果有一套书能够帮助学生按照主题和难度整理好需要的专业词汇,再辅以中英文的说明,帮助学生达到本土学生的理解水平,将大大缩短学生需要适应的时间,学生也可以更加专注在知识积累本身,而不是分心在语言理解上。

唯寻汇聚了一批最优秀的老师,他们是国际课程的亲历者,也是国内最早一批国际教育的从业者。多年来,他们积累了大量的教学经验,深谙教学知识和考试技巧。除了专业的国际课程之外,我们将陆续推出"唯寻国际教育丛书",

帮助广大的国际课程学子。这套词汇书是系列教辅书的第一套,专业词汇的部分老师们按照知识内容和出现顺序进行了编排,并遴选了核心词汇和理解有困难的词汇,再反复揣摩编排逻辑,以帮助学生更好地学习、记忆和查找。

预祝进入国际课程学习的同学们顺利迈过转轨的第一道坎,实现留学梦想!

唯寻国际教育

创始人 & 总经理

2020 年 7 月

前言
PREFACE

当今国际教育在中国百花齐放,同时开设的国际课程多达十几种,其中被大家熟知的有 GCSE 课程、A-Level 课程、IB 课程和 AP 课程。对于中国学生来说,用第二语言英语来学习一门专业学科并和以英语为母语的学生共同竞争,这的确存在很多的困难。对于刚刚开始接触国际课程的学生,很大的难点在于理解题目的意思,记忆专业术语的定义。尤其在经济学的学习中,各个国际课程都很注重对专业术语的记忆、理解和应用,但目前国内并没有专业的词汇书来帮助学生预习和复习学科相关的专业词汇。所以我们希望能够通过唯寻专业团队的努力,帮助同学们在国际课程这条学习道路上走得更顺畅。

为了让学生能够理解考题中文章和题目的意思,并记忆和理解经济学的专业术语,本书将词汇分为通用词汇和高频专业词汇两部分,并对以往所有官方考试卷中评分标准给出的答案里出现的高频词汇进行了挑选,把那些学生需要知道的基础词汇作为通用词汇。具体设置如下:

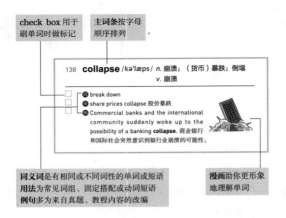

高频专业词汇包括 GCSE 和 IB-MYP、AS 和 A2 三章，每章的主题和词汇均是按照主流教材的顺序来编排。专业词汇的编写专注于词汇的定义，因为往往考试中的第一步就是要求学生定义关键词。对于有些词汇，除了定义之外，书中还做了解释，可以作为考试中对关键词的补充说明。另外，本书为词组类主词条中复杂、不易读的单词添加了音标，不同词组中相同的单词只就近标注一次音标。具体设置如下：

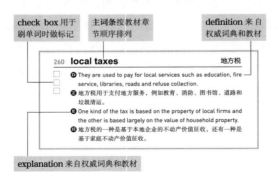

此外，全书的单词均配有标准英音朗读音频，大家可以扫描封面或各节的二维码来收听，如下图：

本书采用便携开本，方便学生随时随地学习和背诵词汇。在使用上，英语基础比较差，理解文章和题目意思有困难的学生，请先背诵一遍通用词汇来加强英语基础。而对于英语基础比较好，理解题目无障碍的学生，可以直接根据自己的年级去背诵相关的专业词汇。

对于刚刚学习经济学的同学，无论是 GCSE 还是 IB-MYP，都可以参考第二部分第一章的词汇来进行课前预习或课后巩固，这部分经济学的基础词汇对于各个国际课程体系是通用的。AS 年级在 GCSE 阶段学过的专业词汇不会重复出现在 AS 章节中，同样，A2 部分的词汇仅为 A2 年级的新增词汇。同学们根据自己的校内进度，可以在上课前花 15 分钟左右的时间预习该章节对应的专业词汇的定义和解释，课后再花 15 分钟左右的时间进行巩固和记忆。长期积累可以打下扎实的学术基础，拿稳考试中的基础分。

不积跬步，无以至千里；不积小流，无以成江海，希望同学们能通过日积月累为美好的未来奠定基石。

编者

2020 年 7 月

目 录
CONTENTS

第一部分 通用词汇 A to Z / 1

A / 2	**N** / 84
B / 16	**O** / 86
C / 23	**P** / 93
D / 39	**Q** / 99
E / 53	**R** / 101
F / 60	**S** / 107
G / 63	**T** / 120
H / 65	**U** / 124
I / 70	**V** / 126
L / 80	**W** / 128
M / 81	

第二部分 高频专业词汇 / 129

第一章 GCSE 和 IB-MYP 高频专业词汇 / 130

第一节 Basic Economic Problems 基础经济问题 / 130

第二节 Allocation of Resources 资源分配 / 134

第三节 Microeconomic Decision Makers 微观经济决定者 / 144

- 第四节 Government and the Macroeconomy 政府和宏观经济 / 167
- 第五节 Economic Development 经济发展 / 188
- 第六节 International Trade and Globalisation 国际贸易和全球化 / 198

第二章 A-Level AS 阶段高频专业词汇 / 207

- 第一节 Basic Economic Ideas and Resource Allocation 基础经济概念和资源分配 / 207
- 第二节 The Price System and the Microeconomy 价格体系和微观经济 / 213
- 第三节 Government Microeconomic Intervention 政府的微观经济干预 / 218
- 第四节 The Macroeconomy 宏观经济 / 220
- 第五节 International Trade 国际贸易 / 224
- 第六节 Government Macroeconomic Intervention 政府的宏观经济干预 / 232

第三章 A-Level A2 阶段高频专业词汇 / 234

- 第一节 Basic Economic Ideas and Resource Allocation 基础经济概念和资源分配 / 234
- 第二节 The Price System and the Microeconomy 价格体系和微观经济 / 237
- 第三节 Government Microeconomic Intervention 政府的微观经济干预 / 249
- 第四节 The Macroeconomy 宏观经济 / 255

第五节　Government Macroeconomic Intervention 政府的宏观经济干预 / 267

附录　高频专业词汇索引 / 269

第一部分
通用词汇 A to Z

A / 2	**N** / 84
B / 16	**O** / 86
C / 23	**P** / 93
D / 39	**Q** / 99
E / 53	**R** / 101
F / 60	**S** / 107
G / 63	**T** / 120
H / 65	**U** / 124
I / 70	**V** / 126
L / 80	**W** / 128
M / 81	

A

扫一扫
听本节音频

001 **abandon** /əˈbændən/ v. 放弃，遗弃；离开

- 用 abandon yourself to sth. 沉溺于某事
- 例 The firm **abandons** its policy of horizontal expansion. 这家公司放弃了其横向扩张的策略。

002 **abolish** /əˈbɒlɪʃ/ vt. 废除，废止

- 用 abolish slavery 废除奴隶制
- 例 What will happen to the number of workers employed by the firm if the minimum wage is **abolished**? 如果废除最低工资，那么公司雇佣的工人数量会发生什么变化？

003 **absorb** /əbˈzɔːb/ vt. 耗费大量（金钱、时间等）；吸收（气体、液体）；吞并

- 用 be absorbed into 使并入
- 例 The new proposals would **absorb** $80 billion of the federal budget. 新提案将占用 800 亿美元的联邦预算。

004 **abuse** /əˈbjuːs/ n. 滥用；虐待
/əˈbjuːz/ v. 滥用；虐待

- 用 drug abuse 药物滥用
- 例 What she did was an **abuse** of her position as manager. 她的所作所为是滥用经理职权。

005 **academia** /ˌækəˈdiːmiə/ n. 学术界，学术生涯

- 用 American academia 美国学术界
- 例 They are all leading figures from **academia**. 他们都是学术界的领军人物。

006 **acceptability** /əkˌseptəˈbɪləti/ *n.* 可接受性；可容许性

- 用 acceptability of sth. to sb. 某人对某事的接受度
- 例 The study aimed to assess the **acceptability** of the new system to patients. 这项研究的目的是评估病人对新系统的接受度。

007 **acceptance** /əkˈseptəns/ *n.* 接纳；赞同

- 用 wide acceptance 广泛认可
- 例 The new laws have gained widespread **acceptance**. 新法律已被广泛接受。

008 **accommodate** /əˈkɒmədeɪt/ *v.* 适应（新情况）；容纳；提供住宿

- 用 accommodate sb. with sth. 给某人提供某物
- 例 A localised strategy is vital to **accommodate** the variation in languages and cultures. 本地化战略对于适应语言和文化的差异来说至关重要。

009 **accompany** /əˈkʌmpəni/ *v.* 伴随，陪伴；伴奏

- 用 accompany sb. on sth. 以某乐器为某人伴奏
- 例 Economic growth, and improved wages that usually **accompany** it, improves happiness and well-being. 经济的增长，还有随之而来的收入提高，能够改善人们的幸福感。

010 **accountable** /əˈkaʊntəbl/ *adj.* 负责的；有解释义务的；可解释的

- 用 be accountable for sth. 对某事负责
- 例 Politicians are ultimately **accountable** to the voters. 政客最终要对选民负责。

011 **accumulate** /əˈkjuːmjəleɪt/ v. 积攒，积累

- 用 accumulate experience 积累经验
- 例 They **accumulate** points by completing an activity within the game. 他们通过完成游戏中的活动来积攒分数。

012 **acknowledge** /əkˈnɒlɪdʒ/ vt. 承认

- 同 recognise, admit (v.), grant
- 用 acknowledge the need for reform 承认改革的必要性
- 例 U.N. officials privately **acknowledge** this is a big number that may be hard to fill. 联合国官员私下承认，这个数字很大，可能很难填补。

013 **acquire** /əˈkwaɪə(r)/ vt. 获得，取得；学到

- 用 acquire knowledge 获得知识
- 例 Giant drug companies are paying large prices to **acquire** drug development firms. 大型制药公司为收购药品研发公司付出了高昂的代价。

014 **adapt** /əˈdæpt/ v. 改编；(使)适应

- 同 accommodate
- 用 adapt oneself to the new environment 某人适应新环境
- 例 The article is **adapted** from *The Independent*. 这篇文章改编自《独立报》。

015 **adaptability** /əˌdæptəˈbɪləti/ n. 适应力

- 用 strong adaptability 适应性强
- 例 Small enterprises generally offer greater **adaptability** than larger firms. 小企业一般比大公司具有更强的适应能力。

016 **adaptable** /əˈdæptəbl/ adj. 适应性强的；可修改的

- 用 be adaptable to do sth. 适应做某事
- 例 Small and medium-sized companies can be flexible and **adaptable**. 中小型企业具有灵活性和适应性。

017 **address** /əˈdres/ *vt.* 设法解决；忙于

- 用 address oneself to sth. 解决某事
- 例 Increased investment is needed to **address** supply-side capacity constraints. 需要增加投资以解决供应方面的产能限制。

018 **adequate** /ˈædɪkwət/ *adj.* 充足的；适当的；胜任的

- 用 adequate food for the weekend 周末有充足的食物
- 例 Lack of **adequate** infrastructure causes distribution costs such as transport and warehousing to rise steeply. 由于缺乏足够的基础设施，运输和仓储等经销成本急剧上升。

019 **admit** /ədˈmɪt/ *v.* 承认；准许进入；可容纳

- 同 acknowledge
- 用 admit to doing sth. 承认某事
- 例 The government **admits** that building a new bridge would bring a positive net benefit to society. 政府承认建造一座新桥将给社会带来正的净效益。

020 **advance** /ədˈvɑːns/ *v.* 发展，进步；前进

- 用 advance on/towards... 朝……前进
- 例 The quality of capital goods is improved as technology **advances**. 资本货物的质量随着技术的进步而提高。

021 **adverse** /ˈædvɜːs/ *adj.* 不利的；相反的

- 用 adverse effect 不利影响
- 例 It is important to consider the possible **adverse** side effects of such measures. 考虑这些措施可能产生的不良副作用很有必要。

022 advocate /ˈædvəkət/ n. 提倡者，拥护者
ˈædvəkeɪt/ vt. 提倡，拥护

- ⊕ an advocate for sth. 某事的倡导者
- 例 NGOs play an important leadership role in acting as **advocates** on public policy issues. 非政府组织在公共政策问题上扮演倡导者的重要角色。

023 affirm /əˈfɜːm/ v. 肯定

- 回 confirm
- ⊕ neither affirm nor deny it 既没有肯定也没有否定这件事
- 例 The government re-**affirmed** the country's commitment to free trade. 政府重申了国家对自由贸易的承诺。

024 affordable /əˈfɔːdəbl/ adj. 负担得起的

- ⊕ affordable price 可承受价格
- 例 Through sales of food at low prices, it can make food more **affordable** to poor people. 低价销售食品可以让穷人能消费得起。

025 aftermath /ˈɑːftəmæθ/ n. 余波，后果

- ⊕ immediate aftermath 直接后果
- 例 Iceland increased interest rates to 18% in the immediate **aftermath** of the crisis to reduce inflation. 冰岛在危机刚发生不久时将利率提高到18%，以降低通货膨胀。

026 agenda /əˈdʒendə/ n. 议程

- ⊕ top of the agenda 首要议程
- 例 Nobel Prize-winning economist suggests a 'five-pronged **agenda**' that would help developing countries gain the potential benefits. 诺贝尔经济学奖获得者提出了一个"五管齐下的议程"，来帮助发展中国家获得潜在的好处。

027 **aggregate** /ˈæɡrɪɡeɪt/ *vt.* 集合；聚集
/ˈæɡrɪɡət/ *n.* 合计，总计
adj. 总数的；总计的

- 用 aggregate demand 总需求
- 例 Along which axis can the market demand curve be **aggregated** from individual demand curves? 市场需求曲线可以沿着哪个轴与个人需求曲线相交？

028 **agreeable** /əˈɡriːəbl/ *adj.* 同意的；令人愉快的；和蔼的

- 用 agreeable climate 气候宜人
- 例 The deal must be **agreeable** to both sides. 交易必须双方都同意。

029 **alleged** /əˈledʒd/ *adj.* 所谓的，声称的；被断言的

- 用 it is alleged that... 声称某事……
- 例 The girl gave evidence in court against her **alleged** attacker. 女孩在法庭上提供了指控攻击她的人的证据。

030 **alleviate** /əˈliːvieɪt/ *vt.* 减轻，缓和

- 用 alleviate suffering 减轻苦恼
- 例 One reason given was that government spending to **alleviate** poverty. 其中一个原因是政府的扶贫支出。

031 **alliance** /əˈlaɪəns/ *n.* 联盟，联合；联姻

- 用 make an alliance 结成联盟
- 例 Three **alliances** cover most of the world's airlines. 三个联盟覆盖了世界上大部分的航空公司。

032 **alongside** /əˌlɒŋˈsaɪd/ *adv.* 与……一起

- 用 lie alongside 并排
- 例 It is best used and most effective when used **alongside** other policies. 当与其他策略一起使用时，它的使用效果最佳且最有效。

033 **alter** /ˈɔːltə(r)/ *v.* 改变，更改

- 用 alter the fact that... 改变……的事实
- 例 A single firm in an industry **alters** production, but its actions have no effect on the market price of the good. 行业内的某一家公司改变了产量，但其行为对市场价格并没有影响。

034 **aluminium** /ˌæljəˈmɪniəm/ *n.* 铝

- 用 aluminium foil 铝箔
- 例 Materials such as **aluminium**, paper and glass can be recycled. 铝、纸和玻璃等材料可以回收利用。

035 **ambition** /æmˈbɪʃn/ *n.* 抱负，雄心

- 用 lifelong ambition 终身的抱负
- 例 She never achieved her **ambition** of becoming a famous entrepreneur. 她从未实现成为著名企业家的抱负。

036 **amount** /əˈmaʊnt/ *n.* 数量，数额

- 用 amount to 总计
- 例 The country spends large **amounts** on foreign aid. 国家在对外援助上花了大量的钱。

037 **analyse** /ˈænəlaɪz/ *vt.* 分析；分解；细察

- 用 analyse the problem 分析问题
- 例 Please **analyse** how productivity influences economic growth. 请分析生产率如何影响经济增长。

038 **analyst** /ˈænəlɪst/ *n.* 分析人士

- 用 a political analyst 政治分析家
- 例 **Analysts** say that the reduced rate of economic growth could have been avoided. 分析人士说，经济增长率的下降本来是可以避免的。

039 **ancient** /ˈeɪnʃənt/ *adj.* 古老的，古代的；过时的

- 用 ancient history 古老的历史
- 例 The term 'economics' is derived from an **ancient** Greek expression. "经济学"一词来源于古希腊语。

040 **angle** /ˈæŋgl/ *n.* 角，角度；视角

- 用 at an angle 倾斜地
- 例 The painting changes slightly when seen from different **angles**. 从不同的角度看，这幅画略有变化。

041 **announce** /əˈnaʊns/ *v.* 宣布，宣告

- 用 announce that... 宣布……
- 例 At a recent UN meeting, the president **announced** reform of the foreign aid programmes. 在最近的一次联合国会议上，总统宣布了国家对外援助计划的改革。

042 **anticipate** /ænˈtɪsɪpeɪt/ *v.* 预料，预期；预见

- 用 anticipate that... 预料……
- 例 It is hard to **anticipate** its impact. 很难预料它的影响。

043 **antique** /ænˈtiːk/ *n.* 古董

- 用 antique shop 古董店
- 例 Priceless **antiques** were destroyed in the fire. 许多无价古董在火灾中被烧毁。

044 **anxiety** /æŋˈzaɪəti/ *n.* 渴望；忧虑

- 🌐 anxiety for the war to end 渴望战争结束
- 📖 Further interest rate cuts were thought unlikely, as there was **anxiety** over the rising price of oil. 由于对油价上涨的担忧，进一步降息被认为是不可能的。

045 **anxious** /ˈæŋkʃəs/ *adj.* 渴望的；担忧的；急切的

- 🌐 be anxious about... 渴望……
- 📖 Governments will be particularly **anxious** to reduce long-term unemployment. 政府特别渴望降低长期失业率。

046 **appalling** /əˈpɔːlɪŋ/ *adj.* 可怕的，令人震惊的

- 🌐 an appalling record 可怕的纪录
- 📖 Mines have been associated with low pay for workers and **appalling** working conditions. 煤矿总是与低薪和可怕的工作条件联系在一起。

047 **apparent** /əˈpærənt/ *adj.* 显然的，明显的

- 🌐 no apparent reason 没有明显的理由
- 📖 With the expansion of trade and the development of markets, the benefits of specialisation became **apparent**. 随着贸易的扩大和市场的发展，专业化的好处越来越明显。

048 **appliance** /əˈplaɪəns/ *n.* （家用）电器，器具；器械；装置；应用

- 🌐 safety appliance 安全装置
- 📖 Steel is used in the construction industry, household **appliances** and many other goods. 钢铁用于建筑业、家用电器和许多其他商品。

049 **applicant** /ˈæplɪkənt/ n. 申请人，申请者；请求者

- 用 job applicant 求职人员
- 例 Because of incomplete information, it takes time for the right **applicants** to get matched up with the right jobs. 由于信息不完整，合适的求职者需要一段时间才能找到合适的工作。

050 **appointment** /əˈpɔɪntmənt/ n. 预约，约定；约会

- 用 business appointment 商务预约
- 例 Hospital **appointments** were cancelled. 医院的预约被取消了。

051 **apprenticeship** /əˈprentɪʃɪp/ n. 学徒期；学徒身份

- 用 apprenticeship system 学徒制度
- 例 A government decides to borrow from the general public in order to finance its extra spending on **apprenticeship** training schemes. 政府决定向公众借款，以资助其在学徒培训计划上的额外开支。

052 **approve** /əˈpruːv/ v. 赞同，同意；为某物提供证据

- 同 acceptance (n.); accept (v.)
- 用 approve of one's doing sth. 同意某人做某事
- 例 The proposal was not **approved**. 提议并没有通过。

053 **approximate** /əˈprɒksɪmət/ adj. 近似的，大概的

- 用 approximate value 近似值
- 例 Cost-benefit analysis is a very rough and **approximate** method used to make choices about public goods. 在选择公共产品时，成本-收益分析法是一种非常粗略且近似的手段。

054 **Argentine** /ˈɑːdʒəntaɪn/ adj. 阿根廷的
n. 阿根廷人

- 例 Originally US $1 may exchange for 8 **Argentine** pesos. 最初 1 美元可以兑换 8 个阿根廷比索。

055 arise /əˈraɪz/ v. 产生；上升；起立

- 搭 arise from... 由某事引起，起因于……
- 例 The problem of sustainability **arises** because of conflicts between environmental and economic goals. 环境目标和经济目标之间的冲突导致可持续问题的产生。

056 armed /ɑːmd/ adj. 武装的；有扶手的

- 搭 armed forces 武装力量
- 例 The government has declared a state of emergency, and food is being transported under **armed** guard. 政府已经宣布进入紧急状态，食品正在武装警卫的护送下运送。

057 artificial /ˌɑːtɪˈfɪʃl/ adj. 人工的，人造的；仿造的

- 搭 artificial lake 人造湖
- 例 More and more countries are adopting **artificial** intelligence. 越来越多国家开始采用人工智能。

058 artwork /ˈɑːtwɜːk/ n. 艺术品

- 搭 a piece of artwork 一件艺术品
- 例 Many original **artworks** have gone missing from the museum. 博物馆里许多原创艺术品都丢失了。

059 assemble /əˈsembl/ v. 集合，聚集；装配

- 近 aggregate
- 搭 the assembled company 聚集的人
- 例 Firms that **assemble** the final product buy components from specialist firms within the industry. 组装最终产品的公司从行业内的专业公司购买零部件。

060 **assembler** /ə'semblə(r)/ *n.* 装配工；汇编程序

- 🌐 assembler language 汇编语言
- 📝 A motorcycle **assembler** employed two hundred workers to make a standardised model. 一家摩托车装配商雇用了 200 名工人制作标准化模型。

061 **assert** /ə'sɜːt/ *vt.* 主张，声称；维护

- 🔄 alleged (adj.)
- 🌐 it is asserted that... 主张……
- 📝 This perspective **asserts** that both trade and aid are important to growth and development. 这种观点认为，贸易和援助对增长和发展都很重要。

062 **assist** /ə'sɪst/ *v.* 帮助，协助

- 🌐 assist sb. in doing sth. 帮助某人做某事
- 📝 SALs were a method used by the World Bank in **assisting** developing countries to adopt economic and trade liberalisation policies. SALs 是世界银行用于帮助发展中国家采取经济和贸易自由化政策的一种方法。

063 **assurance** /ə'ʃʊərəns/ *n.* 担保，保证；信心

- 🌐 quality assurance 品质保证
- 📝 The government provides a kind of **assurance** of protection in the event that financial institutions face difficulties due to poor loan repayments. 在金融机构因无力偿还贷款而面临困难时，政府会提供一种担保来保护它们。

064 **Atlantic** /æt'læntɪk/ *n.* 大西洋

- 🌐 Atlantic ocean 大西洋
- 📝 A quota on fishing was imposed in the **Atlantic** Ocean. 对在大西洋捕鱼实行限额。

065 ATM (automatic teller machine)
abbr. 自动取款机

- 用 ATM system 自动取款机系统
- 例 Can I deposit my money through the **ATM**? 我可以通过自动取款机存钱吗?

066 attraction /əˈtrækʃn/ *n.* 吸引力；有吸引力的人、事物或地点

- 用 tourist attraction 观光胜地
- 例 The use of pollution permits has many **attractions** but carries with critics as well. 使用污染许可证有很多吸引人的地方，但也不乏批评者。

067 auction /ˈɔːkʃn/ *n.* 拍卖

- 用 auction company 拍卖公司
- 例 A classic Rolls-Royce was sold for £25,000 at **auction**. 一辆经典的劳斯莱斯汽车在拍卖会上以 25,000 英镑售出。

068 austerity /ɒˈsterəti/ *n.* 紧缩；节俭

- 用 austerity measures 紧缩措施
- 例 In exchange for help, Iceland was forced to sharply reduce government spending—introducing more **austerity** than the ROI did. 作为援助交换，冰岛被迫大幅削减政府开支——采取了比投资回报率更高的紧缩措施。

069 Australian /ɔːˈstreɪliən/ *adj.* 澳大利亚的
n. 澳大利亚人

- 用 Australian company 澳大利亚公司
- 例 Australia's spending on imports falls and, at the same time, investment abroad by **Australian** firms declines. 澳大利亚的进口支出下降，与此同时，澳大利亚企业的海外投资也在下降。

070 **automotive** /ˌɔːtəˈməʊtɪv/ adj. 汽车的，自动的

- 用 automotive industry 汽车工业
- 例 The iron and steel industry in China was stimulated by strong domestic demand, particularly from the construction, manufacturing and **automotive** industries. 中国的钢铁工业受到了强劲的国内需求的刺激，尤其是来自建筑、制造和汽车行业的需求。

071 **averse** /əˈvɜːs/ adj. 反对的；厌恶的

- 用 be averse to doing sth. 讨厌做某事
- 例 As firms get larger, they become more risk-**averse** by spreading their business activities in a more diversified way. 随着公司规模的扩大，他们通过以更多样化的方式扩展业务活动来规避风险。

072 **aversion** /əˈvɜːʃn/ n. 厌恶；反感的人或物

- 用 aversion therapy 厌恶疗法
- 例 It was suggested that the greatest threat to global economic development was the culture of risk **aversion** among companies. 有人认为，对全球经济发展的最大威胁是企业的风险规避文化。

073 **avocado** /ˌævəˈkɑːdəʊ/ n. 牛油果

- 用 avocado salad 牛油果沙拉
- 例 The table shows the demand schedule for **avocados** in a market on a particular day. 该表显示了在某一天内市场对牛油果的需求表。

074 **avoid** /əˈvɔɪd/ vt. 避免；躲避；消除

- 用 avoid doing sth. 逃避做某事
- 例 To **avoid** a peso collapse, the central bank intervened heavily in the foreign exchange market. 为了避免比索崩溃，中央银行大力干预外汇市场。

B

075 **ballot** /ˈbælət/ n. 投票
v. 投票

- 搭 secret ballot 无记名投票
- 例 Allocation of tickets by **ballot** would be preferable. 最好以投票的方式分配票。

076 **banknote** /ˈbæŋknəʊt/ n. 钞票，纸币

- 搭 banknote detector 验钞机
- 例 What advantage do **banknotes** have over coins? 纸币与硬币相比有什么优势？

077 **bankrupt** /ˈbæŋkrʌpt/ adj. 破产的，倒闭的
vt. 使破产；使枯竭

- 搭 declare bankrupt 宣告破产
- 例 If businesses managed their money as carelessly as they managed their people, most would be **bankrupt**. 如果企业管理资金像管理员工一样粗枝大叶，大多数都会破产。

078 **bankruptcy** /ˈbæŋkrʌptsi/ n. 破产

- 搭 political bankruptcy 政治破产
- 例 It needed $2 million in government aid to avoid **bankruptcy**. 它需要 200 万美元的政府援助以避免破产。

079 **banquet** /ˈbæŋkwɪt/ n. 宴会
v. 宴请

- 搭 state banquet 国宴
- 例 It is a state **banquet** in honour of the visiting president. 这是为欢迎来访的总统而举行的国宴。

080 **basmati** /bæs'mæti/ *n.* 印度香米

- 用 basmati rice recipes 印度香米食谱
- 例 The Indian government replaced the minimum export price that it enforced for non-**basmati** rice with a complete ban on rice exports. 印度政府取消了对非印度香米的最低出口价格，转而全面禁止大米出口。

081 **bauxite** /'bɔːksaɪt/ *n.* 铝土矿，铁矾土

- 用 bauxite resource 铝土矿资源
- 例 The extraction of oil and gas and the mining of iron ore and **bauxite** have grown significantly in recent years. 近年来，石油和天然气的开采以及铁矿石和铝土矿的开采都有了显著增长。

082 **bear** /beə(r)/ *v.* 承受，忍受；结果

- 用 bear risk 承受风险
- 例 If the tax is on the use of domestic fuel, then older members of society may **bear** the greatest effect as they use proportionately more domestic fuel for heating than others in society. 如果对家用燃料征税，老年群体所受影响可能是最大的，因为相对其他社会群体来说，他们取暖使用的民用燃料相应更多。

083 **behalf** /bɪ'hɑːf/ *n.* 代表；利益

- 用 on behalf of 代表
- 例 Financial institutions also speculate on future currency movements on their own **behalf**. 金融机构也会以自己的名义推测未来的货币走势。

084 **beneficiary** /ˌbenɪ'fɪʃəri/ *n.* 受益者

- 用 beneficiary of sth. 某事的受益者
- 例 Gold is perhaps the biggest **beneficiary** in times of inflation and stock market volatility. 在通货膨胀的背景下，黄金或许是最大的受益者，而股票市场则阴晴不定。

085 **beset** /bɪˈset/ vt. 困扰；镶嵌；包围

- 用 beset by enemy 被敌人包围
- 例 To what extent do you think this self-interest is the root cause of the environmental problems that **beset** the human race today? 你认为这种利己主义在多大程度上是当下困扰人类的环境问题的根源？

086 **beverage** /ˈbevərɪdʒ/ n. 饮料

- 用 food and beverage 食品和饮料
- 例 Studies on the consumption of various alcoholic **beverages** have been conducted. 如今已对各种酒精饮料的消费进行了研究。

087 **bid** /bɪd/ v. 出价；叫牌
n. 出价；投标价

- 用 bid for sth. 为某物出价
- 例 The government announced it would allow private companies to **bid** to redevelop the sites. 政府宣布，将允许私人公司竞标重新开发这些地块。

088 **bilateral** /ˌbaɪˈlætərəl/ adj. 双边的

- 用 bilateral talks 双边会谈
- 例 We must make the distinction between regional and **bilateral** trade agreements. 我们必须对区域贸易协定和双边贸易协定做出区分。

089 **blame** /bleɪm/ vt. 责备；归咎于
n. 责备；过失

- 用 blame sb. for sth. 为某事责怪某人
- 例 Some economists **blame** long-term unemployment on globalisation for shifting low-skilled jobs overseas. 一些经济学家将长期失业现象的原因归咎于全球化将低技能工作转移到了海外的。

090 bleak /bliːk/ *adj.* 黯淡的，无希望的；阴冷的

- 用 a bleak prospect 前景黯淡
- 例 Three decades ago, in a **bleak** stretch of the 1970s, an economic phenomenon emerged that was as ugly as its name—stagflation. 30 年前，在 20 世纪 70 年代一段惨淡的时期，出现了一种与其名字一样丑陋的经济现象——滞胀。

091 blind /blaɪnd/ *adj.* 盲目的；瞎的

- 用 go blind 失明
- 例 Markets are **blind** and the direction of change they provide often represents inefficient resource allocation from a society's point of view. 市场是盲目的，从社会的角度来看，市场所提供的改变方向往往表现出效率低的资源分配。

092 block /blɒk/ *vt.* 阻止，限制
n. 街区；大厦

- 用 block the way 挡路
- 例 Please explain why US sugar farmers try to **block** increases in sugar quotas. 请解释为什么美国蔗糖种植户试图阻止增加蔗糖的配额。

093 Boeing /ˈbəʊɪŋ/ *n.* 波音公司

- 用 Boeing airplane 波音飞机
- 例 In 2013, new aircraft, the **Boeing** 787 Dreamliner, was assembled in the United States. 2013 年，美国组装了一架新飞机——波音 787 梦幻客机。

094 Bolivia /bəˈlɪviə/ *n.* 玻利维亚

- 用 Bolivia post office 玻利维亚邮局
- 例 **Bolivia** encouraged investment by foreign firms in order to exploit its oil and gas resources. 玻利维亚鼓励外国公司投资，以开发其石油和天然气资源。

095 **bolster** /ˈbəʊlstə(r)/ *v.* 支持，支撑

- 🌐 bolster up 援助，支持
- 📝 Turkey tried to **bolster** its currency by raising its interest rate to attract funds. 土耳其试图通过提高利率来吸引资金以支撑其货币。

096 **boom** /buːm/ *n.* 繁荣；（某种体育运动、音乐等）突然风靡的时期
v. 使兴旺

- 🌐 economic boom 经济繁荣，经济腾飞
- 📝 A major commodity **boom** occurred in the decade of the 2000s. 21世纪前十年出现了大宗商品的繁荣期。

097 **boost** /buːst/ *v.* 促进，推动

- 🌐 boost one's confidence 提升某人的信心
- 📝 We use local suppliers on construction projects, which **boosts** the local economy. 我们在建设项目中使用当地供应商，这促进了当地经济的发展。

098 **border** /ˈbɔːdə(r)/ *n.* 边境，边界，国界
v. 接近；与……接壤

- 🌐 border trade 边境贸易
- 📝 Under the impetus of the **border** trade, the RMB started circulation abroad spontaneously. 在边境贸易的推动下，人民币开始自发地在境外流通起来。

099 **boredom** /ˈbɔːdəm/ *n.* 厌倦；令人厌烦的事物

- 🌐 relieve boredom 排遣，解闷
- 📝 In modern developed economies the dehumanising impact of production techniques has been acknowledged and procedures introduced to counteract **boredom**. 在现代发达经济体中，人们已经认识到生产技术带来的非人性化的影响，因此引入了程序来消除厌倦情绪。

100 **Botswana** /bɒˈtswɑːnə/ *n.* 博茨瓦纳（非洲中南部国家）

- 用 Botswana tourism 博茨瓦纳旅游业
- 例 In 2012, the rate of inflation in **Botswana** was 7.5%. 2012 年，博茨瓦纳的通胀率为 7.5%。

101 **bottleneck** /ˈbɒtlnek/ *n.* 瓶颈

- 用 traffic bottleneck 交通瓶颈
- 例 As GDP approaches the level of potential output, resource **bottlenecks** begin to cause increases in resource and product prices. 随着 GDP 接近潜在产出水平，资源瓶颈开始导致资源和产品价格上涨。

102 **bound** /baʊnd/ *adj.* 注定的；受约束的；准备去往……的
　　　　　　　　　　 n. 界限
　　　　　　　　　　 v. 限制；束缚

- 用 a north-bound train 一列北行的火车
- 例 Since we all have different experiences, there is **bound** to be great variation between any two individuals' scales of preferences. 由于我们每个人的经历不同，所以任何两个个体之间必然存在很大的差异。

103 **boycott** /ˈbɔɪkɒt/ *n.* 联合抵制
　　　　　　　　　　　 v. 联合抵制；拒绝购买；拒绝参加

- 用 boycott on sth. 抵制某事（物）
- 例 There have been calls for **boycotts** of Chinese goods but they have all failed miserably. 有人呼吁抵制中国商品，但他们都惨败了。

104 **branch** /brɑːntʃ/ *n.* 分支；分公司；树枝

- 用 branch company 分公司
- 例 The number of banks and their **branches** in relation to the population in developing countries is far smaller than in

developed ones. 发展中国家银行及其分支机构的数量相对于人口的比例要远远低于发达国家。

105 brand /brænd/ n. 品牌，商标；类型

- 搭 brand loyalty 品牌忠诚度
- 例 Typical examples are Coca-Cola and Pepsi, both well-known **brands** of cola. 典型的例子是可口可乐和百事可乐，这两个都是著名的可乐品牌。

106 brewery /ˈbruːəri/ n. 啤酒厂

- 搭 Tsingtao brewery 青岛啤酒厂
- 例 Building a local infrastructure, including a **brewery**, requires huge amounts of capital. 建设包括啤酒厂在内的当地基础设施需要大量资金。

107 Bulgaria /bʌlˈɡeəriə/ n. 保加利亚

- 例 Romania and **Bulgaria**, both EU members, are hoping to join the area in 2012. 罗马尼亚和保加利亚都是欧盟成员国，希望在 2012 年加入该地区。

108 bulk /bʌlk/ n. 大量；体积，容量

- 搭 bulk buying 大宗采购
- 例 It's cheaper to buy in **bulk**. 批量购买更便宜。

109 bureaucracy /bjʊəˈrɒkrəsi/ n. 官僚主义

- 搭 excessive bureaucracy 极度官僚主义
- 例 It is considered to be the country with the least amount of **bureaucracy** in the European Union. 它被认为是欧盟国家中官僚风气最小的国家。

110 bureaucratic /ˌbjʊərəˈkrætɪk/ adj. 官僚（主义）的

- 搭 bureaucratic organisations 官僚组织
- 例 It is a **bureaucratic** system of decision-making. 该决策体系具有官僚主义风气。

C

扫一扫
听本节音频

111 **Cambodia** /kæmˈbəʊdiə/ *n.* 柬埔寨

- 用 Cambodia Air 柬埔寨航空
- 例 The Kingdom of **Cambodia** is a Southeast Asian nation. 柬埔寨王国是一个东南亚国家。

112 **campaigner** /kæmˈpeɪnə(r)/ *n.* 活动推动者，竞选者

- 用 seasoned campaigner 老将
- 例 Some anti-smoking **campaigners** are calling for the smoking of cigarettes anywhere to be made illegal. 一些反吸烟人士呼吁立法禁止在任何地方吸烟。

113 **cancer** /ˈkænsə(r)/ *n.* 癌症，恶性肿瘤

- 用 lung cancer 肺癌
- 例 Smokers face an increased risk of developing lung **cancer**. 吸烟者患肺癌的风险增加。

114 **Canon** /ˈkænən/ *n.* 佳能

- 例 **Canon** reportedly sent its 22,000 workers on paid annual leaves during September 17 and 18. 据报道，9月17日至18日，佳能让2.2万名员工休了带薪年假。

115 **capability** /ˌkeɪpəˈbɪləti/ *n.* 能力，才能；容量

- 用 beyond the capabilities 超出能力范围
- 例 Industrial policies include the establishment of a research and development **capability**, as well as the investments in human capital. 产业政策包括建立研究和发展能力，以及对人力资本的投资。

116 **capitalist** /ˈkæpɪtəlɪst/ *n.* 资本家
adj. 资本主义的

- 搭 a famous capitalist 一位著名的资本家
- 例 There are conflicts between **capitalists** and workers. 资本家和工人之间有很多矛盾。

117 **capture** /ˈkæptʃə(r)/ *vt.* 俘获；夺得

- 搭 capture one's attention 捕捉某人的注意力
- 例 The reason why the low-price firm makes much higher profits is that by charging a low price it **captures** a large portion of sales from its rival. 这家低价公司之所以能获得如此高的利润是因为通过低定价，从竞争对手那里抢占了不少销售额。

118 **caretaker** /ˈkeəteɪkə(r)/ *n.* 照顾者，看管人；管理员

- 近 gatekeeper
- 搭 bankrupt caretaker 破产管理人
- 例 In any of India's new shopping malls many of the shop workers, **caretakers** and security staff are employed by companies other than those of the owners of the mall. 在印度的任何一家新购物中心，许多店员、看门人和安保人员都是受雇于商场所有者以外的公司的。

119 **cargo** /ˈkɑːɡəʊ/ *n.* 货物；船装货

- 搭 bulk cargo 大宗货运
- 例 **Cargo** volumes would double and UK competitiveness would increase. 货运量将翻一番，英国的竞争力将增强。

120 **cartel** /kɑːˈtel/ *n.* 卡特尔；企业联合；垄断联盟

- 搭 tariff cartel 关税同盟
- 例 A **cartel** is a formal price or output agreement between firms in an industry to restrict competition. 卡特尔是行业内企业之间为限制竞争而签订的正式价格或产量协议。

121 **categorisation** /ˌkætəgəraɪˈzeɪʃn/ *n.* 分类

- 🈶 historical categorisation 历史分类
- 🈺 Some football clubs also adopt a similar approach with what they call 'price-**categorisation**'. 一些足球俱乐部也采用了类似的方法,他们称之为"价格分类"。

122 **categorise** /ˈkætəgəraɪz/ *vt.* 将……分类

- 🈶 categorise risks 分类风险
- 🈺 In Economics we **categorise** the resources available to us into four types. 在经济学中,我们把可用的资源分为四类。

123 **cease** /siːs/ *v.* 停止,终止

- 🈶 cease doing sth. 停止做某事
- 🈺 What might cause a country's currency notes to **cease** to act as money? 什么原因会导致一个国家停止使用纸币作为其货币?

124 **celebrity** /səˈlebrəti/ *n.* 名人,名声

- 🈶 TV celebrities 电视明星
- 🈺 Some firms attempt to create a favourable image by use of **celebrity** advertising. 一些公司试图通过明星广告代言来建立良好的形象。

125 **centralise** /ˈsentrəlaɪz/ *vt.* 把……集中起来

- center
- 🈶 centralise power 使权力集中
- 🈺 The foreign exchange market is not a **centralised** meeting place, but involves any location where one currency can be exchanged for another. 外汇市场不是一个集中的交易场所,而是一个兑换货币的地方。

126 chain /tʃeɪn/ n. 连锁；束缚；链条

- 搭 a chain of coincidences 一连串的巧合
- 例 In Australia two big supermarket **chains** control up to 80% of grocery sales. 澳大利亚两大连锁超市占据了高达 80% 的零售额。

127 chairman /'tʃeəmən/ n. 主席，会长；董事长

- 搭 honorary chairman 名誉主席
- 例 The **chairman** believes that this is likely to increase domestic prices for Basmati rice by 20%. 主席认为这可能会使印度香米的国内价格上涨 20%。

128 challenge /'tʃælɪndʒ/ vt. 向……挑战
n. 挑战；质疑

- 搭 face challenge 面对挑战
- 例 All countries, including the rich and the poor, have the right to **challenge** each other through the WTO. 所有国家，无论是富裕和贫穷，都有权通过世贸组织相互质疑。

129 challenging /'tʃælɪndʒɪŋ/ adj. 具有挑战性的

- 搭 a challenging career 富有挑战性的职业
- 例 In these **challenging** economic times, critical thinking and self-confident leadership are more important than ever. 在这个充满挑战的经济时代，批判性思维和自信的领导力比以往任何时候都重要。

130 chamber /'tʃeɪmbə(r)/ n. 会馆；居室；议院

- 搭 the upper/lower chamber 上/下议院
- 例 According to data published by the Indonesian **Chamber** of Commerce and Industry, around 17% of a typical company's total expenditure is absorbed by such costs. 根据印尼工商会公布的数据，一家公司大约 17% 的总支出被这些成本所吸收。

131 **channel** /'tʃænl/ v. 提供资金，输送

- 用 channel A through B 通过 B 传递 A
- 例 Why is more and more ODA **channelled** through NGOs? 为什么越来越多的官方发展援助是通过非政府组织提供的？

132 **check** /tʃek/ v. 确认，检查

- 用 check in 登记，报到
- 例 Using this book and the glossary in the student CD, **check** on their meanings. 通过本书和学生CD中的词汇表，检查它们的意思。

133 **chronic** /'krɒnɪk/ adj. 长期的；慢性的

- 用 chronic disease 慢性病
- 例 Many people don't realise that having **chronic** nightmares is a medical problem that can be treated. 许多人并不知道长期的梦魇是一种可以治疗的医学问题。

134 **circulate** /'sɜːkjəleɪt/ v. 流通；传播；循环

- 用 circulate briskly 迅速周转
- 例 When people go to the mall and buy televisions and eat out, their money **circulates** through the economy. 当人们去购物，买电视机，出去吃饭，他们的钱在经济中流通。

135 **classification** /ˌklæsɪfɪ'keɪʃn/ n. 分类

- 同 categorisation
- 用 the classification of sth. 某物的分类
- 例 The **classification** of countries into developing and developed is, therefore, never clear. 把国家分为发展中国家和发达国家的界定从来就不清楚。

136 cocaine /kəʊˈkeɪn/ n. 可卡因

- 搭 cocaine addiction 可卡因成瘾
- 例 They established bans on heroin and **cocaine** consumption. 他们禁止吸食海洛因和可卡因。

137 coincide /ˌkəʊɪnˈsaɪd/ vi. 一致，符合；同时发生

- 搭 coincide with sth. 与某事物一致
- 例 The government increases spending on education, which **coincides** with an increase in wage. 政府增加教育支出，这与工资上涨是一致的。

138 collapse /kəˈlæps/ n. 崩溃；（货币）暴跌；倒塌 v. 崩溃

- 同 break down
- 搭 share prices collapse 股价暴跌
- 例 Commercial banks and the international community suddenly woke up to the possibility of a banking **collapse**. 商业银行和国际社会突然意识到银行业崩溃的可能性。

139 collude /kəˈluːd/ vi. 勾结；串通

- 搭 collude with sb. to do sth. 串通某人做某事
- 例 Firms sometimes act together or **collude**, usually illegally, to acquire greater monopoly power. 公司有时会联合行动或勾结，通常是非法的，以获得更大的垄断势力。

140 commentary /ˈkɒməntri/ n. 评论，注释，说明

- 搭 commentary on sth. 实况报道某事
- 例 Our reporters will give a running **commentary** on the election results as they are announced. 我们的记者将对公布的选举结果作实况追踪报道。

141 commerce /ˈkɒmɜːs/ n. 贸易；商业

- 用 international commerce 国际商务
- 例 We pioneers and leaders of electronic **commerce**, are meeting here to call for changes in patent law. 我们这些电子商务的创始人和领导人在此集会，共同呼吁修改专利法。

142 commission /kəˈmɪʃn/ n. 委员会；委任；犯罪行为

- 用 the commission of a crime 犯罪
- 例 In 2007 the UK Competition **Commission** indicated that failure in the market mechanism would result in both winners and losers. 2007 年，英国竞争委员会指出，市场机制的失败会对赢家和输家都造成一定影响。

143 commitment /kəˈmɪtmənt/ n. 承诺，保证

- 同 assurance
- 用 make a commitment 承诺
- 例 Social scientists, like everyone else, have class interests, ideological **commitments**, and values of all kinds. 社会科学家和其他人一样，有阶级利益、意识形态承诺和各种价值观。

144 common /ˈkɒmən/ adj. 普遍的；通常的；共同的

- 用 in common 共同的
- 例 Inflation is far more **common** than deflation. 通货膨胀比通货紧缩普遍得多。

145 compact /kəmˈpækt/ adj. 袖珍的；紧密的；简明的

- 用 a compact narration 简明的叙述
- 例 The notebook computer is small and **compact** and weighs only 3.6 lb. 这款笔记本电脑体积小巧，重量仅 3.6 磅。

146 compelling /kəmˈpelɪŋ/ adj. 引人注目的；令人信服的

- ⊕ a compelling need 迫切的需要
- 例 You have to write **compelling** abstracts and introductions that hook the reader and make her feel like investing time in your work. 你要写出引人注目的摘要和引言，这是为了吸引读者并且让他们乐于花时间在你的文章上。

147 compensate /ˈkɒmpenseɪt/ v. 补偿，赔偿；弥补

- ⊕ compensate a loss 弥补损失
- 例 Financial investors require much higher interest rates on bonds, in order to **compensate** them for the increased risk. 金融投资者要求更高的债券利率，以补偿他们增加的风险。

148 competitor /kəmˈpetɪtə(r)/ n. 竞争者，对手

- ⊕ strategic competitor 战略竞争对手
- 例 In which market situation will a firm take account of the reactions of its **competitors** before deciding to cut its price? 在什么样的市场情况下，一家公司在做出降价决定前会考虑其竞争对手的反应？

149 complain /kəmˈpleɪn/ v. 抱怨，投诉；控告

- ⊕ complain about sth. 抱怨某事
- 例 Now the governments in developed countries are **complaining** that the transport of products around the world increases pollution and should be limited. 如今发达国家的政府抱怨世界各地的产品运输增加了污染，应加以限制。

150 comply /kəmˈplaɪ/ vi. 遵守，顺从

- ⊕ comply with... 遵守……
- 例 They refused to **comply** with the UN resolution. 他们拒绝遵守联合国决议。

151 **compound** /ˈkɒmpaʊnd/ *adj.* 复合的；混合的；化合的

n. 化合物

- 用 compound fertiliser 复合肥料
- 例 The alternative is to lend the money to a finance company at a **compound** interest rate of 5%. 另一种选择是把钱以 5% 的复合利率借给一家金融公司。

152 **co-ordination** /kəʊˌɔːdɪˈneɪʃn/ *n.* 协调；对等

- 用 in co-ordination with... 与……相协调
- 例 The firm seeks to improve management control and **co-ordination**. 公司寻求改善管理控制和协调。

153 **comprehensive** /ˌkɒmprɪˈhensɪv/ *adj.* 综合的；广泛的；有理解力的

- 用 comprehensive utilisation 综合利用
- 例 Canada and the European Union signed the *Comprehensive Economic and Trade Agreement*. 加拿大与欧盟签署了《全面经济贸易协定》。

154 **comprise** /kəmˈpraɪz/ *vt.* 包括，包含；由……组成

- 用 be comprised of... 由……组成
- 例 The committee is **comprised** of representatives from both the public and private sectors. 委员会由来自政府和私人部门的双方代表组成。

155 **concave** /kɒnˈkeɪv/ *adj.* 凹的

n. 凹形结构

vt. 使……凹陷

- 用 a concave mirror 凹透镜
- 例 Indifference curves are **concave** or bowed inward to the origin. 无差别曲线是向内凹或向原点弯曲的。

156 **concentrate** /ˈkɒnsntreɪt/ v. 集中，全神贯注于

- 用 concentrate on sth. 全神贯注于某事
- 例 We should **concentrate** on improving the use of existing capacity, not building another runway. 我们应该集中精力提高现有资源的性能，而不是建造另一条跑道。

157 **concern** /kənˈsɜːn/ vt. 关系到，涉及，关心

- 用 be concerned with sth. 与某事（物）有关
- 例 The theory of the firm is also **concerned** with how much output a loss-making firm should produce in order to minimise its loss. 企业理论还关心的是一个亏损企业应该有怎样的产出，才能使其损失最小化。

158 **concert** /ˈkɒnsət/ n. 音乐会

- 用 a pop concert 一场流行音乐会
- 例 What is likely to affect the position of the demand curve for tickets to pop **concerts**? 什么因素会影响流行演唱会门票的需求曲线？

159 **condemn** /kənˈdem/ vt. 谴责，声讨；宣判

- 近 damn, doom, sentence
- 用 condemn the killings 谴责屠杀
- 例 Some people have **condemned** efforts to support the currency, arguing that a weaker rouble is good for exports. 一些人谴责支持卢布的做法，认为卢布贬值有利于出口。

160 **confectionery** /kənˈfekʃənəri/ n. 糕点糖果；糖果店

- 用 confectionery warehouse 糖果仓库
- 例 When asked about its role in **confectionery** as well as the weight-loss industry, a Nestle spokesperson said chocolate could be part of a healthy diet. 当被问及其在糕点糖果及减肥行业中扮演的角色时，雀巢公司发言人表示，巧克力可能是健康食品的一部分。

161 conference /ˈkɒnfərəns/ n. 会议

- 用 hold a conference 召开会议
- 例 International **conferences** have been held to discuss the effects of global warming. 已经召开了国际会议来讨论全球变暖的影响。

162 confine /kənˈfaɪn/ vt. 限制；禁闭；局限于……范围之内

- 用 confine sb./sth. to sth. 把某人/某物限制于某处
- 例 The benefits derived from the goods are **confined** to those who consume them. 商品的益处只有其消费者才能享受到。

163 congested /kənˈdʒestɪd/ adj. 拥挤的，堵塞的；充血的

- 同 crowded
- 用 congested city streets 交通拥堵的城市街道
- 例 Victoria Harbour has three privately operated road tunnels, the oldest and most **congested** of which is the Cross Harbour Tunnel. 维多利亚港有三条私人经营的隧道，其中最古老和最拥挤的是海底隧道。

164 conglomerate /kənˈglɒmərət/ n. 企业集团；adj. 综合企业的

- 同 enterprise group
- 用 a media conglomerate 大众传媒联合体
- 例 A diversified **conglomerate** can cover any losses in one activity with the profits from another, an option not open to smaller firms. 一家多元化的企业集团可以用另一项业务的利润来弥补某项业务的任何损失，这一做法对小公司而言是不可行的。

165 conquer /ˈkɒŋkə(r)/ v. 战胜，征服

- 用 conquer fear 战胜恐惧
- 例 Though the motives of these groups—to profit, convert, learn or **conquer**—have usually been selfish, the overall effect of

their actions has been to draw us all closer together. 尽管这些人的动机是自私的——赚钱、改变信仰、求知或征服,但是他们行为的总体效果却将世界联结得更紧密。

166 **consideration** /kənˌsɪdəˈreɪʃn/ n. 考虑;考虑因素

- 用 under consideration 在考虑之中
- 例 There should be careful **consideration** of future economic development. 应该对未来经济发展予以仔细的考虑。

167 **consist** /kənˈsɪst/ vi. 由……组成;存在于,在于

- 用 A consist of B A 由 B 组成
- 例 The car industry **consists** of firms that are car manufacturers. 汽车工业由汽车制造商组成。

168 **consolidate** /kənˈsɒlɪdeɪt/ v. 巩固;合并

- 用 consolidated one's position 巩固某人的地位
- 例 When growth is slow companies often merge and **consolidate**, rather than make risky investments. 当增长缓慢时,公司通常会采取合并的方式,而非风险投资。

169 **contain** /kənˈteɪn/ v. 遏制,控制;容纳

- 近 accommodate, admit
- 用 contain an epidemic 控制传染病
- 例 The ban failed to **contain** inflation, which was among the world's highest throughout President Kirchner's term of office. 这一禁令未能遏制通货膨胀,在基什内尔总统的任期内,阿根廷的通货膨胀率是全球最高的。

170 **contract** /kənˈtrækt/ v. 缩减;定约;染病
/ˈkɒntrækt/ n. 合同

- 用 contract a marriage 订婚
- 例 The long-run supply of rental houses will **contract**. 房屋出租的长期供应将会缩减。

171 **contrast** /ˈkɒntrɑːst/ *n.* 对比；明显不同的人或事
/kənˈtrɑːst/ *v.* 对照；与……形成对比

- ⊕ contrast A with B 将 A 和 B 进行对比
- 例 Developing economies are often keen to encourage industrial development in rural areas. Developed economies, by **contrast**, often prevent industrial development in rural areas. 发展中国家的经济往往热衷于鼓励农村地区的工业发展。相比之下，发达国家的经济往往阻碍农村地区的工业发展。

172 **conventional** /kənˈvenʃənl/ *adj.* 传统的；常见的；惯例的

- ⊕ conventional method 常规方法
- 例 Consumers make irrational decisions, against what might have been predicted by **conventional** economic theory. 消费者会做出非理性的决定，这与传统经济理论的预测相悖。

173 **convex** /ˈkɒnveks/ *adj.* 凸出的

- ⊕ a convex mirror 凸面镜
- 例 Why indifference curves are usually drawn **convex** to the origin? 为什么无差异曲线通常是向原点凸出的？

174 **cooperative** /kəʊˈɒpərətɪv/ *adj.* 合作的；乐于合作的；合作社的

- ⊕ cooperative relationship 合作关系
- 例 What is most likely to result in non-**cooperative** behaviour between producers in an oligopoly market? 在寡头垄断市场中，生产者之间最可能出现的不合作行为是什么？

175 **copyright** /ˈkɒpiraɪt/ *n.* 版权，著作权

- ⊕ copyright law 著作权法
- 例 The authors and publishers acknowledge the following sources of **copyright** material. 作者和出版商承认以下版权资料的来源。

第一部分　通用词汇 A to Z | 35

176 **correct** /kəˈrekt/ v. 纠正；校准
adj. 精准的；得体的

- 🌐 correct errors 改正错误
- 📝 Monetary and supply side policies may **correct** a balance of payments disequilibrium. 货币政策和供应方政策可能会纠正收支不平衡问题。

177 **correspond** /ˌkɒrəˈspɒnd/ vi. 符合，一致

- 📘 coincide (v.)
- 🌐 correspond with sth. 与某物一致
- 📝 Which total revenue curve **corresponds** to this firm's marginal revenue curve? 哪条总收入曲线对应公司的边际收入曲线？

178 **cosmetic** /kɒzˈmetɪk/ adj. 美容的；化妆用的
n. 化妆品；装饰品

- 🌐 cosmetic products 化妆品
- 📝 Purchases of **cosmetic** items, such as skincare products and fragrances, increased in the recession. 在经济萧条期间，护肤品和香水等化妆品的购买量有所增加。

179 **counselling** /ˈkaʊnsəlɪŋ/ n. 辅导；建议

- 🌐 counselling service 咨询服务
- 📝 Communities will decide how and when their members will be offered HIV testing and **counselling**. 社区将决定如何及何时向其成员提供艾滋病毒检测和咨询。

180 **counter** /ˈkaʊntə(r)/ vt. 抵消；对抗
adj. 相反的
adv. 反方向地

- 📘 adverse (adj.)
- 🌐 counter late payments of debts 对付债务逾期
- 📝 Which government policies **countered** the effects of income inequality? 哪些政府政策抵消了收入不平等的影响？

181 **counteract** /ˌkaʊntərˈækt/ *vt.* 抵消；中和

- 同 offset, counter
- 用 counteract the effect 抵消作用
- 例 The European Investment Bank could have considered investments that would **counteract** the effects of budget cuts and tax increases. 欧洲投资银行本可以考虑进行一些投资，以抵消预算削减和增税的影响。

182 **counterfeit** /ˈkaʊntəfɪt/ *vt.* 伪造，仿造；造假
  adj. 假的，伪造的

- 同 artificial (*adj.*)
- 用 counterfeit money 假币
- 例 The notes become harder to **counterfeit**. 纸币越来越难伪造。

183 **crash** /kræʃ/ *n.* 暴跌，崩溃；（交通工具）坠毁

- 同 collapse
- 用 air crash 飞机失事
- 例 Economists warned that the falls in share prices could indicate a downturn for economies with a possible collapse of banks, as happened in the financial **crash** of 2008. 经济学家警告说，股价下跌可能意味着经济下滑，银行可能会倒闭，就像2008年的金融危机一样。

184 **creditor** /ˈkredɪtə(r)/ *n.* 债权人

- 用 ordinary creditor 普通债权人
- 例 A country's foreign debt refers to its level of external debt, meaning the total amount of debt incurred by borrowing from foreign **creditors**. 一国的外债指的是该国的外债水平，即该国向外国债权人借款所产生的债务总额。

185 **credit** /ˈkredɪt/ *n.* 贷款；信用；学分
  vt. 相信，信任；存入金额

- 用 credit card 信用卡
- 例 Poor people do not have access to **credit**. 穷人无法获得贷款。

186 **criticism** /ˈkrɪtɪsɪzəm/ n. 批评

- 用 criticism and praise 批评和赞扬
- 例 The only **criticism** of demand theory is that the consumer is not rational. 对需求理论的唯一批评是消费者不理性。

187 **curb** /kɜːb/ vt. 控制；勒住
n. 抑制物；路缘

- 同 contain
- 用 curb inflation 抑制通货膨胀
- 例 In 1928, FED officials were anxious to **curb** the stock market boom. 1928 年，美联储官员急于抑制股市繁荣。

D

188 **dampen** /ˈdæmpən/ vt. 抑制；减弱；使潮湿

- 同 contain
- 用 dampen one's enthusiasm 减弱某人的热情
- 例 When will taxes be most effective in **dampening** cyclical changes in national output? 什么时候税收能最有效地抑制国民产出的周期性变化？

189 **debit** /ˈdebɪt/ n. 借记，借方
v. 借记，取款

- 用 debit entry 借方分录
- 例 New customers will be able to get their account, chequebook, **debit** and credit cards within 15 minutes. 新客户能在 15 分钟内拿到自己的账户、支票簿、借记卡和信用卡。

190 **deficient** /dɪˈfɪʃnt/ adj. 不足的，有缺陷的

- 用 be deficient in sth. 缺少……
- 例 As an economy with **deficient** demand, China is not a major net contributor to growth outside its borders. 作为一个需求不足的经济体，中国算不上境外经济增长的主要净援助国。

191 **deflator** /dɪˈfleɪtə/ n. 紧缩指数；平减物价指数

- 用 price deflator 平减物价指数
- 例 The GDP **deflator** reflects changes in average prices for the economy as a whole. GDP 平减指数反映了整体经济平均价格的变化。

192 **deforestation** /ˌdiːˌfɔːrɪˈsteɪʃn/ *n.* 毁林，采伐森林

- 用 excess deforestation 过度采伐
- 例 We enjoy the comfort and beauty of our furniture, yet we never bother to think about the serious soil erosion caused by **deforestation**. 我们享受家具的美丽与舒适，但我们从来就不愿去思考过度砍伐带来的严重的土壤侵蚀问题。

193 **delay** /dɪˈleɪ/ *v.* 延期；（使）耽搁
n. 延误；延迟的时间

- 用 without delay 立即
- 例 Foreign companies were **delaying** major investments in Poland because of the uncertainties in the economic climate. 由于经济环境的不确定性，外国公司纷纷推迟在波兰的重大投资。

194 **deliver** /dɪˈlɪvə(r)/ *v.* 分发；传达；交付；发表

- 用 deliver a speech 发表演讲
- 例 Leaflets have been **delivered** to every household. 传单已分发到每家每户。

195 **demographic** /ˌdeməˈɡræfɪk/ *adj.* 人口结构的，人口统计的

- 用 demographic data 人口数据
- 例 In 2014 emerging markets were suffering large capital outflows, partly caused by the stronger US dollar and partly because of **demographic** factors. 2014 年，新兴市场遭遇大规模资本外流，部分是因为美元走强，部分是因为人口因素。

196 **demolish** /dɪˈmɒlɪʃ/ *vt.* 拆除；破坏

- 用 demolish walls 拆墙
- 例 Many homes would have to be **demolished** but the airport said they would pay the owners 25% above the property's market value. 许多房屋将被拆除，但机场方面表示，他们将向业主支付比房产市值高出 25% 的费用作为赔偿。

197 demonstrate /ˈdemənstreɪt/ v. 证明；展示；论证

- 用 demonstrate sth. to sb. 向某人证明某事
- 例 What is **demonstrated** in these values? 这些价值证明了什么？

198 demotivated /ˌdiːˈməʊtɪveɪtɪd/ adj. 消极的，失去动力的

- 用 a demotivated person 一个消极的人
- 例 The workforce of the new airline lacks morale and is **demotivated**. 这家新航空公司的员工缺乏士气，消极怠工。

199 denomination /dɪˌnɒmɪˈneɪʃn/ n. 面额，面值

- 用 denomination value 票面价值
- 例 The notes are issued in smaller **denominations**. 这些纸币是以更小的面值发行的。

200 denote /dɪˈnəʊt/ vt. 表示；表明，意为

- mean
- 用 denote time 表示时间
- 例 The plus sign denotes credits and the minus sign **denotes** debits. 加号表示贷方，减号表示借方。

201 dense /dens/ adj. 稠密的；浓厚的

- 用 dense population 稠密的人口
- 例 The development would destroy **dense** forests. 开发会破坏茂密的森林。

202 dentistry /ˈdentɪstri/ n. 牙科学；牙医业

- 用 dentistry diagnosis 牙科诊断
- 例 Gold is demanded for its use in industrial production, in **dentistry**, as jewellery and as a store of value. 黄金被用于工业生产、牙科材料、珠宝原料和保值手段。

203 **depict** /dɪˈpɪkt/ v. 描绘，描画；描述

- 🌐 depict sb./sth. as sb./sth. 将某人（事）描绘成某人（事）
- 📖 Which diagram **depicts** the shape of the firm's corresponding total revenue (TR) curve? 哪个图描述了企业总收益曲线的形态？

204 **deplete** /dɪˈpliːt/ vt. 耗尽，用尽；使衰竭

- 🌐 deplete resources 耗尽资源
- 📖 In Africa, industrial methods of agriculture **deplete** the soil, pollute water tables and fail to benefit small-scale farmers. 在非洲，工业化的农业手段耗尽了土壤，污染了地下水，不能让小农受益。

205 **depositor** /dɪˈpɒzɪtə(r)/ n. 存款人

- 🌐 small depositor 小额存户
- 📖 When a **depositor** cashes a check, he reduces the amount of deposits and increases the amount of currency held by the public. 一旦储户兑现支票，其存款数额就会减少，公众所持有的货币量就会增加。

206 **depressed** /dɪˈprest/ adj. 萧条的；沮丧的

- 🌐 depressed economy 经济萧条
- 📖 What would be likely to reduce the mobility of labour between a **depressed** and a prosperous region of a country? 什么因素会减少一个国家的劳动力在萧条地区和繁荣地区之间的流动？

207 **deregulate** /ˌdiːˈreɡjuleɪt/ vt. 解除对……的管制

- 🌐 deregulate interest rates 推进利率市场化
- 📖 The wisest response to high unemployment is to **deregulate** labour markets. 应对高失业率最明智的措施是放松对劳动力市场的监管。

208 **designate** /ˈdezɪgneɪt/ adj. 指定的
vt. 指定

- 回 assigned (adj.)
- 用 designate the floor as a no-smoking area 指定该楼层为无烟区
- 例 The government introduces a congestion charge on motorists who drive their vehicles within a **designate** urban zone. 政府对在指定城区内驾驶车辆的司机征收拥堵费。

209 **descend** /dɪˈsend/ v. 下降

- 用 descend from 由……传下来；起源于
- 例 Which combination in the diagram could represent the consumer's order of preference in **descending** order? 图中哪个组合由高到低表示了消费者的偏好？

210 **destination** /ˌdestɪˈneɪʃn/ n. 目的地，终点

- 用 tourist destination 旅游目的地
- 例 The proposal would allow the airport to be connected to more emerging markets and enable 40 new **destinations** to be served directly. 该提议将允许机场与更多的新兴市场连接，并新增 40 个直飞目的地。

211 **destruction** /dɪˈstrʌkʃn/ n. 破坏，毁灭

- 用 weapons of destruction 毁灭性武器
- 例 In some regions of the world, land appropriate for agriculture is shrinking due to environmental **destruction**. 在世界上一些地区，由于环境破坏，农业用地越来越少。

212 **detached** /dɪˈtætʃt/ adj. 分离的，脱节的；不带感情的

- 用 be detached from 脱离……
- 例 Staff feel **detached** from the overall undertaking. 员工们感觉与整个工作脱节。

213 **detergent** /dɪˈtɜːdʒənt/ *n.* 清洁剂
adj. 去污的

- 用 laundry detergent 洗衣粉
- 例 In 2011, two soap and **detergent** firms, Unilever and Procter & Gamble, were fined a total of €315 for fixing the price of washing powder in eight European countries. 2011 年，联合利华和宝洁这两家肥皂和清洁剂公司因在 8 个欧洲国家操纵洗衣粉价格，被处以总计 315 欧元的罚款。

214 **deter** /dɪˈtɜː(r)/ *vt.* 制止，阻止

- 近 block
- 用 deter sb. from doing sth. 阻止某人做某事
- 例 Mexico also suffered from deep problems of its own, for example, a poor education system and a rise in violent crime, **deterring** tourists and investors. 墨西哥也面临着自身的深层次问题，例如，糟糕的教育体系和暴力犯罪的增加，阻碍了游客和投资者。

215 **devastating** /ˈdevəsteɪtɪŋ/ *adj.* 毁灭性的

- 用 devastating illness 重病
- 例 There were thousands of job losses at three major steel factories which was **devastating** news for UK steel workers and the regional economies. 三大钢铁厂数千人失业，这对于英国所有钢铁工人和地区经济而言是一个毁灭性的消息。

216 **diabetes** /ˌdaɪəˈbiːtiːz/ *n.* 糖尿病

- 用 elderly diabetes 老年糖尿病
- 例 Life expectancy has steadily increased due to improved healthcare, decreased deaths from heart disease, cancer, **diabetes** and chronic respiratory disease. 由于医疗护理的改善，因心脏病、癌症、糖尿病和慢性呼吸道疾病死亡的人数越来越少，预期寿命稳步提高。

217 **differentiate** /ˌdɪfəˈrenʃieɪt/ v. 区分，区别

- 🌐 differentiate varieties of plants 区分不同植物
- 🌐 What **differentiates** the *Millennium Declaration* from statements of earlier years is that it establishes specific goals known as the Millennium Development goals. 《千年宣言》与前几年声明的不同之处在于，它确立了被称为千年发展目标的具体目标。

218 **disadvantageous** /ˌdɪsædvənˈteɪdʒəs/ adj. 不利的；不便的

- 🔄 adverse
- 🌐 disadvantageous status 弱势地位
- 🌐 Due to historical and practical reasons, some developing countries are at a **disadvantageous** position in competition. 由于历史原因和现实因素，一些发展中国家在竞争当中处于相对不利的地位。

219 **disaster** /dɪˈzɑːstə(r)/ n. 灾难，灾祸；不幸

- 🌐 natural disaster 自然灾害
- 🌐 Humanitarian aid involves aid extended in regions where there are emergencies caused by natural **disasters** such as floods and earthquakes. 人道主义援助包括向发生水灾、地震等自然灾害的地区提供援助。

220 **disastrous** /dɪˈzɑːstrəs/ adj. 灾难性的；损失惨重的

- 🌐 disastrous accident 严重事故
- 🌐 Rice and wheat prices will double again in the next 20 years with **disastrous** consequences for the poor. 未来20年，大米和小麦的价格将再次翻倍，给穷人带来灾难性的后果。

221 **discard** /dɪˈskɑːd/ v. 丢弃；抛弃
n. 被抛弃的人或物；不要的牌

- 同 abandon (v.)
- 用 discard old beliefs 抛弃旧观念
- 例 10% of the data was **discarded** as unreliable. 10% 的数据因为不可靠而被丢弃。

222 **discharge** /dɪsˈtʃɑːdʒ/ v. 释放；排出；准许（某人）离开

- 用 discharge sb. from sth. 允许某人离开
- 例 A food processing firm **discharges** waste water into the lake next to its factory. 一家食品加工公司将废水排放到工厂旁边的湖里。

223 **discipline** /ˈdɪsəplɪn/ n. 约束，纪律，惩罚

- 用 classroom discipline 课堂纪律
- 例 The stock market can exert effective **discipline** on the industry. 股票市场可以对这个行业加以有效的约束。

224 **discredit** /dɪsˈkredɪt/ vt. 不信；使……丢脸

- 同 disbelieve
- 用 a discredit policy 失去信誉的政策
- 例 Strong government intervention in the market has been mostly **discredited** as a strategy for economic growth and development. 作为经济增长和发展的一种战略，政府对市场强有力的干预基本上已被证明是不可信的。

225 **discriminate** /dɪˈskrɪmɪneɪt/ v. 歧视，区别

- 用 discriminate against sb. 歧视，排斥某人
- 例 A country's trade policy cannot **discriminate** between its trading partners. 一个国家的贸易政策不能区别对待其贸易伙伴。

226 **disguise** /dɪsˈɡaɪz/ *vt.* 掩饰；假装；隐瞒

- 用 in the disguise of 假扮成……；以……为借口
- 例 Emerging economies had been helped by cheap money from the advanced countries but this **disguised** the need of fundamental reforms in some countries. 新兴经济体曾得到发达国家廉价资金的帮助，但这掩盖了一些国家进行根本性改革的必要性。

227 **dishonest** /dɪsˈɒnɪst/ *adj.* 不诚实的

- 反 honest (*adj.*) 诚实的
- 用 dishonest traders 奸商
- 例 Some banks have been accused of having a control over the market that enabled them to get away with poor service and **dishonest** claims about free banking. 一些银行被指控操纵市场，使它们得以在服务质量差的情况下逃脱惩罚，并在自由银行业的问题上做出不诚实的声明。

228 **disinflation** /ˌdɪsɪnˈfleɪʃ(ə)n/ *n.* 反通货膨胀，通货紧缩

- 反 inflation *n.* 通货膨胀
- 用 disinflation situation 通缩状况
- 例 To some extent, this helps contain global **disinflation**. 在某种程度上来说，这有助于抑制全球经济通货紧缩。

229 **dismantle** /dɪsˈmæntl/ *vt.* 拆除；取消；解散

- 同 demolish
- 用 dismantle the engine 拆开机器
- 例 Japan has already provided around 20 billion yen to help **dismantle** more than 70 retired nuclear submarines. 日本已经提供了约 200 亿日元，帮助拆除 70 多艘已退役的潜水艇。

230 **dismiss** /dɪsˈmɪs/ vt. 解雇；解散；不予考虑

- 用 dismiss sb. from 解雇某人
- 例 It will increase the losses that workers will incur if they are **dismissed** for not working hard enough. 如果工人因工作不够努力而被解雇，将会增加损失。

231 **disorder** /dɪsˈɔːdə(r)/ n. 混乱；骚乱

- 用 in disorder 状态混乱
- 例 The government hopes the policy will reduce public **disorder** offences and cut the cost of alcohol-related ill health. 政府希望这项政策能减少公共秩序混乱的犯罪行为，并降低与酒精有关的健康问题的成本。

232 **dispense** /dɪˈspens/ vt. 分配，分发 vi. 特许；豁免

- 同 distribute (vt.)
- 用 dispense sth. to sb. 给某人分发某物
- 例 Some hospitals have turned to robotic pharmacies to help **dispense** medication. 一些医院已经开始采用机器人来分发药物。

233 **display** /dɪˈspleɪ/ vt. 显示；陈列 n. 展览；展示

- 同 demonstrate (vt.)
- 用 on display 展览
- 例 **Display** information in a diagrammatic or logical form. 以图表或逻辑形式显示信息。

234 **dispute** /dɪˈspjuːt/ n. 辩论；意见不同 vt. 对……提出质疑；争执

- 同 challenge (vt.)
- 用 dispute about sth. 有关某事（物）的争辩
- 例 It handles trade **disputes**. 它处理贸易争端。

235 **disruption** /dɪsˈrʌpʃn/ *n.* 崩溃；分裂，瓦解

- 同 crash, collapse
- 用 cause serious disruptions 造成严重的混乱
- 例 A war or violent conflict can result in destruction of physical capital and **disruption** of the economy. 战争或暴力冲突会导致物质资本毁灭和经济崩溃。

236 **distinctive** /dɪˈstɪŋktɪv/ *adj.* 独特的，有特色的；与众不同的

- 用 distinctive capabilities 特殊能力
- 例 The other **distinctive** feature of this screen is the rounded rectangles. 此屏幕的另一个独特之处是它的圆角矩形。

237 **distort** /dɪˈstɔːt/ *vt.* 歪曲，曲解；扭曲

- 同 contort
- 用 distort the voice 声音失真
- 例 Newspapers are often guilty of **distorting** the truth. 报纸新闻经常犯歪曲事实的错误。

238 **distress** /dɪˈstres/ *n.* 危难，不幸；贫困

- 同 disaster
- 用 finance distress 财务危机
- 例 The auto industry and retailing remain in **distress**. 汽车业和零售业继续处于困境。

239 **distribute** /dɪˈstrɪbjuːt/ *vt.* 散布；分发；配给

- 同 dispense
- 用 distribute sth. to sb. 把某物分给某人
- 例 High rates of unemployment, particularly when they are unequally **distributed**, can lead to serious social problems. 高失业率，特别是当失业率分布不均时，会引发严重的社会问题。

240 **disturbance** /dɪˈstɜːbəns/ *n.* 干扰；骚乱；障碍

- 同 disorder
- 搭 a disturbance of the public peace 扰乱治安
- 例 A government school is built by private builders in a residential neighbourhood. The builders ignore the effects of noise and **disturbance**. 开发商将学校建在住宅区内，却忽视了噪音和干扰会带来的影响。

241 **diversify** /daɪˈvɜːsɪfaɪ/ *v.* 使多样化；多元化；从事多种经营

- 搭 diversify our products 使我们的产品多样化
- 例 A number of developing economies have adopted import substitution policies and sought to **diversify** their economies. 许多发展中国家采取了进口替代政策，并设法使其经济多样化。

242 **divert** /daɪˈvɜːt/ *v.* 转移；使改道；使分心

- 搭 divert attention from... 将注意力从……转移
- 例 Whether **diverting** expenditure to the car industry might conflict with other macroeconomic government objectives? 将支出转移到汽车行业是否会与政府的其他宏观经济目标相冲突？

243 **divisibility** /dɪˌvɪzəˈbɪləti/ *n.* 可分性

- 同 separability
- 搭 a divisibility problem 可分性问题
- 例 **Divisibility** is a key property of money. 可分性是货币的一个重要特性。

244 **doctrine** /ˈdɒktrɪn/ *n.* 主义；学说；信条

- 搭 the Monroe Doctrine 门罗主义
- 例 The United States President stated that the 'America First' **doctrine** means increased protectionism. 美国总统表示，"美国优先"主义意味着保护主义加剧。

245 **dominate** /ˈdɒmɪneɪt/ v. 控制，支配；占优势

- 用 dominate the market 主导市场，控制市场
- 例 In some countries supermarkets **dominate** food shopping. 在一些国家，超市主宰了食品购买。

246 **domination** /ˌdɒmɪˈneɪʃn/ n. 控制；支配

- 用 market domination 市场主导
- 例 England's **domination** over Wales, Scotland and Ireland introduced the English language to these regions, but with the devastating consequence of the downfall of the local languages. 英格兰对威尔士、苏格兰及爱尔兰的统治将英语引入了这些地区，却令当地语言衰落，造成了毁灭性的后果。

247 **downturn** /ˈdaʊntɜːn/ n. 衰退

- 用 the continuing economic downturn 经济持续低迷
- 例 Due to a cyclical **downturn**, a government is experiencing a budget deficit. 由于周期性的衰退，政府正面临预算赤字。

248 **dramatic** /drəˈmætɪk/ adj. 急剧的，激烈的；引人注目的

- 同 compelling
- 用 a dramatic increase 急剧增加
- 例 In February 2016 there were **dramatic** changes in both financial and commodity markets across the world. 2016 年 2 月，全球金融和商品市场都发生了巨变。

249 **draw** /drɔː/ v. 推断出结论；画画；拉

- 用 draw up 草拟
- 例 Which conclusion may be **drawn** from the graphs? 这些图表可以得出怎样的结论？

250 **drought** /draʊt/ *n.* 干旱

- 用 drought region 干旱地区
- 例 The country experienced two years of severe **drought**. 这个国家经历了两年严重的旱灾。

251 **Dubai** /ˈdjuːbaɪ/ *n.* 迪拜

- 例 These include markets like New Delhi, **Dubai** and Hong Kong, which continue to grow at soaring rates. 包括新德里、迪拜、中国香港等的市场在以飞快的速度增长。

252 **duplication** /ˌdjuːplɪˈkeɪʃn/ *n.* 重复；复制

- 用 duplication of effort 重复劳动
- 例 It avoids the wasteful **duplication** of resources. 这避免了资源的重复浪费。

253 **dweller** /ˈdwelər/ *n.* 居民，居住者

- 用 town dweller 城镇居民
- 例 The life of a modern city **dweller**, surrounded by strangers, is an evolutionary novelty. 现代城市居民的生活总是被陌生人围绕，这是进化过程中出现的新事物。

254 **dynamism** /ˈdaɪnəmɪzəm/ *n.* 活力

- 同 vitality
- 用 a zone of dynamism 充满活力的地区
- 例 New businesses have **dynamism** and vigour. 新企业充满活力与生机。

E

255 **electrify** /ɪˈlektrɪfaɪ/ *vt.* 使电气化；使激动

- 用 electrify the audience 使观众兴奋不已
- 例 In 2015, a company **electrified** the main railway line between two cities in order to decrease the journey time. 2015 年，一家公司为了缩短旅程时间，对两座城市之间的主要铁路线进行了电气化改造。

256 **embargo** /ɪmˈbɑːɡəʊ/ *n.* 禁止，贸易禁运
　　　　　　　　　　　　vt. 禁止或限制贸易

- 用 embargo on sth. 禁运某物
- 例 It is an **embargo** and will worsen Russia's balance of trade. 这是一项禁运令，将恶化俄罗斯的贸易差额。

257 **embark** /ɪmˈbɑːk/ *v.* 着手，从事

- 用 embark on/upon 着手……，开始……
- 例 Which trade-off do governments face when they **embark** upon the privatisation of a state monopoly? 当政府着手对国有垄断企业进行私有化时，他们面临着怎样的取舍？

258 **embed** /ɪmˈbed/ *v.* 使嵌入，使插入，植入

- 用 embed A in B 把 A 植入 B
- 例 You could **embed** one type of document in another. 你可以在一个类型的文件中嵌入另一个。

259 **embody** /ɪmˈbɒdi/ *vt.* 体现，表现

- 用 be embodied in sth. 体现在某物中
- 例 Improved capital goods are capital goods that **embody** a new technology. 改良生产资料是体现新技术的生产资料。

260 **emit** /ɪˈmɪt/ vt. 发出；发射；表达

- 搭 emit heat 发热
- 例 No pollution can be **emitted** without a permit. 未经许可，不能排放任何污染物。

261 **empirical** /ɪmˈpɪrɪkl/ adj. 实证的，经验主义的，根据经验的

- 搭 empirical results 经验性结论
- 例 The **empirical** evidence suggests that tax increases or decreases do not have a very significant effect on labour supplied. 经验证明，增税或减税对劳动力供应没有显著影响。

262 **employability** /ɪmˌplɔɪəˈbɪləti/ n. 就业能力，受聘价值

- 搭 improve one's employability 提升就业能力
- 例 No matter what your industry is, whether it's IT, entertainment or engineering, your **employability** can be enhanced by knowledge of a second language. 不论你从事何种行业，IT、娱乐或是工程，掌握一门第二外语能够提升你的就业能力。

263 **enclosed** /ɪnˈkləʊzd/ adj. 封闭的；与外界隔绝的

- 搭 enclosed sea 内海
- 例 European countries are increasingly banning smoking in **enclosed** public areas and workplaces. 欧洲国家加大了禁止在封闭的公共场合及工作场所吸烟的监管力度。

264 **endorse** /ɪnˈdɔːs/ vt. 认可，赞同；签署

- 近 approve (v.)
- 搭 endorse a ban on 签署……的禁令
- 例 This was **endorsed** by a conference in Mali in 2015. 2015 年在马里举行的一次会议中签署了它。

265 **endowment** /ɪnˈdaʊmənt/ *n.* 天资，禀赋；捐资

- 用 natural endowments 自然天赋
- 例 Countries differ vastly with respect to their natural resource **endowments**. 各国的自然资源禀赋差别很大。

266 **enormous** /ɪˈnɔːməs/ *adj.* 庞大的，巨大的

- 用 enormous amount of immigrants 大量移民
- 例 The scale of the multinational corporations are **enormous** in size. 大型跨国公司在规模上是庞大的。

267 **ensure** /ɪnˈʃʊə(r)/ *vt.* 确保，保证

- 用 ensure one's success 确保某人的成功
- 例 The Kenyan government reintroduced price controls to **ensure** that commodities were sold to the citizens at reasonable prices. 肯尼亚政府重新实施价格管制，以确保商品以合理价格出售给公民。

268 **enthusiast** /ɪnˈθjuːziæst/ *n.* 狂热分子，爱好者

- 用 a football enthusiast 橄榄球爱好者
- 例 A hacker is a computer expert or **enthusiast**. 黑客是计算机专家或计算机狂热者。

269 **entrepreneurship** /ˌɒntrəprəˈnɜːʃɪp/ *n.* 企业家精神

- 用 social entrepreneurship 社会企业家精神
- 例 Poland's growth has been based on skilled labour and **entrepreneurship**, not on natural resources. 波兰的经济增长是基于熟练的劳动力和企业家精神，而非自然资源。

270 **environmental** /ɪnˌvaɪrənˈmentl/ *adj.* 环境的

- 用 environmental conservation 环境保护
- 例 There is a reduction in **environmental** pollution. 环境污染有所减少。

271 equate /ɪˈkweɪt/ v. 使同等；视为同等

- 搭 equate A with B 把 A 和 B 同等看待
- 例 If we **equate** satisfying the customer with quality, then process can potentially have a negative effect on quality. 如果我们将满足顾客的需求与质量同等看待，那么过程就会对质量产生潜在的负面影响。

272 equitable /ˈekwɪtəbl/ adj. 公平的，公正的

- 搭 equitable solution 公平的解决
- 例 When will a society have achieved an **equitable** distribution of income? 一个社会何时才能实现收入的公平分配？

273 eradication /ɪˌrædɪˈkeɪʃn/ n. 根除；消灭

- 搭 the eradication of a disease 根除疾病
- 例 We will set our sights on the **eradication** of extreme poverty in our time. 我们将力争在当下这个时代根除极端贫困的现象。

274 erosion /ɪˈrəʊʒn/ n. 侵蚀，腐蚀

- 搭 surface erosion 地表侵蚀
- 例 Agriculture produces more greenhouse gases than all methods of transport put together, and contributes to a host of other problems, like soil **erosion**. 农业产生的温室气体比所有交通方式加起来还要多，并且还进一步造成了许多其他问题，例如土壤侵蚀。

275 establishment /ɪˈstæblɪʃmənt/ n. 成立，确立，制定

- 搭 organisational establishment 组织机构建立
- 例 The **establishment** of a new firm increases the general level of wage rates in the area. 一家新公司的成立提升了这个地区的平均工资水平。

276 **estimation** /ˌestɪ'meɪʃn/ n. 估计，评估；评估的结果

- 用 cost estimation 成本估算
- 例 Each team can apply whatever **estimation** method most appropriate to their part of the work. 每个团队都可以采用最适合他们那部分工作的评估手段。

277 **ethical** /'eθɪkl/ adj. 道德的，伦理的

- 用 ethical problems 道德问题
- 例 The business has fallen behind competitors and needs to improve its **ethical** standards. 该公司已经落后于其竞争对手，需要提高道德标准。

278 **exaggerated** /ɪɡ'zædʒəreɪtɪd/ adj. 夸张的，言过其实的

- 用 an exaggerated laugh 夸张的笑声
- 例 The power of Finance Ministers to make a difference to an economy is **exaggerated**. 财政部长的职权对于经济的影响力被夸大了。

279 **exception** /ɪk'sepʃn/ n. 例外

- 用 make an exception 破例
- 例 Discuss why there might be **exceptions** to this normal response. 讨论一下为什么这个正常的反应可能会有例外。

280 **exclude** /ɪk'skluːd/ vt. 排除，排斥

- 用 exclude A from B 把 A 从 B 中排除出去
- 例 Official financing is **excluded** from the financial account. 官方资金不包括在财务账户内。

281 **exclusive** /ɪk'skluːsɪv/ adj. 独有的；排外的

- 用 be exclusive of sb. 不包括某人
- 例 Professional sports leagues create a local monopoly by signing long-term contracts with the best players and securing

exclusive use of sports stadiums. 职业体育联盟通过与最优秀的运动员签订长期合同，并确保体育场馆的独家使用权，因而形成了垄断。

282 **exert** /ɪɡˈzɜːt/ *vt.* 施加影响；竭力，努力

- 用 exert oneself 努力，尽力
- 例 The stock market can **exert** effective discipline on the industry. 股票市场可以对这个行业施加有效的约束。

283 **exhibition** /ˌeksɪˈbɪʃn/ *n.* 展览，展出；表演，显示

- 同 display
- 用 on exhibition 展出中
- 例 A study found that demand for tickets for **exhibitions** at a major art gallery had unitary price elasticity. 一项研究发现，大型画展的门票需求具有单一的价格弹性。

284 **existent** /ɪɡˈzɪstənt/ *adj.* 现存的，存在的
　　　　　　　　　　　　　　　　　n. 存在的事物

- 反 non-existent *adj.* 不存在的
- 用 an existent problem 现存问题
- 例 In tax havens, which include Dubai, Hong Kong, Singapore and Switzerland, taxes are either non-**existent** or levied at a low rate. 在迪拜、中国香港、新加坡和瑞士等避税天堂，税收要么不存在，要么税率很低。

285 **exotic** /ɪɡˈzɒtɪk/ *adj.* 异国的，异域风情的；外来的

- 用 exotic plant 外来植物
- 例 Postcards brought the world a little closer, at a time before air travel was possible to the **exotic** East. 当飞机还不能将你送达到充满异域风情的东方世界时，是明信片把世界连接得更紧密些的。

286 **expense** /ɪkˈspens/ *n.* 消费；价钱
v. 付钱，承担费用

- 用 at the expense of 以……为代价
- 例 This money can provide food, clothing, housing, and pay for educational **expenses** or for investment in small enterprises. 这笔钱可用于购买食物、衣服、支付房租、教育经费或投资于小型企业。

287 **expire** /ɪkˈspaɪə(r)/ *vi.* 期满；终止；逝世

- 同 cease (*v.*), run out
- 用 an expired passport 过期的护照
- 例 Copyrights on the product have **expired**. 产品的版权已经过期。

288 **exploration** /ˌekspləˈreɪʃn/ *n.* 探测，探究

- 用 gas exploration 天然气勘探
- 例 It is an oil **exploration** company. 这是一家石油勘探公司。

289 **explosive** /ɪkˈspləʊsɪv/ *adj.* 爆发性的；爆炸性的

- 用 an explosive device 爆炸装置
- 例 In the last two to three decades their growth has been **explosive**. 在过去的二三十年里，它们的增长是爆发式的。

290 **expose** /ɪkˈspəʊz/ *vt.* 使受影响；使曝光；揭发

- 用 expose sth. to sb. 向某人揭发/透露某事
- 例 A firm **exposed** to market forces is more likely to be efficient. 受市场力量影响的企业的效率有可能更高。

291 **extend** /ɪkˈstend/ *vt.* 给予；提供 *vi.* 延长

- 用 extend a warm welcome to visitors 向来访者表示热烈欢迎
- 例 The US government is determined to **extend** economic opportunity for US workers, farmers and businesses. 美国政府决心为美国工人、农民和企业提供更多的经济机会。

F

扫一扫
听本节音频

292 **facilitate** /fə'sɪlɪteɪt/ *vt.* 促进；帮助

- 回 boost
- 用 facilitate economic growth 促进经济增长
- 例 What is likely to **facilitate** the growth of large firms in an economy? 在一个经济体中，什么可以促进大公司的增长？

293 **facility** /fə'sɪləti/ *n.* 设备；手段；场所；才能

- 回 endowment
- 用 a great facility for languages 很强的语言天赋
- 例 The hotel has conference **facilities** for rent. 这家酒店有会议设施出租。

294 **fairness** /'feənəs/ *n.* 公平，公正

- 回 equitable (*adj.*)
- 用 judicial fairness 司法公正
- 例 Consumer Commission is required to monitor the supermarkets to ensure **fairness**. 消费者委员会会被要求监督超市以确保公平。

295 **faltering** /'fɔːltərɪŋ/ *adj.* 蹒跚的；犹豫的

- 用 faltering economy 摇摇欲坠的经济
- 例 Mexico saw lower growth, partly because it was tied to a **faltering** United States economy. 墨西哥的经济增长放缓，部分原因是与日渐衰退的美国经济有关。

296 fault /fɔːlt/ n. 错误；弱点；故障 v. 发现错误

- 用 one's fault for doing sth. 某人做错了某事
- 例 Many small shops have closed. How can they blame for that be the **fault** of the supermarket? 许多小商店都关门了，这怎么能怪超市呢？

297 felicity /fəˈlɪsəti/ n. 幸福，快乐

- 近 happiness
- 用 joy and felicity 快乐幸福
- 例 America is desperately trying to create a brave new world of persistent good fortune, joy without pain, **felicity** with no penalty. 美国正拼命地创造一个美丽新世界，那里财富永存、喜悦无忧、快乐无碍。

298 fetch /fetʃ/ v. 售卖；去拿来

- 用 fetch and carry for sb. 为某人打杂，跑腿
- 例 On the black market in Malaysia sugar was sold at 1.70 ringgit per kilogramme, while it **fetched** 2.90 ringgit in neighbouring Thailand. 在马来西亚的黑市上，每公斤糖的售价为1.70林吉特，而在邻国泰国，每公斤糖的售价为2.90林吉特。

299 fluctuate /ˈflʌktʃueɪt/ v. 波动；涨落；动摇

- 用 fluctuate between A and B 在A与B之间摇摆
- 例 Why prices might **fluctuate** less in an oligopoly market than in a perfectly competitive market? 为什么在寡头垄断市场中，价格波动可能比在完全竞争市场中要小？

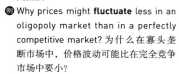

300 **forecast** /ˈfɔːkɑːst/ v. 预测，预报
n. 天气预测，预报

- 回 anticipate (v.)
- 用 weather forecast 天气预报
- 例 42.6 million people are expected to enter the labour market every year but the **forecast** is that only 40 million net new jobs will be created. 预计每年有 4,260 万人进入劳动力市场，但预测只会产生 4,000 万个新工作岗位。

301 **fragmented** /fræɡˈmentɪd/ adj. 碎片化的

- 用 a fragmented society 支离破碎的社会
- 例 **Fragmented** markets and ever more diverse tastes of consumers threaten the dominance of the old brands. 分散的市场和越来越多样化的消费者口味对老品牌的主导地位构成了威胁。

G

302 gender /ˈdʒendə(r)/ n. 性别

- 用 gender differences 性别差异
- 例 The government aims to better promote **gender** equality and empower women. 政府的目标是更好地促进性别平等，赋予妇女权力。

303 globalisation /ˌɡləʊbəlaɪˈzeɪʃn/ n. 全球化

- 用 economic globalisation 经济全球化
- 例 In an age of **globalisation**, global powers have to be economic titans. 在一个全球化的时代，世界大国还应是经济巨人。

304 gloomy /ˈɡluːmi/ adj. 黯淡的；阴沉的；令人沮丧的

- 同 bleak
- 用 a gloomy outlook 前景黯淡
- 例 The outlook was also **gloomy**, with concerns regarding the global economy and domestic economic policy. 由于对全球经济和国内经济政策的担忧，前景也不容乐观。

305 govern /ˈɡʌvn/ vt. 管理，支配；统治

- 同 dominate, regulate
- 用 govern the colony 管理殖民地
- 例 Many corporate executives seem to believe that they can lay down rules to **govern** every eventuality. 许多企业管理者似乎认为他们可以靠制定规则来管控一切。

greenhouse /ˈgriːnhaʊs/ n. 温室

- greenhouse effect 温室效应
- There have been accusations of deforestation, reduction of biodiversity, harm to wildlife and increasing emissions of **greenhouse** gases. 森林砍伐、生物多样性减少、对野生动物的危害以及温室气体排放的增加都受到了指责。

H

307 hamper /ˈhæmpə(r)/ vt. 妨碍；束缚
n. 大篮子

- 用 hamper development 妨碍发展
- 例 One feature of Indonesia's economy that has been **hampering** its economic and social development is the lack of quality and quantity of its infrastructure. 印度尼西亚经济和社会发展受到阻碍的一个原因就是其基础设施的质量和数量都不过关。

308 handmade /ˌhændˈmeɪd/ adj. 手工的

- 用 handmade crafts 手工艺品
- 例 Fine **handmade** lace is still made in Belgium, Slovenia, and elsewhere, but chiefly as souvenirs. 比利时、斯洛文尼亚以及其他地方仍在做一些精细的手工花边，但主要用作纪念品。

309 harbour /ˈhɑːbə(r)/ n. 海港
v. 怀有，心怀；包含

- 用 harbour a grudge 怀恨在心
- 例 Historically, public sector projects, such as building roads, **harbours**, airports, schools, hospitals and other infrastructure, have been financed out of the government budget. 历史上，公共部门项目资金来自政府预算，如道路、港口、机场、学校、医院和其他基础设施建设。

310 hardly /ˈhɑːdli/ adv. 表示不大可能；几乎不；刚刚

- 用 hardly surprising 并不令人惊讶
- 例 This is **hardly** surprising, since trade protection policies are usually undertaken with a view to protecting domestic

production and domestic employment. 这并不奇怪，因为贸易保护政策的目的通常是保护国内生产和就业。

311 **hardware** /ˈhɑːdweə(r)/ *n.* 硬件；五金制品

- ⊕ computer hardware 计算机硬件
- ⑩ We need to produce lots of military **hardware** to improve our defences. 我们需要生产大量的军事装备来提高我们的防御能力。

312 **harvest** /ˈhɑːvɪst/ *n.* 收获；产量
                                       v. 收割

- ⊕ good harvest 丰收
- ⑩ The **harvest** in 2011 was the smallest in 30 years, mostly due to heavy rains in the main coffee-producing regions. 2011 年的收成是 30 年来最低的，主要是咖啡主产区的暴雨所致。

313 **headline** /ˈhedlaɪn/ *n.* 大标题；内容提要

- ⊕ headline news 新闻头条
- ⑩ A newspaper **headline** stated that the Australian car industry has been affected by the strength of the Australian dollar. 一家报纸的头条新闻说，澳大利亚的汽车工业受到了澳元走强的影响。

314 **headquarters** /ˌhedˈkwɔːtəz/ *n.* 总部

- ⊕ general headquarters 陆军总司令部
- ⑩ Multinational corporations have their **headquarters** mostly in developed countries. 跨国公司的总部主要设在发达国家。

315 **heated** /ˈhiːtɪd/ *adj.* 激烈的，兴奋的；热的

- ⓘ dramatic
- ⊕ a heated debate 激烈的争论
- ⑩ If foreign direct investment forms only a small share of total private investment in developing countries, why is it the

subject of **heated** discussions? 如果外国直接投资只占发展中国家私人投资总额的一小部分，为什么它会成为激烈讨论的主题？

316 **heatwave** /ˈhiːtweɪv/ *n.* 热浪

- 🌐 bring a heatwave 带来热浪
- 📝 Droughts and **heatwaves** in 2012 reduced production in some of the world's leading cereal producers such as US, Ukraine and Australia. 2012 年的干旱和热浪导致美国、乌克兰和澳大利亚等世界主要谷物生产国减产。

317 **herd** /hɜːd/ *n.* 兽群，畜群
        v. 放牧

- 🌐 a herd of 一群
- 📝 Farmers will increase the size of their dairy **herds** to supply more milk. 农民们将增加奶牛的数量以提供更多牛奶。

318 **heroin** /ˈherəʊɪn/ *n.* 海洛因

- 🌐 heroin addiction 毒瘾
- 📝 **Heroin** use rose in New York during the 1960s. 20 世纪 60 年代，海洛因在纽约的使用量增加。

319 **highlight** /ˈhaɪlaɪt/ *vt.* 突出，强调
          n. 最精彩的部分

- 🔁 affirm, emphasise
- 🌐 the highlight in his speech 他演讲中最精彩的部分
- 📝 This **highlights** the important role that advertising and promotions play in this market structure. 这突出了广告和促销在这个市场结构中的重要作用。

320 **hinder** /ˈhɪndə(r)/ *v.* 阻碍，打扰

- 🔁 hamper, deter, block
- 🌐 hinder sb./sth. from doing sth. 阻碍……的发生
- 📝 Higher interest rates threatened to **hinder** economic growth

by raising the cost of borrowing. 高利率会提高借贷成本，从而抑制经济增长。

321 **hint** /hɪnt/ *n.* 暗示，线索
v. 暗示，示意

- 用 drop sb. a hint about sth. 给了某人一个……暗示
- 例 Any **hint** of abnormal profits being made should be a signal for the entry of new firms. 任何异常盈利的迹象都应该是新公司进入的信号。

322 **historic** /hɪˈstɒrɪk/ *adj.* 有历史意义的

- 用 historic sites 历史古迹
- 例 We can understand the reasons behind the use of these terms if we put the natural rate concept in **historic** perspective. 如果我们从历史的角度来理解自然速率的概念，我们就能理解这些术语背后的原因。

323 **homogeneity** /ˌhəʊməʊdʒəˈniːəti/ *n.* 同质

- 同 homogeneousness
- 用 cultural homogeneity 文化同质性
- 例 Any one unit of money is as good as any other, and indeed it is precisely for its **homogeneity**, divisibility, and recognisability that the market chooses gold as money in the first place. 一块钱到哪里都是一块钱，正是由于其高度的同质性、可分割性、易识别性才使市场优先选择了黄金作为货币。

324 **homogeneous** /ˌhɒməˈdʒiːniəs/ *adj.* 同质的

- 用 a homogeneous population 同类人群
- 例 The firms in an industry all produce a **homogeneous** product, but each firm is able to influence the price it charges for its own product. 行业内的公司都生产同类产品，但每个公司都能影响自己产品的价格。

325 **housemaid** /ˈhaʊsmeɪd/ *n.* 女佣，女仆

- 回 maidservant
- 用 take sb. as housemaid 把某人当作女佣
- 例 Doctors go abroad to work as nurses; teachers go to work as **housemaids**. 医生出国当护士；教师们去当女佣。

326 **housework** /ˈhaʊswɜːk/ *n.* 家务事

- 用 do housework 做家务
- 例 People move from unpaid **housework** to paid employment. 人们从无偿的家务劳动转向有偿的工作。

327 **hurricane** /ˈhʌrɪkən/ *n.* 飓风

- 回 cyclone
- 用 hurricane-force winds 飓风级大风
- 例 **Hurricanes** can occur in some parts of the world. 在世界的某些地方会发生飓风。

328 **hydroelectric** /ˌhaɪdrəʊɪˈlektrɪk/ *adj.* 水力发电的

- 用 hydroelectric stations 水电站
- 例 A cost-benefit analysis is carried out on the construction of a **hydroelectric** power station. 对某水电站的建设进行了成本效益分析。

329 **hypermarket** /ˈhaɪpəmɑːkɪt/ *n.* 大型超市

- 回 supermarket
- 用 local hypermarket 本土超市
- 例 Tesco **hypermarkets** in Malaysia reacted to this price by rationing customers to 2 kilograms per customer. 马来西亚的一家大型综合超市（特斯科）对这一价格做出反应，对每位顾客限量供应 2 公斤。

I

扫一扫
听本节音频

330 **iceberg** /ˈaɪsbɜːg/ *n.* 冰山；显露部分

- 搭 iceberg theory 冰山理论
- 例 This figure represents only the tip of the **iceberg**, since as many as 90% of cases go unreported. 这个数字只是冰山一角，因为多达 90% 的案例没有被报告出来。

331 **idealise** /aɪˈdiːəlaɪz/ *v.* （使）理想化

- 搭 an idealised view of 关于……的一种理想化观点
- 例 Economic theory produces a precise equilibrium outcome, often in an **idealised** market situation. 经济理论产生的精确结果通常是应用在理想化市场情况下的。

332 **illegal** /ɪˈliːgl/ *adj.* 非法的，违法的
　　　　　　　　　　　　n. 非法移民，非法劳工

- 搭 illegal income 非法所得
- 例 An organisation buys up the total supply at the maximum price and then resells it to gain maximum **illegal** revenue. 一个组织以最高价格全部买下所有（商品），然后转售，以获得最大非法利润。

333 **illustrate** /ˈɪləstreɪt/ *vt.* 阐明 *vi.* 举例说明

- 搭 illustrate A with B 用 B 说明 A
- 例 Which function of money is best **illustrated** by this transaction? 这种交易最能说明货币的哪一种功能？

334 **immigrant** /ˈɪmɪgrənt/ *n.* 移民
adj. 移民的

- 用 illegal immigrant 非法移民
- 例 Canada wanted a smaller number of highly educated skilled **immigrants**. 加拿大需要降低受过高等教育的技术移民的数量。

335 **immunisation** /ˌɪmjunaɪˈzeɪʃn/ *n.* 免疫

- 用 boost immunisation 加强免疫
- 例 Improved labour quality is the result of investments in human capital, including spending to provide medical services and **immunisation**. 劳动力质量的提高是人力资本投资的结果，这包括医疗服务及免疫接种疫苗的费用支出。

336 **impede** /ɪmˈpiːd/ *vt.* 阻碍，妨碍，阻止

- 同 hamper, hinder, deter, block
- 用 impede the process 阻碍进程
- 例 Regulation should enhance the effectiveness of competitive markets, not **impede** them. 监管应当强化竞争市场的效率，而不是阻碍它们。

337 **implement** /ˈɪmplɪment/ *vt.* 执行；实现
/ˈɪmplɪmənt/ *n.* 工具，器具

- 用 implement a plan 执行计划
- 例 What is the most effective policy the government could **implement**? 政府能够实施的最有效的政策是什么？

338 **imply** /ɪmˈplaɪ/ *vt.* 说明，表明；暗示，暗指

- 同 denote, hint
- 用 it is implied that... 意味着……
- 例 What does this statement **imply** about the coastal region? 这句话对沿海地区意味着什么？

339 impress /ɪmˈpres/ v. 留下印象；使意识到重要性

- 用 impress sb. with... 某人给人留下深刻印象
- 例 They do bad work because they want to take it easy and still get paid. They work really hard because they want to **impress** someone. 他们工作差劲是因为他们想轻松完成任务而又可以得到报酬，而非常努力工作是因为想让某人对他们印象深刻。

340 imprisonment /ɪmˈprɪznmənt/ n. 监禁，关押

- 用 false imprisonment 非法监禁
- 例 In 2005, Yahoo was roundly criticised for handing over information that led to the arrest and **imprisonment** of a Chinese journalist. 2005年，雅虎因为处理信息不当导致一名中国新闻工作者被逮捕和关押而饱受指责。

341 inaccessible /ˌɪnækˈsesəbl/ adj. 难达到的；难接近的

- 用 be inaccessible to sb. 某人无法达到的
- 例 The problem is compounded by the fact that most affected people live in relatively **inaccessible** parts of the mountainous north. 这一问题影响深远，因为许多受灾民众身处北部偏远山区那些相对难以接近的地区。

342 inadequacy /ɪnˈædɪkwəsi/ n. 不足，不够好；能力不足

- 同 deficient (adj.), insufficiency
- 例 In order to develop trade relationship between our province and Russia, we must start from reality and reassess the advantage and **inadequacy**. 为加快发展对俄贸易，我们必须从实际出发，重新定位自己的优势和不足。

343 incline /ɪnˈklaɪn/ v. 倾向于，有……的趋势

- 田 incline to do sth. 倾向做某事
- 例 Currency traders were less **inclined** to deal with countries that they regarded as being poorly governed. 外汇交易员不太愿意与他们认为管理不善的国家打交道。

344 inconvertible /ˌɪnkənˈvɜːtɪb(ə)l/ adj. 不能兑换的

- 同 unconvertible
- 田 inconvertible loan stocks 不能兑换的债券
- 例 A country that has exchange controls has an **inconvertible** currency. 一个实行外汇管制的国家有不可兑换的货币。

345 incorporate /ɪnˈkɔːpəreɪt/ v. 体现；包含；吸收

- 同 embody, comprise
- 田 incorporate A in/into/within B 把 A 包含于 B
- 例 Go over the reading again and see if you can do the self-assessment tasks that are **incorporated** into the topic. 再复习一遍阅读材料，看看你是否能完成与主题相关的自我评估任务。

346 increment /ˈɪŋkrəmənt/ n. 增加；增量

- 田 rate of increment 增长率
- 例 Although we live bathed in a sea of background radiation, people treat any **increment** as a dire risk. 虽然我们生活在一个充满辐射的世界，但人们把任何辐射的增加都当成致命的危险。

347 incur /ɪnˈkɜː(r)/ vt. 带来（成本、花费）

- 田 incur damages 遭受损失
- 例 You risk **incurring** bank charges if you exceed your overdraft limit. 如果超出了透支限额，就会带来银行加收费用的风险。

348 **independence** /ˌɪndɪˈpendəns/ n. 独立性

- economic independence 经济独立
- Domestic policy retains its **independence** under floating exchange rates. 国内政策在浮动汇率制度下保持独立性。

349 **indicate** /ˈɪndɪkeɪt/ vt. 表明，指出；预示，暗示

- imply, denote, hint, suggest, show
- The numerical value **indicates** the strength of their relationship. 数值表明了它们之间关系的强度。

350 **individual** /ˌɪndɪˈvɪdʒuəl/ n. 个人，个体
adj. 单独的，个别的

- individual enterprise 私人企业
- **Individuals** are free to choose the number of hours they work. 个人可以自由选择他们工作多少个小时。

351 **induce** /ɪnˈdjuːs/ vt. 引诱，诱导；劝说

- induce sb. to do sth. 诱导某人做某事
- An increase in price **induces** consumers to spend more on the product. 价格的上涨诱使消费者在产品上花更多的钱。

352 **industrialisation** /ɪnˌdʌstrɪəlaɪˈzeɪʃn/ n. 工业化

- industrialisation policy 产业化政策
- The reasons behind the better performance of resource-poor countries can be found in their earlier **industrialisation**. 资源匮乏的国家表现较好的原因在于他们较早地进行了工业化。

353 **inefficient** /ˌɪnɪˈfɪʃnt/ adj. 无效率的，效率低的

- inefficient market 无效市场
- **Inefficient** government policies mean that the market system will be better at resource allocation. 政府政策的低效意味着市场体系在资源配置方面会更好。

354 **inequitable** /ɪnˈekwɪtəbl/ *adj.* 不公平的

- 同 unfair
- 用 inequitable distribution of wealth 财富分配不公平
- 例 Underground markets are **inequitable**. 地下市场是不公平的。

355 **infection** /ɪnˈfekʃn/ *n.* 感染，传染

- 用 virus infection 病毒感染
- 例 The immunisation of children against smallpox reduces the danger of the risk of **infection** to others. 对儿童进行天花疫苗接种可减少感染他人的危险。

356 **infer** /ɪnˈfɜː(r)/ *vt.* 推断，下结论；意指

- 同 draw, conclude
- 用 infer from your remarks 从你的话中推断
- 例 If we can observe and measure Y, then we can **infer** some characteristics about X. 如果我们能观察和测量 Y，那么我们就能推断出 X 的一些特征。

357 **inflexible** /ɪnˈfleksəbl/ *adj.* 不可变的；顽固的

- 用 inflexible prices 非浮动价格
- 例 Prices were **inflexible** in the downward direction even in the face of steep recession. 即使在经济严重衰退的情况下，价格在下行方向上也是不变的。

358 **influence** /ˈɪnfluəns/ *vt.* 影响
　　　　　　　　　　　　　n. 影响，有影响的人或事

- 用 have influence on sth. 对某物构成影响
- 例 Government policies on labelling also **influence** how the markets for food develop. 政府的标签政策也影响着食品市场的发展。

359 innovative /ˈɪnəveɪtɪv/ adj. 创新的，革新的

- 用 innovative thinking 创新思维
- 例 New businesses have dynamism and vigour. They are more productive and more **innovative**. 新企业充满活力，更有效率，更有创造力。

360 insecurity /ˌɪnsɪˈkjʊərəti/ n. 不安全

- 同 unsafety
- 用 job insecurity 工作无保障
- 例 Reducing protection results in lower incomes for some workers and increased job **insecurity**. 减少保护措施会导致一些工人收入下降，工作不安全感增加。

361 insignificant /ˌɪnsɪɡˈnɪfɪkənt/ adj. 无关紧要的，微不足道的

- 同 negligible
- 用 an insignificant difference 微不足道的差别
- 例 The levels of chemicals in the river are not **insignificant**. 河水中的化学物质含量不容忽视。

362 insist /ɪnˈsɪst/ v. 坚持做，执意做

- 用 insist on doing sth. 坚持做某事
- 例 One supermarket, which started as a small shop, **insisted** on selling only high quality products. 一家超市，开始时只是一家小店，坚持只卖高质量的产品。

363 inspection /ɪnˈspekʃn/ n. 检查

- 同 check (v.)
- 用 carry out an inspection 开展检查
- 例 Whenever a good is imported from another country, it must go through a number of customs procedures involving **inspections**, valuation and others. 当从国外进口一件货物时，它必须通过一系列海关手续，包括检查、估价和其他手续。

364 **institution** /ˌɪnstɪˈtjuːʃn/ *n.* 机构；风俗习惯；制定

- 近 establishment
- 搭 academic institution 学术机构
- 例 The firm is owned by a small number of financial **institutions**. 这家公司为少数几家金融机构所有。

365 **integrate** /ˈɪntɪgreɪt/ *v.* 使……完整，结合；成为一体

- 搭 integrate A with B 整合 A 和 B
- 例 In view of this risk, some micro-credit schemes try to **integrate** credit with the provision of education. 鉴于这种风险，一些小额信贷计划试图将信贷与教育服务结合起来。

366 **intensify** /ɪnˈtensɪfaɪ/ *v.* 加强，强化

- 搭 intensify supervision 加大监督力度
- 例 Economists generally do not look upon price controls favourably, because these **intensify** problems of resource misallocation. 经济学家通常不看好价格控制，因为这加剧了资源配置不当的问题。

367 **intentional** /ɪnˈtenʃənl/ *adj.* 故意的，蓄意的

- 搭 intentional injury 故意伤害
- 例 Is this advertisement a clever and funny stunt or a malicious and **intentional** effort to harm? 这则广告是一个讨巧有趣的噱头，还是一种恶意的蓄意伤害？

368 **interaction** /ˌɪntərˈækʃn/ *n.* 相互作用

- 搭 interaction between A and B A 和 B 相互作用
- 例 The level of activity in an economy is determined by the **interaction** of aggregate demand and aggregate supply. 一个经济体的活动水平是由总需求和总供给的相互作用决定的。

369 **interpretation** /ɪnˌtɜːprəˈteɪʃn/ n. 解释，说明；演绎

- 用 judicial interpretation 司法解释
- 例 The laws themselves may be vague, allowing much room for different **interpretations**. 法律本身可能是模糊的，给不同的解释留有很大的空间。

370 **interruption** /ˌɪntəˈrʌpʃn/ n. 中断，干扰

- 同 disturbance
- 用 without interruption 不中断
- 例 Since the 1990-1991 recession ended, the economy has moved ahead without **interruption**. 自1990-1991年的经济衰退结束以来，经济一直在稳步前进。

371 **invalidate** /ɪnˈvælɪdeɪt/ vt. 使无效；证明……错误

- 用 invalidate the guarantee 使担保无效
- 例 If the ruling stands, it would **invalidate** more than 600 board decisions issued over the past year. 如果该裁决成立，将使过去一年发布的600多项董事会决定失效。

372 **invariably** /ɪnˈveəriəbli/ adv. 总是；不变地

- 用 invariably divide into two 总是一分为二
- 例 The opportunity to compete is **invariably** crucial in determining efficiency in a market. 竞争机会始终是决定市场效率的关键。

373 **invasion** /ɪnˈveɪʒn/ n. 入侵，侵略

- 用 invasion of privacy 侵犯个人隐私
- 例 Following the threat of **invasion** the country prepared for war. 在受到入侵的威胁后，这个国家做好了战争的准备。

374 **inverse** /ˌɪnˈvɜːs/ *adj.* 相反的，反向的

- 同 counter, adverse
- 用 inverse ratio 反比
- 例 Once you have found a new equation, enter it into the calculator and ask it to graph the **inverse** function. 一旦你发现一个新方程，把它输入计算器，让它画出反函数的图像。

375 **investigation** /ɪnˌvestɪˈɡeɪʃn/ *n.* 调查研究

- 用 investigation into sth. 调查某事
- 例 It is a method of **investigation** used in all the social and natural sciences. 这是所有社会科学和自然科学中使用的一种调查方法。

376 **irresponsible** /ˌɪrɪˈspɒnsəbl/ *adj.* 不负责任的

- 用 an irresponsible attitude 不负责任的态度
- 例 **Irresponsible** drinking costs the UK taxpayer £21 billion a year, with nearly a million alcohol-related crimes. 不负责任的饮酒行为每年给英国纳税人造成 210 亿英镑的损失，并导致近 100 万起与饮酒有关的犯罪。

377 **irrigation** /ˌɪrɪˈɡeɪʃn/ *n.* 灌溉

- 用 drip irrigation 滴灌
- 例 The lack of water for **irrigation** is limiting rice output in Australia and Sri Lanka. 缺乏灌溉用水限制了澳大利亚和斯里兰卡的水稻产量。

L

378 **levy** /ˈlevi/ v. 征收,征集

- 用 levy tax 征税
- 例 Inflation was also made worse by **levying** a new tax. 征收新税也加剧了通货膨胀。

M

379 macaroni /ˌmækəˈrəʊni/ n. 通心粉

- 🔵 Italian macaroni 意大利通心粉
- 🟢 We all need flour because we all need to eat bread, **macaroni** and dough. 我们都需要面粉，因为我们都需要吃面包、通心粉、生面团。

380 malnutrition /ˌmælnjuˈtrɪʃn/ n. 营养不良

- 🔵 dystrophy
- 🔵 chronic malnutrition 慢性营养不良
- 🟢 People in developing countries suffer from **malnutrition** and poverty. 发展中国家的人民饱受营养不良和贫困之苦。

381 manipulate /məˈnɪpjuleɪt/ vt. 操作，处理；操纵

- 🔵 manipulate sb. into sth. 操纵某人做某事
- 🟢 You will be assessed on your understanding of the concept rather than your ability to **manipulate** difficult figures. 评估的是你对概念的理解，而不是你处理复杂数字的能力。

382 margarine /ˌmɑːdʒəˈriːn/ n. 人造黄油

- 🔵 melt the margarine 融化人造黄油
- 🟢 Palm oil is used in the production of many goods, including cooking oil, **margarine**, ice cream, soap and shampoo. 棕榈油被用于许多商品的生产，包括食用油、人造奶油、冰淇淋、肥皂和洗发水。

383 **meltdown** /ˈmeltdaʊn/ *n.* 暴跌；彻底垮台；核反应炉熔毁

- collapse, crash
- financial meltdown 金融危机
- The move is likely to cause the biggest currency depreciation since Argentina's economic **meltdown** in 2002. 此举可能导致自 2002 年阿根廷经济崩溃以来最大的货币贬值。

384 **meritorious** /ˌmerɪˈtɔːriəs/ *adj.* 值得称赞的；有价值的

- praiseworthy
- meritorious service 功勋，功劳
- She showed **meritorious** loyalty to the family firm. 她对家族企业表现出值得称赞的忠诚。

385 **migrate** /maɪˈgreɪt/ *v.* 鸟类迁移；移居

- migrating birds 候鸟
- Labour from developing countries often **migrates** to developed countries and finds jobs. 发展中国家的劳动力经常去往发达国家并在那里找工作。

386 **miraculous** /mɪˈrækjələs/ *adj.* 不可思议的；奇迹般的

- unimaginable
- miraculous healing 奇迹般的痊愈
- This small island nation has made **miraculous** economic growth thanks to the efforts of all Japanese citizens. 在所有日本国民的努力下，这个小小的岛国创造出了奇迹般的经济增长。

387 **misallocate** /ˌmɪsˈæləkeɪt/ v. 错误分配

- 用 misallocate capital and labour 资金与劳动配置错误
- 例 The market system **misallocates** resources. 市场体系错配了资源。

388 **miserable** /ˈmɪzrəbl/ adj. 悲惨的；痛苦的；令人不愉快的

- 用 a miserable life 悲惨的生活
- 例 If water has the capacity to enhance life, its absence has the capacity to make it **miserable**. 如果水有能力改善生命，那么没有水就会变得悲惨。

389 **morale** /məˈrɑːl/ n. 士气，斗志

- 用 boost/raise/improve morale 提升士气
- 例 The workforce of the new airline lacks **morale** and is demotivated. 这家新航空公司的员工缺乏斗志，士气低落。

390 **mortality** /mɔːˈtæləti/ n. 死亡率

- 用 operative mortality 手术死亡率
- 例 The infant **mortality** rate has risen. 婴儿死亡率上升。

391 **myth** /mɪθ/ n. 神话；虚构的人或事

- 用 an ancient myth 远古神话
- 例 Economies of scale are a **myth** in many industries, especially newer sectors such as technology and services. 在许多行业，规模经济是一个神话，尤其是在技术和服务等较新的行业。

N

392 **narrow** /ˈnærəʊ/ *adj.* 狭窄的，有限的
v. 变窄

- 用 narrow down 缩小
- 例 The diagram shows changes in broad and **narrow** measures of money supply between 2004 and 2006. 图表显示了 2004 年至 2006 年间广义和狭义货币供应量的变化。

393 **nationalise** /ˈnæʃnəlaɪz/ *vt.* 收归国有，使国有化

- 用 nationalise the industry 产业国有化
- 例 What is not likely to represent a strong case for an industry to be **nationalised**? 什么不太可能成为一个行业被国有化的有力理由？

394 **negotiation** /nɪˌɡəʊʃiˈeɪʃn/ *n.* 谈判

- 用 business negotiation 商务谈判
- 例 Which situation would have helped the trade union in the **negotiations**? 在谈判中什么情况对工会有利？

395 **neutral** /ˈnjuːtrəl/ *adj.* 中立的；中性的

- 用 neutral attitude 中立态度
- 例 The participants who are **neutral** on prices are waiting for better signals to enter the market. 对价格持中立态度的市场参与者正在等待更好的信号以进入市场。

nutritious /njuˈtrɪʃəs/ *adj.* 有营养的

- 用 nutritious foods 营养食品
- 例 Agro-ecological methods are by contrast more sustainable for the farmers and more **nutritious** for consumers. 相比之下，农业生态方法对农民来说更可持续，对消费者来说更有营养。

O

397 **obstacle** /ˈɒbstəkl/ *n.* 障碍，干扰，妨碍

- 同 interruption, disturbance
- 用 overcome the obstacles 克服障碍
- 例 The report said that **obstacles** which prevented customers switching accounts to rival banks meant that the banking industry was not competitive. 报告称，设置障碍阻止客户将账户转至对手银行意味着银行业缺乏竞争力。

398 **occupant** /ˈɒkjəpənt/ *n.* 居住者，占有者；汽车内的乘坐者

- 同 dweller
- 用 the occupant of this house 房屋居住者
- 例 The current **occupant** of 10 Downing Street hardly needs reminding of the need to focus on growth and employment. 如今，唐宁街10号的主人几乎不需要提醒人们关注增长和就业的必要性。

399 **oilfield** /ˈɔɪlfiːld/ *n.* 油田

- 用 offshore oilfield 海上油田
- 例 CNPC is providing services for Iraq's biggest **oilfield**, in conjunction with BP and an Iraqi group. 中石油正与英国石油和一个伊拉克集团合作，为伊拉克最大油田提供服务。

400 **omit** /əˈmɪt/ *vt.* 省略；遗漏；忽略

- 用 be omitted from the team 从队伍里除名
- 例 Key actions have been **omitted** from the process. 关键步骤在过程中被省略了。

401 **ongoing** /ˈɒngəʊɪŋ/ *adj.* 持续不断的；不断前进的；正在进行的

- 用 ongoing task 进行中的任务
- 例 The factors that restrict growth included **ongoing** dry weather conditions causing lower output of agricultural goods. 制约经济增长的因素包括导致农产品产量下降的持续的干旱天气。

402 **operational** /ˌɒpəˈreɪʃənl/ *adj.* 经营的；操作的；有效的

- 同 in effect, in operation
- 用 operational efficiency 经营效率
- 例 The new company set up better **operational** strategies, laying emphasis on quality and improving its packaging. 新公司制定了更好的经营策略，注重质量以及改进包装。

403 **opponent** /əˈpəʊnənt/ *n.* 反对者，对手
adj. 对立的，敌对的

- 同 competitor
- 用 a political opponent 政敌
- 例 **Opponents** to the 5/20 rule argue that it seriously discriminates against Indian airline operators by not allowing them to compete in a free market. 5/20 规则的反对者认为，该规则不允许印度航空公司在自由市场参与竞争，这是对印度航空公司的严重歧视。

404 **opt** /ɒpt/ *vi.* 选择，挑选

- 用 opt to do sth. 选择做某事
- 例 In terms of allocative mechanisms, some economies, such as Singapore and Hong Kong **opted** for a strong focus on the market. 就分配机制来说，一些经济体，比如新加坡和中国香港，在分配资源时都会着重关注市场。

405 **ounce** /aʊns/ n. 盎司

- 用 $5 per ounce 每盎司五美元
- 例 Gold is selling at $930 an **ounce** this day. 黄金这天的价格是 930 美元每盎司。

406 **organic** /ɔːˈɡænɪk/ adj. 有机的；器官的

- 用 organic agriculture 有机农业
- 例 Now, in supermarkets, they have the benefit of a wide choice, reasonable prices, international dishes, and **organic** produce. 如今在超市，人们有更多的选择，价格更合理，可以享用到更多的进口食品以及有机农产品。

407 **oriented** /ˈɔːriɛntɪːd/ adj. 重视……的；以……为方向的

- 用 customer oriented 以客户为导向
- 例 Malaysia has a market-**orientated** economy. 马来西亚的经济以市场为导向。

408 **outbreak** /ˈaʊtbreɪk/ n. 疾病的发作；战争的爆发

- 用 the outbreak of World War I 第一次世界大战爆发
- 例 In 2014, there was an **outbreak** of Ebola, a deadly disease, in West Africa. 2014 年，西非爆发了致命疾病——埃博拉病毒。

409 **outlay** /ˈaʊtleɪ/ n. 支出，开支，费用

- 用 capital outlay 资本支出
- 例 Rival firms respond by increasing their advertising **outlays**. 竞争对手则以增加广告支出作为回应。

410 **outline** /ˈaʊtlaɪn/ vt. 概述；描画……的轮廓
n. 轮廓；大纲

- 回 depict
- 甲 general outline 大纲，概要
- 例 Please **outline** the functions of the enterprises in a modern economy. 请概述企业在现代经济中的作用。

411 **outperform** /ˌaʊtpəˈfɔːm/ vt. 胜过；做得比……好

- 甲 outperform one's rivals 表现优于竞争对手
- 例 Since 1925, market data indicate that small-cap stocks **outperform** the broader stock market in January. 自1925年以来，市场数据显示，一月份小盘股的表现要优于大盘。

412 **outweigh** /ˌaʊtˈweɪ/ vt. 在重量上比……重；比……重要，比……有价值

- 甲 gains outweigh losses 利大于弊
- 例 For inferior goods, the substitution effect **outweighs** the income effect. 对于劣质商品，替代效应大于收入效应。

413 **overcome** /ˌəʊvəˈkʌm/ vt. 克服，战胜

- 回 conquer
- 甲 overcome difficulties 克服困难
- 例 Clothes design firms need to **overcome** high barriers to enter into the industry. 服装设计公司需要克服进入这个行业的高门槛。

414 **overdraft** /ˈəʊvədrɑːft/ n. 透支

- 甲 pay off an overdraft 付清透支
- 例 A consumer takes advantage of an **overdraft** facility to buy a car. 消费者利用透支这一手段购买汽车。

415 **overestimate** /ˌəʊvərˈestɪmeɪt/ v. 估计、评价过高
/ˌəʊvərˈestɪmət/ n. 估计、评价过高

- 搭 overestimate oneself 自不量力
- 例 Official statistics may **overestimate** true unemployment. 官方统计数据可能高估了真实的失业率。

416 **overexploitation** /ˌəʊvəˌreksplɔɪˈteɪʃən/
n. 过度开采；过度利用

- 搭 overexploitation of natural resources 对自然资源的过度开采
- 例 Poverty is the most important cause of environmental destruction, due to the **overexploitation** by poor people of their scarce environmental resources. 贫穷是造成环境破坏的最重要原因，因为穷人对其稀少的环境资源进行了过度开发。

417 **overflow** /ˌəʊvəˈfləʊ/ v. 挤满人；（液体）溢出
n. 泛滥

- 搭 a heart overflowed with love 心里充满了爱
- 例 Property prices had soared and hotels **overflowed**. 房地产价格飙升，酒店人满为患。

418 **overheat** /ˌəʊvəˈhiːt/ v. 过热
n. 过热，激烈

- 搭 cause the economy to overheat 引发经济过热
- 例 The officials have devoted considerable effort to slowing growth in some sectors to alleriate their **overheat**. 为了避免经济过热，官员们想方设法来减缓经济增长的速度。

419 **overlap** /ˌəʊvəˈlæp/ v. 部分重叠

- 回 repeat
- 搭 overlap each other 上下交叠
- 例 Lack of co-ordination of such projects results in **overlapping** and duplication of some projects. 由于这些项目之间缺乏合作，导致了一些项目的重叠。

420 **overproduction** /ˌəʊvəprəˈdʌkʃn/ n. 生产过剩

- 搭 prevent overproduction 避免生产过剩
- 例 The subsidy has caused **overproduction** relative to what is socially desirable. 相对于社会需求而言，这种补贴导致了生产过剩。

421 **override** /ˌəʊvəˈraɪd/ vt. 推翻；凌驾于某物；不顾

- 搭 override objections 不顾反对
- 例 By signing the order the president would **override** the democratic process and rule by decree. 通过签署该命令，总统将推翻民主程序，并通过法令统治国家。

422 **overspecialise** /ˌəʊvəˈspeʃəlaɪz/ v. 使过于专业化

- 搭 tend to overspecialise 趋于过度专业化
- 例 Instead of being vexed by **overspecialised** terminology, experts conversed excitedly! 专家们并没有被过于专业的术语弄得心烦意乱，而是兴奋地交谈着！

423 **overtake** /ˌəʊvəˈteɪk/ v. 超过，赶上；突然发生

- 回 outperform
- 搭 be overtaken by bad weather 突遇恶劣天气
- 例 We musn't let ourselves be **overtaken** by our competitors. 我们决不能让竞争对手超过我们。

424 **overturn** /ˌəʊvəˈtɜːn/ v. 颠覆，推翻，倾覆

- 🔄 override
- 🔗 overturn a decision 推翻决定
- 📖 A WHO report warned that all of that progress could be **overturned** within a generation if the unhealthy lifestyle of many Europeans is not addressed. 世界卫生组织的一份报告说，如果许多欧洲人不健康的生活方式得不到解决，那么所有取得的进步将在一代人的时间内被颠覆。

425 **overwhelm** /ˌəʊvəˈwelm/ vt. 淹没；击败；情感充溢

- 🔗 be overwhelmed by feelings of guilt 被内疚淹没
- 📖 Vietnam is enjoying rapid growth but its small businesses are being **overwhelmed** by a huge influx of cheap goods from other countries in Asia. 越南经济正快速增长，但来自亚洲其他国家的大量廉价商品正在淹没其小企业。

P

426 **partnership** /ˈpɑːtnəʃɪp/ n. 合伙，合伙企业，合作关系

- 用 strategic partnership 战略伙伴关系
- 例 Unilever, a multinational global food manufacturer, has announced a **partnership** with Oxfam. 跨国全球食品制造商联合利华宣布与英国慈善组织乐施会合作。

427 **patent** /ˈpeɪtnt/ n. 专利
v. 获取专利

- 用 apply for a patent 申请专利
- 例 The firm has a **patent** on an essential process. 该公司拥有一项重要工艺的技术专利。

428 **penalise** /ˈpiːnəlaɪz/ vt. 置于不利地位；惩罚，处罚

- 用 penalise sb. for sth. 为某事惩罚某人
- 例 The children are **penalised** for life, as they grow into adulthood lacking skills, and condemned to low productivity and low incomes. 孩子们在成长过程中会因缺乏技能而终生受累，并注定会陷入低效和低薪的境地。

429 **pensioner** /ˈpenʃənə(r)/ n. 领养老金者

- 用 tax threshold for a pensioner 领退休金的纳税起征点
- 例 The ratio of workers to **pensioners** is declining. 工作的人与养老金领取者的比例正在下降。

430 **perish** /ˈperɪʃ/ v. 腐烂；灭亡，毁灭

- 回 destruction (n.)
- 扩 perish the thought 打消念头
- 例 The apples on the desk slowly **perished** and the smell hung over the room. 桌子上的苹果慢慢腐烂了，气味笼罩着房间。

431 **persuasive** /pəˈsweɪsɪv/ adj. 有说服力的，令人信服的

- 回 compelling
- 扩 persuasive arguments 令人信服的论点
- 例 Consumers do not see the rival firm's product as a close substitute on account of extensive **persuasive** advertising. 由于大量的说服性广告，消费者并不认为竞争对手的产品是一个强有力的替代品。

432 **peso** /ˈpeɪsəʊ/ n. 比索

- 扩 peso's purchasing power 比索的购买力
- 例 In 2004 union officials and businessmen in Argentina agreed to increase the minimum wage from 350 to 450 **pesos**. 2004年，阿根廷工会官员和商人同意将最低工资从350比索提高到450比索。

433 **pesticide** /ˈpestɪsaɪd/ n. 杀虫剂

- 扩 chemical pesticide 化学农药
- 例 Currently, six companies supply 60% of the world's commercial seed market and 11 companies supply 98% of the world's **pesticide** market. 目前，全球商业种子市场60%的货源是由6家公司提供的，全球杀虫剂市场98%的货源是由11家公司提供的。

434 **pharmaceutical** /ˌfɑːməˈsuːtɪkl/ *adj.* 制药（学）的
n. 药物

- 用 pharmaceutical products 药物制品
- 例 In 2014 an American multinational **pharmaceutical** developer and supplier made a bid to take over a Swedish-British multinational **pharmaceutical** company. 2014 年，一家美国跨国制药品开发商和供应商出价收购一家瑞典和英国合资的跨国制药公司。

435 **poisonous** /ˈpɔɪzənəs/ *adj.* 有毒的；令人讨厌的

- 用 poisonous gas 有毒气体
- 例 Some people have become concerned about the amount of **poisonous** gases and carbon emissions being produced. 有些人已经开始关注有毒气体和碳的排放量了。

436 **polisher** /ˈpɒlɪʃə(r)/ *n.* 抛光机，磨光机

- 用 a floor polisher 地板上光机
- 例 Mines were shut in Southern Africa and Canada, diamond cutters and **polishers** in India lost their jobs and retail jewellers went out of business in the US. 南非和加拿大的钻石矿被关闭，印度的钻石切割工和抛光工失业，美国的珠宝零售商破产。

437 **politician** /ˌpɒləˈtɪʃn/ *n.* 政客，政治家

- 同 statesman
- 用 most skillful politician 最有手腕的政治家
- 例 The information refers to rising house prices and **politicians** sometimes say such a rise is a sign of an improvement in the economy. 这些信息指的是不断上涨的房价，政客们有时会说这样的上涨是经济好转的迹象。

438 **polluter** /pəˈluːtər/ n. 污染者,制造污染的人或组织

- 🌐 legitimate polluter 合法排污者
- 📖 In the case of emissions of industrial production, they force **polluters** to cut emissions. 在工业生产的排放方面,它们迫使污染者减少排放。

439 **populate** /ˈpɒpjuleɪt/ vt. 居住于,构成人口;殖民于

- 🌐 a heavily populated country 人口稠密的国家
- 📖 Hong Kong is a very densely **populated** city of over seven million people. 香港是一个人口稠密的城市,人口超过 700 万。

440 **portability** /ˌpɔːtəˈbɪləti/ 可携带性;可移植性

- 🔄 transportability
- 🌐 increase the portability 增强可携带性
- 📖 The new light cover increases this model's **portability**. 新型的轻质外壳使这种型号携带更轻便。

441 **predict** /prɪˈdɪkt/ v. 预言,预知,预测

- 🔄 forecast, anticipate
- 🌐 it is predicted that... 可预言……
- 📖 The Quantity Theory of Money **predicts** that changes in money supply can cause inflation. 货币数量理论预测货币供应的变化会引起通货膨胀。

442 **preferential** /ˌprefəˈrenʃl/ adj. 优惠的,优先的,优待的

- 🌐 preferential treatment 优待
- 📖 A **preferential** trade agreement is an agreement between two or more countries to lower trade barriers between each other on particular products. 优惠贸易协定是两个或多个国家之间就特定产品降低贸易壁垒的协议。

443 prestige /preˈstiːʒ/ n. 声望，声誉

- 同 reputation
- 用 personal prestige 个人声誉
- 例 Economic growth may increase a country's international **prestige** and power. 经济增长可以提高一个国家的国际声望和力量。

444 pretend /prɪˈtend/ v. 假装，佯装；自认为

- 同 disguise
- 用 pretend to be asleep 假装睡着
- 例 No one should **pretend** to know where or who the next Apple will be. 没有人应该假装知道下一个苹果公司会在哪里或谁会成为下一个苹果公司。

445 privatise /ˈpraɪvətaɪz/ v. 使私有化

- 用 privatise a company 使公司私有化
- 例 A government decides to **privatise** a state monopoly. 政府决定将国有垄断企业私有化。

446 prohibit /prəˈhɪbɪt/ vt. 阻止；禁止

- 同 impede, hamper, hinder, deter, block
- 用 prohibit sb. from doing sth. 阻止某人做某事
- 例 In many countries, laws exist which **prohibit** firms from copying innovations introduced by other firms. 在许多国家，法律禁止公司复制其他公司引进的创新。

447 propensity /prəˈpensəti/ n.（行为方面）倾向，习性

- 同 incline (v.)
- 用 marginal propensity 边际倾向
- 例 The rich also have a lower marginal **propensity** to consume and a higher marginal propensity to save than the poor. 与穷人相比，富人的边际消费倾向较低，而边际储蓄倾向较高。

第一部分　通用词汇 A to Z | 97

448 **property** /ˈprɒpəti/ *n.* 财产；性质，性能

- 用 damage other people's property 毁坏他人财产
- 例 In 2009 there were huge fires in Australia which destroyed much **property** and countryside. 2009 年澳大利亚发生了大火，烧毁了许多财产和村落。

449 **proposition** /ˌprɒpəˈzɪʃn/ *n.* 主张，观点；提议

- 用 an attractive proposition 一个有吸引力的主张
- 例 Do you agree with the **propositions** that markets and government intervention should complement each other in developing countries? 对于发展中国家的市场和政府干预应该互为补充的主张，你是否同意？

450 **province** /ˈprɒvɪns/ *n.* 省份；知识范围，领域

- 用 outside my province 不归我管
- 例 It requires the agreement of all EU members and the approval of Canada's **provinces**. 这需要所有欧盟成员国的同意和加拿大各省的批准。

Q

451 **qualified** /ˈkwɒlɪfaɪd/ adj. 合格的，有资格的，符合条件的

- 用 a qualified employee 称职的员工
- 例 The problem is clearest in the technology industry because of the incredible shortage of **qualified** workers. 这个问题在科技行业最为明显，因为合格工人少得令人难以置信。

452 **qualitative** /ˈkwɒlɪtətɪv/ adj. 质量的；定性的；性质的

- 用 qualitative differences 质的区别
- 例 Why is it important to use **qualitative** data as well as quantitative GDP data when considering whether a country is developed or developing? 为什么在考虑一个国家是发达国家还是发展中国家时，定性数据和定量 GDP 数据同样重要？

453 **quantify** /ˈkwɒntɪfaɪ/ vt. 量化，为……定量

- 用 quantify the risks 量化风险
- 例 What information might an economist use to **quantify** the relative importance of the government? 经济学家会使用什么信息来量化政府的相对重要性呢？

454 **quarry** /ˈkwɒri/ n. 采石场；猎物；敌人

- 用 limestone quarry 石灰石采矿场
- 例 The diagram shows the supply of limestone from **quarry** X and **quarry** Y at two prices. 该图显示了采石场 X 和采石场 Y 以两种价格供应的石灰石。

455 **quote** /kwəʊt/ v. 报价；引用；挂牌

- 🟡 quote a passage from the speech 从讲话中引用一段话
- 🟠 Prices are **quoted** in terms of common monetary units. 价格是以通用货币为单位报价的。

R

456 **random** /ˈrændəm/ adj. 随意的，任意的；未经首先考虑的

- ⊕ random order 随机顺序
- ⊚ We conclude from the data from 1927–2012 that the pattern of returns is **random**. 我们从1927–2012年的数据中得出结论，回报率的模式是随机的。

457 **rapeseed** /ˈreɪpsiːd/ n. 油菜籽

- ⊕ rapeseed oil 油菜籽油
- ⊚ He had harvested his **rapeseed** but not rice. 他收获了油菜籽，但是没有收获大米。

458 **rationalise** /ˈræʃənəlaɪz/ v. 使合理化，使有经济效益；对……加以科学地说明

- ⊕ rationalise high house prices 对高房价加以科学地说明
- ⊚ Research and development costs can be pooled, and production plants can be **rationalised**. 研发成本可以分摊，生产工厂可以进行合理化改革。

459 **rationality** /ˌræʃəˈnæləti/ n. 合理性

- ⊕ economic rationality 经济合理性
- ⊚ Discuss how the idea of **rationality** is used in the indifference curve theory of consumer behaviour. 请讨论一下合理性概念是如何应用在消费者行为无差异曲线理论中的。

460 **rations** /ˈræʃnz/ *vt.* 定量供应
n. 口粮，配给量，定量

- 用 on short rations 短缺
- 例 If these products have a high price, the market mechanism will automatically result in a type of **rationing** occurring. 如果这些产品的价格很高，市场机制将自动导致某种形式的定量供应发生。

461 **realistic** /ˌriːəˈlɪstɪk/ *adj.* 现实的

- 用 a realistic assessment 现实的评价
- 例 Whether the assumptions underlying consumer equilibrium are **realistic**? 消费者均衡的假设是否现实？

462 **rebate** /ˈriːbeɪt/ *n.* 折扣；退还款

- 用 a tax rebate 退税
- 例 Buyers are offered a cash **rebate**. 购买者享受现金折扣。

463 **recruit** /rɪˈkruːt/ *v.* 聘用，征募

- 用 recruit sb. to do sth. 招聘某人做某事
- 例 When does the firm find it difficult to **recruit** new labour? 公司什么时候发现很难招到新人？

464 **rebel** /ˈrebl/ *n.* 反叛者
/rɪˈbel/ *vi.* 反叛，反抗

- 用 rebel against sth. 反抗某事
- 例 In early March, Raqqa became the first urban center to fall entirely under **rebel** control. 三月初，拉卡成为第一个完全落入叛军控制的城市中心。

465 **recipient** /rɪˈsɪpiənt/ *n.* 受方，接受者

- 用 the recipient of awards 领奖人
- 例 Some benefit **recipients** misspend the money they receive. 有些受惠者将他们收到的钱挥霍了。

466 **reconcile** /ˈrekənsaɪl/ vt. 使调和，使一致

- 用 reconcile disputes 调解纠纷
- 例 The objective of growth maximisation **reconciles** the interests of both owners and managers, because both groups have much to gain from a growing firm. 增长最大化的目标调和了所有者和管理者双方的利益，因为这两个群体都能从一个增长中的公司获得很多利益。

467 **redeployment** /ˌriːdɪˈplɔɪmənt/ n. 调换，调动

- 用 staff redeployment 人员调动
- 例 We have fully assessed opportunities for **redeployment** within the company but there appears to be no suitable alternative jobs available at present. 我们充分评估了公司内部调动的机会，但目前似乎没有其他合适的岗位。

468 **redistribute** /ˌriːdɪˈstrɪbjuːt/ vt. 重新分配

- 用 redistribute sth. to sb. 将某物重新分配给某人
- 例 The government **redistributed** all income taken from the rich to the poor. 政府将富人的所有收入重新分配给穷人。

469 **refine** /rɪˈfaɪn/ vt. 精炼，去除杂质；改进，改善

- 用 the process of refining oil 炼油的程序
- 例 Many foods are now **refined** to such an extent that the natural fibre is lost. 许多食品经过加工都失去了天然纤维。

470 **regime** /reɪˈʒiːm/ n. 管理体制；统治制度，政权

- 用 military regime 军事政权
- 例 Often aid has been used to support **regimes** in developing countries that are considered to be 'friendly' to the interests of the donor governments. 援助经常被用来支持发展中国家的体制，这些体制被认为对捐助国政府的利益"友好"。

471 **reliant** /rɪˈlaɪənt/ adj. 依赖的，依靠的

- 搭 be reliant upon charity 依靠赞助
- 例 A dependence on primary products for export revenues means that developing countries are **reliant** on the industrialised world for their economic performance. 出口收入依赖初级产品意味着发展中国家的经济表现依赖于工业化国家。

472 **reluctant** /rɪˈlʌktənt/ adj. 不情愿的，勉强的

- 搭 be reluctant to help 不情愿帮忙
- 例 A survey by the Polish central bank indicated that companies were very **reluctant** to start new investments. 波兰央行的一项调查显示，企业非常不愿意开始新的投资。

473 **rely** /rɪˈlaɪ/ vi. 依赖，依靠；信任，信赖

- 搭 rely on your own judgement 相信你的判断
- 例 Developing countries should become self-sufficient and not **rely** on aid. 发展中国家应该自给自足，而不是依赖援助。

474 **resentment** /rɪˈzentmənt/ n. 不满，愤恨，怨恨

- 搭 feel resentment against sb. 对某人感到怨恨
- 例 This can lead to **resentment** and can impede economic growth. 这可能导致不满情绪，并可能阻碍经济增长。

475 **resistance** /rɪˈzɪstəns/ n. 抵制，反抗；阻力

- 联 rebel (v.)
- 搭 resistance to the new law 抵制新法律
- 例 In brief, *The Economist* misinterprets the **resistance** of developing countries to a new round. 简言之，《经济学人》误解了发展中国家对新一轮谈判的抵制。

476 **respiratory** /rəˈspɪrətri/ adj. 呼吸的

- 搭 respiratory system 呼吸系统
- 例 Life expectancy has steadily increased due to improved healthcare, decreased deaths from heart disease, cancer,

diabetes and chronic **respiratory** disease. 由于医疗保健的改善，心脏病、癌症、糖尿病和慢性呼吸道疾病的死亡人数减少，预期寿命稳步提高。

477 **resumption** /rɪˈzʌmpʃn/ *n.* 恢复，重新开始；继续进行

- 🔗 the resumption of peace talk 恢复和谈
- 📖 China is by far the largest source of visitors, but there has been a **resumption** of growth from Russia. 到目前为止，来自中国的游客人数最多，但来自俄罗斯游客的数量也恢复了增长。

478 **retaliatory** /rɪˈtæliətri/ *adj.* 报复性的

- 🔗 retaliatory action 报复行动
- 📖 Mexico was proposing to impose **retaliatory** duties on some US products imported into Mexico. 墨西哥提议对一些进口到墨西哥的美国产品征收报复性关税。

479 **retention** /rɪˈtenʃn/ *n.* 保留；保持；记忆力

- 🔗 heat retention 保温
- 📖 The new system of remuneration will improve staff **retention**. 新的薪酬制度将提升人员保留率。

480 **retire** /rɪˈtaɪə(r)/ *v.* 退休；退役
　　　　　　　　　　　　　　 n. 退休

- 🔗 retire from teaching 从教师岗位退休
- 📖 **Retired** citizens pay no tax on their pensions. 退休公民的退休金不用交税。

481 **reveal** /rɪˈviːl/ *vt.* 揭示，透露；显出，露出

- 🔁 expose
- 🔗 it is revealed that... 据透露……
- 📖 In 2015, the vast and growing gap between rich and poor was **revealed** in a report from the charity Oxfam. 2015 年英国慈善

机构乐施会的一份报告揭示了贫富差距巨大,而且差距还在不断扩大。

482 **revival** /rɪ'vaɪvl/ *n.* 复苏,振兴;再流行

- 用 an economic revival 经济复苏
- 例 There was some **revival** in consumer confidence. 消费者信心有所恢复。

483 **riot** /'raɪət/ *n.* 暴乱,骚乱;丰富多样
        v. 发生骚乱

- 同 disturbance, disorder
- 用 run riot 撒野,肆意妄为
- 例 These price rises caused food **riots** in developing countries. 这些价格上涨在发展中国家引发了食品骚乱。

484 **rivalrous** /'raɪv(ə)lrəs/ *adj.* 竞争性的,敌对性的

- 同 competitive
- 用 rivalrous competition 争胜竞争
- 例 We have to make some indispensable compromise in order to survive in such a **rivalrous** industry. 为了在激烈的市场竞争中幸存下来,我们不得不在某些方面做一定程度的妥协。

485 **rupiah** /ruː'piːə/ *n.* 卢比

- 用 a few hundred rupiahs 几百卢比
- 例 Indonesian **rupiah** weakens to the lowest level in almost four years. 印尼卢比跌至近四年来的最低水平。

S

扫一扫
听本节音频

486 **sack** /sæk/ *vt.* 解雇；破坏
n. 一大袋；抢劫

- 同 demolish
- 用 be sacked for refusing to work 因拒绝工作而被解雇
- 例 The IMF would probably tell Greece to **sack** thousands of public-sector workers and cut pensions sharply. 国际货币基金组织可能会要求希腊解雇数千名公共部门员工，并大幅削减养老金。

487 **sanitation** /ˌsænɪˈteɪʃn/ *n.* 卫生

- 用 food sanitation 食品卫生
- 例 Education, housing, health, **sanitation** and employment are all part of life satisfaction. 教育、住房、健康、卫生和就业都是生活满意度的组成部分

488 **satellite** /ˈsætəlaɪt/ *n.* 人造卫星；卫星

- 用 a satellite broadcast 卫星广播
- 例 The **satellite** was launched into orbit around the moon. 卫星进入环月轨道。

489 **shelter** /ˈʃeltə(r)/ *n.* 居所，住处；避难所
v. 保护

- 用 take shelter from the rain 躲雨
- 例 We can all identify certain basic needs that must be satisfied if we are to stay alive. These include the obvious essentials of food, **shelter** and clothing. 如果我们想要生存下去，我们是可以确定哪些基本需求是必须得到满足的，包括食物、住所和衣服等显而易见的必需品。

490 shipwreck /'ʃɪprek/ vt. 遭遇海难，船只失事
n. 海难

- 用 a shipwrecked sailor 遭遇海难的水手
- 例 Some people are **shipwrecked** on a tropical island and allocate their time for gathering coconuts and fishing. 有些人在一个热带岛屿上遭遇海难，他们把时间分配在采集椰子和捕鱼上。

491 silicon /'sɪlɪkən/ n. 硅；硅元素

- 用 silicon valley 硅谷
- 例 The company pioneered the use of the **silicon** chip. 这家公司是最早使用硅芯片的。

492 simplify /'sɪmplɪfaɪ/ vt. 使简化，使简易

- 用 a simplified version 简化版
- 例 We need to **simplify** and generalise about the factors that can influence supply in most industries. 我们需要对影响大多数行业供应的因素进行简化和概括。

493 simultaneously /ˌsɪml'teɪniəsli/ adv. 同时发生地

- 用 proceed simultaneously 同步进行
- 例 The economy of a country is **simultaneously** experiencing a balance of payments deficit, a budget deficit and unemployment. 这个国家在同一时间出现了国际收支赤字、预算赤字和失业的现象。

494 slump /slʌmp/ n. 骤降，猛跌；萧条期
vi. 价格数量等骤降

- 同 collapse, crash, meltdown (n.)
- 用 a slump in sales 销售量锐减
- 例 By November 2007, there were increased signs of a housing market **slump**. 到2007年11月，有越来越多的迹象表明房地产市场正在大步下滑。

495 soar /sɔː(r)/ vi. 猛增,急升;高飞

- 用 soaring prices 飞涨的物价
- 例 By mid-2012, the figure had **soared** to 125 million. 截止到 2012 年年中,这一数字已飙升至 1.25 亿。

496 souvenir /ˌsuːvəˈnɪə(r)/ n. 纪念品,礼物

- 用 a souvenir shop 纪念品商店
- 例 The organisers of a major sporting event produce official **souvenir** products. 大型体育赛事的组织者会制作官方纪念品。

497 sovereign /ˈsɒvrɪn/ adj. 有主权的,完全独立的; 有至高无上权利的

- 用 a sovereign ruler 最高统治者
- 例 Independence and **sovereign** equality among states is a fundamental principle of international law. 国家的独立和主权平等是国际法上的一项根本原则。

498 soyabean /ˈsɔɪəbiːn/ n. 大豆

- 用 soyabean farmer 大豆种植者
- 例 It competes with other vegetable oils, made from **soyabeans**, rapeseed, sunflowers and groundnuts. 它的竞争对手是由大豆、油菜籽、向日葵和花生制成的其他植物油。

499 sparse /spɑːs/ adj. 稀少的,稀疏的

- 用 the sparse population 零星的人口
- 例 Many slopes are rock fields with **sparse** vegetation. 澳大利亚北领地是一个幅员辽阔、人烟稀少的地区。

500 specialist /ˈspeʃəlɪst/ adj. 专门的
n. 专家

- 用 specialist shops 专卖店
- 例 Firms that assemble the final product buy components from **specialist** firms within the industry. 组装最终产品的公司从行业内的专业公司购买零部件。

501 **specification** /ˌspesɪfɪˈkeɪʃn/ *n.* 规格，规范，说明书

- 用 product specification 产品规格
- 例 The product **specification** demanded by each customer is different. 每个客户要求的产品规格都有所不同。

502 **specify** /ˈspesɪfaɪ/ *v.* 具体说明，明确规定

- 用 specify your plan 详细说明你的计划
- 例 The contract clearly **specifies** who can operate the machinery. 合同明确规定了谁能操作这台机器。

503 **speculate** /ˈspekjuleɪt/ *v.* 投机；推测，猜测

- 用 speculate on the stock market 炒股
- 例 Financial institutions **speculate** on future currency movements on their own behalf. 金融机构以自己的名义对未来的货币走势投机。

504 **spiral** /ˈspaɪrəl/ *n.* 螺旋形；逐渐加速上升或下降 *v.* 盘旋上升或下降

- 用 the spiralling cost of health care 急剧上涨的保健费
- 例 A deflationary **spiral** involves a process where deflation sets into motion a series of events that worsen the deflation. 通货紧缩螺旋指的是通货紧缩引发一系列事件使得通货紧缩更加恶化的过程。

505 **spoil** /spɔɪl/ *v.* 破坏，糟蹋；溺爱；变坏

- 同 sack, demolish
- 用 spoil the appetite 破坏食欲
- 例 Mining them produces undesirable side-effects, such as radioactivity, air pollution and **spoilt** landscapes. 开采它们会产生不良的副作用，如放射性污染、空气污染以及景观破坏。

506 **spokesman** /ˈspəʊksmən/ n. 发言人

- 用 news spokesman 新闻发言人
- 例 A **spokesman** from the Turkish Currency Exchange said that the Turkish economy was not strong enough. 土耳其货币交易所发言人称,土耳其经济不够强劲。

507 **sponsorship** /ˈspɒnsəʃɪp/ n. 赞助,资助

- 用 a $50 million sponsorship deal 一项 5000 万美元的赞助协议
- 例 Certainly the brand has had some black moments in its **sponsorship** of athletes. 当然,这个品牌在赞助运动员的过程中也有一些不光彩的时刻。

508 **spray** /spreɪ/ n. 喷雾(剂);浪花
v. 喷洒;扫射

- 用 a can of insect spray 一罐杀虫剂
- 例 The bamboo grows into the garden of his neighbour, who removes the bamboo with a chemical **spray**. 竹子长在了邻居的花园里,所以邻居用化学喷雾剂把竹子清除掉了。

509 **stabilise** /ˈsteɪbɪlaɪz/ v. 使……稳定,稳固

- 用 stabilise prices 稳定物价
- 例 As international inflationary pressures remained weak, the terms of trade were expected to **stabilise** during 2013. 由于国际通胀压力依然疲弱,预计 2013 年贸易条件将趋于稳定。

510 **stagnation** /stægˈneɪʃn/ n. 停滞

- 用 economic stagnation 经济停滞
- 例 **Stagnation** comes because there isn't anything that excites you enough to take action. 停滞的到来是因为没有任何东西足够让你产生兴趣去采取行动。

511 **stainless** /ˈsteɪnlɪs/ *adj.* 不锈的，防锈的

- 用 stainless steel 不锈钢
- 例 Indonesia has started a ban on exports of nickel, which is used to make **stainless** steel. 印尼开始禁止镍的出口，镍被用来制造不锈钢。

512 **staple** /ˈsteɪpl/ *n.* 主食；某国的支柱产品
adj. 主要的

- 用 staple food 主食
- 例 A government may wish to make a food **staple** more affordable to low income earners, and can do so by granting a subsidy to producers of the good. 政府可能希望让低收入者更能负担得起某种主食，为此会向食品生产商提供一些补贴。

513 **steady** /ˈstedi/ *adj.* 稳固的；沉稳的
v. 使平稳

- 用 a steady job 稳定的工作
- 例 A government aims to achieve **steady** and stable growth, in line with the economy's long-run increase in productivity. 政府的目标是实现稳定的增长，这与经济生产率的长期增长相一致。

514 **steep** /stiːp/ *adj.* 急剧的，大起大落的；陡峭的
v. 浸泡

- 用 a steep decline in the birth rate 出生率骤降
- 例 In contrast, a **steeper** rise in unemployment between 2007 and 2009 saw inflation only fall from 2.4% to 1.7%. 相比之下，2007 年至 2009 年间失业率陡增，通货膨胀却仅从 2.4% 降到了 1.7%。

515 **steeply** /ˈstiːpli/ *adv.* 大幅度地；陡峭地；险峻地

- 用 falling steeply 急剧下跌
- 例 Lack of adequate infrastructure causes distribution costs such as transport and warehousing to rise **steeply**. 由于缺乏足够的基础设施，因此运输和仓储等配送成本急剧上升。

516 **steelmaker** /ˈstiːlmeɪkə(r)/ n. 钢铁制造商

- 用 steelmaker association 钢铁制造商协会
- 例 The Luxembourg government, the **steelmaker's** largest shareholder with a 5.6% stake, rejected the bid Tuesday. 卢森堡政府是这家钢铁公司的最大股东,持有该公司 5.6% 的股份,于周二拒绝了这一报价。

517 **stickiness** /ˈstɪkinəs/ n. 粘性

- 用 price stickiness 价格粘性
- 例 The model suggests price **stickiness** is within a certain range of marginal costs. 该模型表明,价格粘性是在一定的边际成本范围内的。

518 **stifle** /ˈstaɪfl/ v. 扼杀,压制;使窒息

- 用 stifle a cry 忍住不哭
- 例 The downside could be that a high tax rate **stifles** the incentive to work. 不利的一面可能是高税率打消了工作的积极性。

519 **stipulate** /ˈstɪpjuleɪt/ v. 规定,明确要求

- 同 specify
- 用 be stipulated in the contract 在合同中明确要求
- 例 This **stipulates** that Indian-owned airline operators must have a minimum number of aircraft. 这一规定要求印度所有的航空公司运营商所拥有的飞机数量不得低于最低数量。

520 **storage** /ˈstɔːrɪdʒ/ n. 存储;仓库;贮藏所

- 用 food storage 食物储藏
- 例 The petrol **storage** tanks are full. 汽油罐已经满了。

521 **straightforward** /ˌstreɪt'fɔːwəd/ *adj.* 简单的；坦率的

- 搭 a straightforward operation 简单的操作
- 例 The situation is not as **straightforward** as they suggest. 情况并不像他们所说的那样简单。

522 **strain** /streɪn/ *n.* 重负，情感方面的压力；张力
v. 损伤

- 搭 under great strain 重压之下
- 例 These repayments are putting a **strain** on our finances. 偿还这些债务对我们的财务状况形成了压力。

523 **straits** /streɪts/ *n.* 困难（常用于复数）；海峡

- 搭 financial straits 经济困难
- 例 The factory is in dire **straits**. 这家工厂陷入困境。

524 **strand** /strænd/ *v.* 使滞留，使搁浅
n. 观点、计划等的一部分

- 搭 be stranded at the airport 滞留在机场
- 例 A group of tourists become **stranded** on a deserted island. 一群游客被困在一座荒岛上。

525 **strategic** /strə'tiːdʒɪk/ *adj.* 战略上的

- 搭 strategic management 战略管理
- 例 **Strategic** trade policy is a new argument in favour of trade protection that appeared in the 1980s. 战略贸易政策是 20 世纪 80 年代出现的新论据，以支持贸易保护主义。

526 **streetlight** /'striːtlaɪt/ *n.* 路灯

- 搭 dim streetflight 昏暗的路灯
- 例 We are one of the largest manufacturer, supplier and exporter of LED **streetlight**. 我们是全球最大的 LED 路灯生产商、供应商和出口商之一。

527 **strike** /straɪk/ *n.* 罢工或罢课；击
v. 击打；因疾病等痛苦

- 🌐 be stricken with diseases 被病魔折磨
- 📝 The trade union for transport workers decided to call a **strike** unless its members were awarded a higher rate of pay. 运输工人工会决定举行罢工，除非其成员能获得更高的工资。

528 **struggle** /ˈstrʌgl/ *v. & n.* 奋斗，努力；艰难地行进

- 🌐 struggle against cancer 同癌症抗争
- 📝 India has **struggled** to provide enough electricity to power its industry. 印度一直难以为其工业提供足够的电力。

529 **subdue** /səbˈdjuː/ *vt.* 控制，抑制，克制

- 🔁 curb, contain
- 🌐 subdue the rebels 镇压反叛者
- 📝 Why did inflationary pressures remain **subdued** in Fiji despite higher growth? 为什么斐济的通货膨胀压力在经济高速增长的情况下仍然受到抑制？

530 **substitute** /ˈsʌbstɪtjuːt/ *n.* 替代品；替补
v. 取代，替代

- 🌐 substitute A for B 用 A 替代 B
- 📝 The firms produce close **substitutes**. 这些公司生产相似的替代品。

531 **substitutable** /ˈsʌbstɪtjuːtəbl/ *adj.* 可替换的

- 🔁 replaceable
- 🌐 easily substitutable 易替换的
- 📝 The greater the number of substitute products and the more closely **substitutable** those products are, the more we would expect consumers to switch away from a particular product when its price goes up. 可替代产品的数量越多以及这些产品的替代性越强，消费者在物价上涨时就越有可能放弃这种商品而选择其他。

532 subtract /səb'trækt/ vt. 减去

- ⊕ subtract from sth. 从某物中减去
- ⓔ The balance of trade in goods is calculated by **subtracting** imports from exports. 货物贸易差额是用出口减去进口来计算的。

533 subtraction /səb'trækʃn/ n. 减法，减少

- ⊕ be tested on addition and subtraction 加减法测试
- ⓔ Leadership is not about isolation, but aggregation, not addition or **subtraction**, but multiplication. 领导力不是孤立，而是聚集，不是加减，而是倍增。

534 suffer /'sʌfə(r)/ v. 受苦，受难；容忍

- ⊕ suffer from asthma 被哮喘折磨
- ⓔ Venezuela is **suffering** the worst economic crisis in its history. 委内瑞拉正遭受有史以来最严重的经济危机。

535 sufficient /sə'fɪʃnt/ adj. 足够的，充分的

- ⓢ adequate
- ⓐ insufficient adj. 不够的
- ⊕ sufficient storage of stock 不足的存货
- ⓔ Donor funds are neither **sufficient**, nor reliable enough, to be able to cover interest rate subsidies. 捐赠资金既不充足也不可靠，因此不足以支付利率补贴。

536 suited /'suːtɪd/ adj. 适合的，相配的；穿着……套装的

- ⊕ a grey-suited technician 身着灰色套装的技术人员
- ⓔ Its climate is not so **suited** to producing olives but the olives can be sold for a higher price per sack. 那里的气候不太适合生产橄榄，因此抬高了橄榄的单价。

537 **summit** /ˈsʌmɪt/ n. 首脑会议；最高点；极点

- 同 peak, climax, pinnacle, culmination
- 用 a summit conference 峰会
- 例 The cooperation was on display at the first G20 **summit** in an Asia Pacific nation. 这种合作在亚太国家举行的20国集团首次峰会上得到了体现。

538 **superior** /suːˈpɪəriə(r)/ adj. 更好的；级别上更高的；有优越感的
n. 上级

- 用 superior knowledge 更丰富的知识
- 例 Sales taxes are always **superior** to income taxes as a means of raising revenue for the government. 作为提高政府收入的一种手段，销售税总是优于所得税。

539 **supervision** /ˌsuːpəˈvɪʒn/ n. 管理，监督

- 用 under strict supervision 在严苛的监管之下
- 例 The IMF recommended that the Indian government and central bank should raise interest rates, reduce the budget deficit and improve bank **supervision**. 国际货币基金组织建议印度政府和中央银行提高利率、减少预算赤字并加强银行监管。

540 **suppose** /səˈpəʊz/ v. 假定；推断，认为

- 同 infer
- 用 be supposed to do sth. 应当做某事
- 例 **Suppose** the average consumer's expenditure is divided between bread, meat, milk and vegetables in the ratio 4:3:2:1 假设消费者在面包、肉类、牛奶和蔬菜上的消费比例为4:3:2:1。

541 **surge** /sɜːdʒ/ v. 激增；涌动
n. 数量急剧上升；强烈感情的突发

- 回 soar
- 串 prices surge 物价飞涨
- 例 Statistics reported that Egypt's annual inflation rate **surged** to 32.9% in April 2017. 数据显示，埃及 2017 年 4 月的通货膨胀率飙升至 32.9%。

542 **surgical** /'sɜːdʒɪkl/ adj. 外科的，外科手术的

- 串 surgical gloves 手术手套
- 例 In 2008, makers of **surgical** products and rubber gloves, increased profits by 2.6%. 2008 年，外科手术产品和橡胶手套制造商的利润增长了 2.6%。

543 **surprise** /sə'praɪz/ n. 突然的事；惊奇
vt. 使诧异；使措手不及

- 串 take sb. by surprise 出乎某人意料
- 例 The change in consumer spending habits caught retailers and manufacturers by **surprise**. 消费者消费习惯的变化让零售商和制造商措手不及。

544 **sustainability** /səˌsteɪnə'bɪləti/ n. 可持续性

- 串 economic sustainability 经济可持续性
- 例 Urban **sustainability** solutions do not just benefit the environment and people's quality of life; they are often highly profitable. 城市的可持续性解决方案不仅有利于改善环境和提高人们的生活质量，而且这种解决方案的利润也很高。

545 **sustain** /sə'steɪn/ vt. 维持，保持；遭受损失；证实

- 回 retention (n.)
- 串 sustain losses 遭受损失
- 例 The USA's current account deficit in 2005 reached 6.2% of GDP and by 2013 it had fallen to 2.5%, a level it could **sustain**. 2005

年美国的经常账户赤字占 GDP 的 6.2%，到 2013 年这一数值下降到 2.5%，才达到可以维持的水平。

546 **swift** /swɪft/ *adj.* 迅速的，马上做出的；敏捷的
n. 雨燕

- 搭 a swift decision 迅速做出的决定
- 例 This led to a **swift** reaction from consumers who reduced spending and increased savings. 这导致消费者迅速做出反应，他们减少支出，增加储蓄。

547 **synthetic** /sɪn'θetɪk/ *adj.* 人造的，人工合成的
n. 合成纤维

- 同 artificial
- 搭 synthetic fabrics 合成织物
- 例 The bigger fear is that **synthetic** biology could be the end of us all. 更大的担忧是合成生物学可能是我们所有人的末日。

T

548 tax /tæks/ n. 税，税赋，负担

- ⊕ tax increase 税收增加
- ⓔ On taxes, the report emphasised the need to end the use of tax **havens** to hide large amounts of money. 在税收方面，该报告强调有必要停止使用避税天堂来隐藏大量资金。

549 temporary /ˈtemprəri/ adj. 临时的，暂时的
n. 临时雇员

- ⊕ temporary work 临时工作
- ⓔ In 2008, Chinese government imposed **temporary** maximum price controls on energy and transport. 2008 年，中国政府对能源和交通运输实施了临时的最高价格管制。

550 tenant /ˈtenənt/ n. 佃户，租户
v. 居住，工作

- ⊕ tenant farmers 佃农
- ⓔ The rent paid to a land owner by a **tenant** farmer is a transfer payment. 佃农支付给土地所有者的租金是一种转让性支付。

551 territory /ˈterətri/ n. 领土，领地；某人负责的地区

- ⊕ enemy territory 敌方领土
- ⓔ Eleven years later, Iraq became the first mandated **territory** to obtain independence. 11 年后，伊拉克成为第一个获得独立的托管领土。

552 **tournament** /ˈtʊənəmənt/ *n.* 锦标赛

- 用 world tournament 世界锦标赛
- 例 Tiger Woods announces that his final golf appearance will be at the next US Open **Tournament**. 泰格·伍兹宣布他的最后一场高尔夫比赛将在下一次美国公开赛上举行。

553 **transatlantic** /ˌtrænzətˈlæntɪk/ *adj.* 横渡大西洋的

- 用 a transatlantic flight 横跨大西洋的飞行
- 例 Cunard is a company that operates large passenger liners providing **transatlantic** crossings between the US and the UK. 丘纳德公司是一家经营大型客机的公司,提供横跨大西洋的美英航线。

554 **transferable** /ˌtrænsˈfɜːrəbl/ *adj.* 可转移的,可转让的

- 用 provide students with transferable skills 使学生掌握可用于不同工作的技术
- 例 There are many similarities that are **transferable** from coaching a team to leading an organisation. 指导团队和领导组织有许多相似之处。

555 **transferability** /ˌtrænsˌfɜːrəˈbɪləti/ *n.* 可转移性,可转让性

- 同 assignability
- 用 possess transferability 具有可转让性
- 例 If analysed from the angle of economics, **transferability** should also be an important feature of property right. 若从经济学角度来分析,可转让性也应是物权的重要特征。

556 **transform** /trænsˈfɔːm/ v. 使改变形态；使改观

- 用 transform sth. into sth. 把某物转变成某物
- 例 A combination of the internet and computer revolutions is **transforming** the world economy which has led to economic growth. 互联网和计算机革命的结合正在改变世界经济，并带来了经济增长。

557 **transit** /ˈtrænzɪt/ v. 经过
n. 运输

- 用 in transit 在运输中
- 例 The ship is currently **transiting** the Gulf of Mexico. 这艘船正穿越墨西哥湾。

558 **transmission** /trænzˈmɪʃn/ n. 传导；传输；传播

- 用 the transmission of the disease 疾病的传播
- 例 The diagram outlines the monetary **transmission** mechanism following an expansionary central bank intervention. 该图概述了扩张性央行干预后的货币传导机制。

559 **transmit** /trænzˈmɪt/ v. 传输；传播，传染

- 用 transmit signals 传递信号
- 例 An important feature of the poverty cycle is that poverty is **transmitted** from generation to generation. 贫穷循环的一个重要特征是它代代相传。

560 **trigger** /ˈtrɪɡə(r)/ vt. 触发；启动
n. 扳机；不良反应的起因

- 用 the trigger for the strike 触发罢工的原因
- 例 China's recent devaluation of its currency, the Chinese yuan, **triggered** fears of China overwhelming Vietnam with even cheaper goods. 人民币近来贬值引发了一种担忧，担心中国会以更便宜的商品打击越南。

561　**trillion** /ˈtrɪljən/ *n.* 万亿；大量，无数

- 用 a mistake made trillions of times before 一个犯了太多次的错误
- 例 China has attempted to keep the Chinese yuan–US dollar exchange rate relatively stable, costing more than $2 **trillion** of its official foreign exchange reserves. 中国一直试图保持人民币兑美元汇率相对稳定，动用了超过 2 万亿美元的官方外汇储备。

562　**tropical** /ˈtrɒpɪkl/ *adj.* 热带的

- 用 tropical rainforest 热带雨林
- 例 Some people are shipwrecked on a **tropical** island. 有些人在热带岛屿上遭遇海难。

563　**tycoon** /taɪˈkuːn/ *n.* 企业大亨，巨头

- 用 a business tycoon 产业大亨
- 例 **Tycoon** offered help as cheap Chinese goods overwhelm Vietnam's economy. 当廉价的中国商品充斥越南经济时，富商巨头们伸出了援手。

U

564 **undermine** /ˌʌndəˈmaɪn/ vt. 使减少效力；逐渐地（偷偷地）损害

- 🌐 undermine one's adversary's reputation 损害其对手的名誉
- 例 Very low interest rates **undermine** the profitability of commercial banks. 极低的利率削弱了商业银行的盈利能力。

565 **undervalue** /ˌʌndəˈvæljuː/ vt. 低估，轻视

- 反 overvalue vt. 高估
- 🌐 undervalue the art 低估艺术的价值
- 例 An **undervalued** currency is one whose value is too low relative to its equilibrium free market value. 被低估的货币是指其价值相对于其均衡自由市场价值而言过低的货币。

566 **undisclosed** /ˌʌndɪsˈkləʊzd/ adj. 未披露的，未公开的

- 🌐 undisclosed information 未公开的信息
- 例 The exchange rate is allowed to move within an **undisclosed** trading band but not to move outside of it. 汇率可以在一个未披露的交易区间内波动，但不能超出这个区间。

567 **unionise** /ˈjuːniənaɪz/ v. 使加入工会，成立工会

- 🌐 a unionised workforce 加入工会的劳动人口
- 例 **Unionised** labour frequently succeeds in securing high wage increases. 加入工会的工人经常能在争取高工资增长上取得胜利。

568 **unique** /ju'niːk/ *adj.* 独具的，特有的；独一无二的

- 圆 distinctive
- 用 a unique talent 奇才
- 例 Singapore has a **unique** exchange rate system. 新加坡有特有的汇率制度。

569 **unsustainable** /ˌʌnsəˈsteɪnəbl/ *adj.* 不可持续的

- 用 unsustainable growth 难以持续的增长
- 例 Environmentalists say it is **unsustainable** for economies to focus on increasing their GDP. 环保人士说，经济体把重点放在增加国内生产总值上是不可持续的。

V

570 **vaccination** /ˌvæksɪˈneɪʃn/ *n.* 接种疫苗

- 用 vaccination against polio 接种小儿麻痹疫苗
- 例 Certain groups have even questioned the utility of **vaccination**, in spite of its ongoing necessity to control disease. 尽管接种疫苗对控制疾病很有必要，但一些团体还是会质疑免疫接种的用途。

571 **validity** /vəˈlɪdəti/ *n.* 有效性，合法性

- 用 period of validity 有效期
- 例 A law is a concise statement of an event that is supposed to have universal **validity**. 法律是对一个被认为具有普遍有效性的事件的简明陈述。

572 **vendor** /ˈvendə(r)/ *n.* 供应商；小贩，摊贩

- 用 a street vendor 街头小贩
- 例 A **vendor** will provide online tools to assist in the planning. 一供应商会提供有助于进行计划的在线工具。

573 **volatility** /ˌvɒləˈtɪləti/ *n.* 波动性，不稳定性

- 同 fluctuate (v.)
- 用 volatility of prices 价格波动
- 例 **Volatility** of primary product prices has serious negative consequences for producers and for the economy as a whole. 初级产品价格的波动对生产者和整个经济都有严重的消极后果。

574 **voyage** /ˈvɔɪɪdʒ/ *n.* 航行，航海

- 搭 maiden voyage 首航
- 例 Passengers purchasing the **voyage** in the US pay a much lower price than ones purchasing the **voyage** in the UK. 在美国购买航程的乘客比在英国购买航程的乘客支付的价格要低得多。

575 **vulnerability** /ˌvʌlnərəˈbɪləti/ *n.* 脆弱性

- 搭 political vulnerability 政治上的脆弱性
- 例 Given their **vulnerability** in times of severe external payment difficulties, countries are forced to accept harsh conditions that run counter to their development objectives. 鉴于这些国家在面临严重的外部支付困难时所表现出来的脆弱性，它们不得不接受那些与其发展目标背道而驰的苛刻条件。

576 **warehouse** /ˈweəhaʊs/ n. 仓库，货仓

- 同 storage
- 用 warehouse supervisor 仓库管理员
- 例 The US officials said the airstrike apparently hit a **warehouse**, but gave no other details. 美国官员说，空袭击中了一个仓库，但没有透露其他细节。

577 **warship** /ˈwɔːʃɪp/ n. 军舰

- 同 warcraft
- 用 serving on a warship 在军舰上服役
- 例 The British sent a **warship** to help with the evacuation of British citizens from Libya. 英国派出一艘军舰帮助从利比亚撤离英国公民。

578 **wholesale** /ˈhəʊlseɪl/ adj. 批发的；大规模的

- 用 wholesale prices 批发价格
- 例 There is a fall in the world price of tea traded on **wholesale** international markets. 在国际批发市场上交易的世界茶叶价格下降了。

第二部分
高频专业词汇

第一章　GCSE 和 IB-MYP 高频专业词汇 / 130

第二章　A-Level AS 阶段高频专业词汇 / 207

第三章　A-Level A2 阶段高频专业词汇 / 234

第一章 GCSE 和 IB-MYP 高频专业词汇

第一节
Basic Economic Problems 基础经济问题

扫一扫
听本节音频

001 **economic** /ˌiːkəˈnɒmɪk/ **good** 经济商品

- ☐ **D** a product which requires resources to produce it and therefore has an opportunity cost
- ☐ 定 一种需要资源来生产它并因此具有机会成本的产品

002 **free good** 免费商品

- ☐ **D** a product which does not require any resources to make it and therefore does not have an opportunity cost
- ☐ 定 一种不需要任何资源即可生产的产品，因此没有机会成本

003 **resource** /rɪˈsɔːs/ *n.* 资源

- ☐ **D** inputs available for the production of goods and services
- ☐ 定 可用于生产商品和服务的投入物
- ☐ **E** land, labour, capital, entrepreneur
- 释 自然资源、人力资源、资本、企业家

004 **needs** /niːdz/ *n.* 需求

- ☐ **D** basic requirements for survival
- ☐ 定 生存的基本需求
- ☐ **E** examples: food, water, shelter
- 释 例子：食物、水、庇护所

005 **wants** /wɒnts/   *n.* 欲望

- 🇩 needs that are not always realised
- 🇨 并非总能实现的需求

006 **scarcity** /ˈskeəsəti/   *n.* 稀缺性

- 🇩 a situation in which wants are in excess of the resources available
- 🇨 欲望超出可用资源的情况

007 **choice** /tʃɔɪs/   *n.* 选择

- 🇩 It underpins the concept that resources are scarce so choices have to be made by consumers, firms and governments.
- 🇨 它巩固了资源稀缺的概念,因此消费者、企业和政府必须做出选择。

008 **fundamental** /ˌfʌndəˈmentl/ **economic problem**
基本经济问题

- 🇩 How to allocate scarce resources to satisfy unlimited needs and wants.
- 🇨 如何分配稀缺的资源以满足无限的需求和欲望。

009 **chain of production** /prəˈdʌkʃn/   生产链

- 🇩 It describes how businesses from the primary, secondary and tertiary sectors work interdependently to make a product and sell it to the final customer.
- 🇨 它描述了第一、第二和第三产业中的企业如何相互依存地合作制造出产品并将其出售给最终客户。

010 **factors of production**   生产要素

- 🇩 anything that is useful in the production of goods and services
- 🇨 在生产商品和服务时发挥作用的任何东西
- 🇪 land, labour, capital, entrepreneur
- 🇰 自然资源、人力资源、资本、企业家

第二部分　高频专业词汇

011 **land** /lænd/ — *n.* 自然资源

- Ⓓ one of the natural resources in an economy, such as minerals, oil reserves, underground water, forests, rivers and lakes
- 㝎 经济体中的自然资源,如矿产、石油储量、地下水、森林、河流和湖泊

012 **labour** /ˈleɪbə(r)/ — *n.* 劳动力

- Ⓓ human resources available in an economy
- 㝎 经济体中可用的人力资源

013 **capital** /ˈkæpɪtl/ — *n.* 资本

- Ⓓ a large amount of money that is invested or used to start a business
- 㝎 投资或用于创业的大量资金

014 **entrepreneur** /ˌɒntrəprəˈnɜː(r)/ — *n.* 企业家

- Ⓓ an individual who is able to manage other three factors of production and is willing to take risks
- 㝎 能够管理其他三个生产要素并愿意冒险的个人

015 **opportunity** /ˌɒpəˈtjuːnəti/ **cost** — 机会成本

- Ⓓ the value of the next best alternative foregone
- 㝎 被放弃的下一个最佳替代品的价值

016 **labour force** — 劳动力

- Ⓓ the amount of working age population who are willing and able to work
- 㝎 愿意且能够工作的劳动年龄人口数量

017 **factor mobility** /məʊˈbɪləti/ — 生产要素流动性

- Ⓓ the ease by which factors of production can be moved around
- 㝎 生产要素可转移的难易程度

018 occupational /ˌɒkjuˈpeɪʃənl/ mobility 职业流动性

- **D** the ability of labour to switch between different occupations
- **定** 劳动力在不同职业之间转换的能力

019 geographic /ˌdʒɪəˈɡræfɪk/ mobility 地域流动性

- **D** the ability to move factors of production to different locations
- **定** 使生产要素转移到不同地点的能力

020 labour productivity /ˌprɒdʌkˈtɪvəti/ 劳动生产率

- **D** output per worker hour
- **定** 每工时产量

021 investment /ɪnˈvestmənt/ *n.* 投资

- **D** firms' spending on capital goods
- **定** 企业在资本货物上的支出

022 depreciation /dɪˌpriːʃiˈeɪʃn/ *n.* 折旧

- **D** the decrease in the value of capital goods that have worn out or become obsolete
- **定** 由磨损或过时所造成的资本货物价值的减少

023 net investment /ɪnˈvestmənt/ 净投资

- **D** gross investment minus depreciation
- **定** 总投资减去折旧

024 production possibility curve 生产可能性曲线

- **D** It shows all the possible combination of two goods which gives the maximum level of output that an economy can produce when using its existing resources and technology.
- **定** 生产可能性曲线是用来表示经济社会在既定资源和技术条件下所能生产的两种商品最大数量的组合。

第二节
Allocation of Resources 资源分配

025 **economic** /ˌiːkə'nɒmɪk/ **agent** /'eɪdʒənt/ 经济人

- Ⓓ the person who undertakes economic activities and makes economic decisions
- Ⓔ 从事经济活动并做出经济决定的人

026 **market** /'mɑːkɪt/ n. 市场

- Ⓓ It is any set of arrangements that brings together all the producers and consumers of a good or service so they may engage in exchange.
- Ⓔ 市场把商品或服务的所有生产者和消费者安排聚集在一起，以便他们可以进行交换。

027 **economic system** 经济体制

- Ⓓ the means by which choices are made in an economy
- Ⓔ 指在一个国家制定并执行经济决策的各种机制的总和

028 **market economy** 市场经济

- Ⓓ The government will play a less important role in the allocation of scarce resources and that free-market forces, through the operation of the price mechanism and the interaction of the influences of demand and supply, will play a more important role.
- Ⓔ 政府在稀缺资源的分配中发挥较小的作用，而通过价格机制的运作以及供给和需求的影响之间的相互作用，自由市场力量将发挥更为重要的作用。

029 **planned economy** 计划经济

- **D** An economy where resource allocation decisions are taken by a government
- 定 一个由政府决定资源分配的经济体制

030 **mixed economy** 混合经济

- **D** an economy where market forces and government, private and public sectors are involved in resource allocation decisions
- 定 一种市场力量与政府、私人和公共部门共同参与资源分配的经济体制

031 **market mechanism** 市场机制

- **D** a mechanism where decisions on price and quantity are made on the basis of demand and supply alone
- 定 仅根据供应和需求来决定价格和数量的机制

032 **capital-intensive** /ˈkæpɪtəlɪnˌtensɪv/
adj. 资本密集型的

- **D** using a high proportion of capital relative to labour in the production process
- 定 在生产过程中使用大量资本（同劳动力相比）

033 **labour-intensive** /ˌleɪbərɪnˈtensɪv/
adj. 劳动密集型的

- **D** using a high proportion of labour relative to capital in the production process
- 定 在生产过程中使用大量劳动力（同资本相比）

034 **demand** /dɪˈmɑːnd/
n. 需求

- **D** the willingness and the ability of customers to pay a given price to buy a good or service
- 定 客户支付一定价格购买商品或服务的意愿和能力

035 **complements** /ˈkɒmplɪments/   *n.* 互补品

- **D** products that are demanded for their use together with other products
- **定** 互补品是需要与其他产品一起使用的产品。

036 **substitutes** /ˈsʌbstɪtjuːts/   *n.* 替代品

- **D** products that are in competitive demand as they can be used in place of each other
- **定** 替代品是可以相互替代使用的、具有竞争需求的产品。

037 **equilibrium** /ˌiːkwɪˈlɪbriəm/   *n.* 平衡点

- **D** It occurs when the quantity demanded for a product is equal to the quantity supplied of the product.
- **定** 平衡点出现在产品的需求量等于产品的供应量时。

038 **market demand**   市场需求

- **D** total demand for a product
- **定** 某一产品的总需求

039 **extension** /ɪkˈstenʃn/ **in demand**   需求增长

- **D** a rise in the quantity demanded caused by a fall in the price of the product itself
- **定** 产品本身价格下跌导致该产品需求量增加。

040 **contraction** /kənˈtrækʃn/ **in demand**   需求缩减

- **D** a fall in the quantity demanded caused by a rise in the price of the product itself
- **定** 产品本身价格上涨导致该产品需求量下降。

041 **normal goods**   正常商品

- **D** products whose demand increases when income increases and decreases when income falls
- **定** 当收入增加时需求增加，而收入减少时需求减少的产品。

042 **inferior** /ɪnˈfɪəriə(r)/ **goods** 劣等商品

- **D** products whose demand decreases when income increases and increases when income falls
- **定** 当收入增加时需求减少，而收入减少时需求增加的产品。

043 **supply** /səˈplaɪ/ *n.* 供给

- **D** the willingness and ability of a producer to sell a product at a given price
- **定** 生产者以一定价格出售某产品的意愿和能力。

044 **market supply** 市场供给

- **D** total supply of a product
- **定** 某一产品的总供应

045 **extension in supply** 供给增长

- **D** a rise in the quantity supplied caused by a rise in the price of the product itself
- **定** 产品本身价格上涨导致供应数量增加

046 **contraction in supply** 供给缩减

- **D** a fall in the quantity supplied caused by a fall in the price of the product itself
- **定** 产品本身价格下跌导致供应量下降

047 **excess** /ˈekses/ **demand** 需求过剩

- **D** It occurs when the demand for a product exceeds the supply of the product at certain price levels. This happens when the price is set below the equilibrium price, resulting in shortages.
- **定** 在一定价格水平时，产品的需求超过产品供应就会发生这种情况。当价格低于均衡价格时这种情况就会发生，从而导致短缺。

048 **excess supply** 供给过剩

- **D** It occurs when the supply of a product exceeds the demand at certain price levels. This results in a surplus because the price is too high. (i.e. above the market equilibrium price)
- **C** 在一定价格水平时,产品的供应超过需求就会发生这种情况。由于价格太高,导致盈余,即高于市场均衡价格。

049 **taxes** /ˈtæksɪz/ *n.* 税收

- **E** charges imposed by governments on incomes, profits and some types of consumer goods and services to fund their expenditure
- **C** 政府对于收入、利润以及各种消费品和服务,征收的为财政支出提供资金支持的费用

050 **direct taxes** 直接税

- **D** taxes on the income and wealth of individuals and firms
- **C** 对个人和企业的收入和财富的征税。

051 **indirect taxes** 间接税

- **D** taxes on the consumption of goods and services
- **C** 针对消费商品和服务的征税。

052 **subsidy** /ˈsʌbsədi/ *n.* 补贴

- **D** a payment by a government to encourage the production or consumption of a product
- **C** 政府为鼓励产品生产或消费而支付的款项。

053 **disequilibrium** /ˌdɪsˌiːkwɪˈlɪbriəm/ *n.* 非平衡点

- **D** a situation where demand and supply are not equal
- **C** 供需不平等的情况

054 **price discrimination** /dɪˌskrɪmɪˈneɪʃn/ 价格歧视

- **D** It occurs when firms charge different customers different prices for essentially the same product for reasons not related to costs.
- **定** 当公司针对本质上相同的产品向不同客户收取不同价格，而该行为出于与成本无关的原因时，就是价格歧视。

055 **price elasticity** /ˌiːlæˈstɪsəti/ **of demand (PED)**
需求的价格弹性

- **D** a measure of the responsiveness of the quantity demanded to a change in price
- **定** 衡量需求量对价格变化的反应程度。

056 **price elasticity of supply (PES)**
供给的价格弹性

- **D** a measure of the responsiveness of the quantity supplied to a change in price
- **定** 衡量供应量对价格变化的反应程度。

057 **unitary** /ˈjuːnətri/ **price elasticity**
单位需求（或供应）价格弹性

- **D** It occurs when the percentage change in the quantity demanded (or supplied) is proportional to the change in the price, so there is no change in the sales revenue.
- **定** 当需求（或供应）数量的百分比变化与价格变化成比例时，就会发生这种情况，因此销售收入不会发生变化。

058 **private sector** 私营部门

- **D** business organisations which are owned by shareholders or individuals
- **定** 股东或个人所有的商业组织

059 **public sector** 国营部门；公共部门

- the part of the economy controlled by the government
- 由政府控制的经济部分

060 **privatisation** /ˌpraɪvətaɪˈzeɪʃn/ *n.* 私有化

- the policy of selling off state-owned assets (such as property or public-sector businesses) to the private sector, if they can be run more efficiently
- 如果可以更有效地运行国有资产（例如房地产或公共部门企业），则将国有资产销售给私营部门的政策。

061 **nationalisation** /ˌnæʃnəlaɪˈzeɪʃn/ *n.* 国有化

- moving the ownership and control of an industry from the private sector to the government
- 将某行业的所有权及控制权从私营部门转移到政府手上。

062 **market failure** 市场失灵

- market forces resulting in an inefficient allocation of resources
- 市场力量导致资源分配效率低下。

063 **free rider** 搭便车

- someone who consumes a good or service without paying for it
- 消费商品或服务但无须付费的人

064 **allocative** /ˌæləˈketɪv/ **efficiency** 配置效率

- This occurs when resources are allocated in a way that maximises consumers' satisfaction. This means that firms produce the products that consumers demand, in the right quantities.
- 当以最大程度满足消费者的方式分配资源时，就会发生这种情况。这意味着企业可以按正确的数量生产出消费者所需的产品。

065 **productively** /prəˈdʌktɪvli/ **efficient** 生产效率的

- **D** when products are produced at the lowest possible cost and making full use of resources
- **定** 以可能的最低成本生产产品并充分利用资源

066 **dynamic** /daɪˈnæmɪk/ **efficiency** 动态效率

- **D** efficiency occurring overtime as a result of investment and innovation
- **定** 投资和创新造成的较长时期内的效率。

067 **third party** 第三方

- **D** people who are not involved in producing or consuming a product
- **定** 不参与生产或消费产品的人

068 **social benefits** 社会利益

- **D** the total benefits to a society of an economic activity, which is the total of private benefits and external benefits
- **定** 社会经济活动的总利益,包含了私人利益和外部利益。

069 **social costs** 社会成本

- **D** the total costs to a society of an economic activity, which is the total of private costs and external costs
- **定** 社会经济活动的总成本,包含了私人成本和外部成本。

070 **private benefits** 私人利益

- **D** benefits received by those directly consuming or producing a product
- **定** 直接消费或生产产品的人获得的利益。

071 **external** /ɪkˈstɜːnl/ **benefits** 外部利益

- **D** benefits enjoyed by those who are not involved in the consumption and production activities of others directly
- **定** 未直接参与生产或消费的第三方所获得的经济利益

072 **private costs** 私人成本

- costs borne by those directly consuming or producing a product
- 直接消费或生产产品的人承担的费用

073 **external costs** 外部成本

- costs imposed on those who are not involved in the consumption and production activities of others directly
- 未直接参与生产或消费的第三方所承担的经济损失

074 **socially optimum /ˈɒptɪməm/ output** 社会最优产量

- the level of output where social cost equals social benefit and society's welfare is maximised
- 当社会成本等于社会利益时的产出水平,此时社会福利达到最大化。

075 **merit /ˈmerɪt/ goods** 有益品

- They are products which the government considers consumers do not fully appreciate how beneficial they are and so which will be under-consumed if left to market forces. Such goods generate positive externalities.
- 政府认为消费者没有完全意识到该类产品的益处,因此,如果仅任市场力量作用,它们会消费不足。这些商品可产生正外部效应。

076 **demerit /diːˈmerɪt/ goods** 无益品

- They are products which the government considers consumers do not fully appreciate how harmful they are and so which will be over-consumed if left to market forces. Such goods generate negative externalities.
- 政府认为消费者并未完全意识到该类产品的危害性,因此,如果任由市场力量作用,它们会被过度消费。这些商品可产生负外部效应。

077 **public good** 公共物品

- **D** a product which is non-rival and nonexcludable and hence needs to be financed by taxation
- **定** 同时具有非竞争性和非排他性的产品,因此需要政府用税收收入来支付

078 **private good** 私人物品

- **D** a product which is both rival and excludable
- **定** 既有竞争性也有排他性的产品

079 **monopoly** /məˈnɒpəli/ *n.* 垄断

- **D** A monopoly refers to when a company and its product offerings dominate a sector industry
- **定** 垄断指一个公司及其产品独占一个行业的情况。

080 **price fixing** 限定价格

- **D** when two or more firms agree to sell a product at the same price
- **定** 当两个或多个企业同意以相同价格出售某一产品

081 **ration** /ˈræʃn/ *n.* 配给

- **D** limit the amount that can be consumed to solve shortages
- **定** 对于可用于解决短缺问题的消耗量的限制

082 **multinational** /ˌmʌltɪˈnæʃnəl/ **companies (MNCs)** 跨国企业

- **D** companies which produce in more than one country
- **定** 在多个国家生产产品的企业

第三节

Microeconomic Decision Makers 微观经济决定者

扫一扫
听本节音频

083 **money** /ˈmʌni/   *n.* 货币

- 定 an item which is generally acceptable as a means of payment
- 定 被广为接受的付款方式
- 例 coins, notes and bank account
- 释 硬币、纸币和银行账户

084 **self-sufficient** /ˌselfsəˈfɪʃnt/   *adj.* 自给自足的

- 例 Individuals or small communities would produce all the things they needed or wanted for themselves.
- 释 个人或小型社区可以生产所需的或想要的所有东西。

085 **durability** /ˌdjʊərəˈbɪləti/   *n.* 耐久性

- 例 Money should be fairly long lasting yet easily replaced if it becomes worn.
- 释 钱币按理应具有长久性，但一旦磨损应便于更换。

086 **acceptability** /əkˌseptəˈbɪləti/   *n.* 可接受性

- 例 Money is widely recognised and accepted as a medium of payment for goods and services.
- 释 货币被广泛认可并被认为是消费商品和服务的付款方式。

087 **functions of money**   货币的职能

- 定 the role that money plays in the economy
- 定 货币在经济中扮演的角色
- 例 Money is a medium of exchange, a store of value, a unit of account and a method of deferred payment.
- 释 货币是交换媒介、贮藏手段、价值尺度和支付手段。

088 **central bank** 中央银行

- 定 a government-owned bank which provides banking services to the government and commercial banks and operates monetary policy
- 定 国有银行，为政府和商业银行提供银行服务并执行货币政策

089 **saving** /ˈseɪvɪŋ/ *n.* 储蓄

- 定 deferred consumption or the accumulation of wealth
- 定 延期消费或财富累积

090 **disposable** /dɪˈspəʊzəbl/ **income** 可支配收入

- 定 income after income tax has been deducted and state benefits are received
- 定 扣除所得税和国家福利后剩余的收入

091 **wealth** /welθ/ *n.* 财富

- 定 It is measured by the value of assets a person owns minus their liabilities.
- 定 用一个人拥有的资产价值减去其负债来衡量。
- 举 money held in bank accounts, shares in companies, government bonds, cars and property
- 释 银行账户、公司股份、政府债券、汽车和房地产中的资金

092 **rate of interest** 利息

- 定 a charge for borrowing money and a payment for lending money
- 定 由于借（入）钱而产生的费用和由于借（出）钱而产生的收款

093 **average propensity** /prəˈpensəti/ **to consume** /kənˈsjuːm/ 家庭消费比例

- 定 the proportion of household disposable income which is spent
- 定 支出占家庭可支配收入的比例

094 **consumption** /kən'sʌmpʃn/   *n.* 消费

- **D** expenditure by households on consumer goods
- **定** 家庭消费支出

095 **contractual** /kən'træktʃuəl/ **saving**   合约储蓄

- **D** people sign a contract, agreeing to save a certain amount on a regular basis
- **定** 人们签订合同，同意定期储存一定金额。
- **E** The main forms of contractual saving are insurance policies and pension schemes.
- **释** 合约储蓄的主要形式是保险单和养老金计划。

096 **saving ratio** /'reɪʃiəʊ/   储蓄占比

- **D** the proportion of disposable income that is not spent
- **定** 未花费的收入占可支配收入的比例

097 **target** /'tɑːgɪt/ **savers**   目标储蓄者

- **D** people who save to gain a particular sum of money for a particular purpose
- **定** 为了特定目的存钱而获得特定款项的人

098 **average propensity** /prə'pensəti/ **to save**   家庭储蓄占比

- **D** the proportion of household disposable income that is saved
- **定** 储蓄收入占家庭可支配收入的比例

099 **mortgage** /'mɔːgɪdʒ/   *n.* 抵押贷款

- **D** a secured loan for the purchase of property
- **定** 购置房产用的有担保的贷款

100 earnings /'ɜːnɪŋz/ — n. 收入

- **D** wages plus other payments to workers
- 定 工资加上支付给工人的其他款项

101 salary /'sæləri/ — n. 工资

- **D** an annual rate of pay, often paid to employees in professional and other non-manual occupations
- 定 以年计算的薪水,通常支付给专业职业和其他非手工职业的员工
- **E** Salaries are paid monthly at a fixed value, so are fixed costs.
- 释 工资按固定值每月支付,固定成本费用也同样按月支付。

102 profit-related /'prɒfɪt rɪ'leɪtɪd/ pay — 以利润为基础的收入

- **D** payment related to the profits earned by a firm
- 定 与公司赚取的利润有关的收入

103 demand /dɪ'mɑːnd/ for labour — 劳动力需求

- **D** the number of workers that firms are willing and able to employ at a given wage rate
- 定 在给定的工资率下公司愿意并能够雇用的工人数量。

104 share options /'ɒpʃnz/ — 认股权

- **D** the shares provided to workers to encourage them to work hard
- 定 提供给工人的股份,以此鼓励工人努力工作。

105 wage rate — 工资率

- **D** the return for labour services
- 定 劳务报酬
- **E** Wages are paid hourly or weekly, so they are variable costs to firms.
- 释 工资按每小时或每周支付,因此对公司来说是可变成本。

106 **overtime pay** 加班费

- **D** It is paid to workers who work in excess of the standard working week.
- 定 该费用支付给超出标准工作周时间的工人。

107 **bonus** /ˈbəʊnəs/ *n.* 奖金

- **D** an extra payment to workers who produce above a standard amount, finish a project ahead of time or contribute to higher profit
- 定 由于工人生产超出标准数量、提前完成项目或贡献更高利润而向他们提供的额外付款

108 **commission** /kəˈmɪʃn/ *n.* 佣金

- **D** It involves the sales people receiving a proportion of the value of the sales they make.
- 定 销售人员获取他们销售的产品价值的一部分。

109 **national minimum** /ˈmɪnɪməm/ **wage** 国家最低工资

- **D** the lowest amount a firm should pay its workers and it is set by the government
- 定 企业需支付给工人的最低工资,该工资数额由政府设定。

110 **wage differential** /ˌdɪfəˈrenʃl/ 薪资差异

- **D** differences in wages earned by different groups of workers
- 定 不同工人群体赚取不同的工资
- **E** Public opinion tends to consider that jobs which involve long periods of study and training should be highly rewarded.
- 译 舆论倾向于认为需要长期学习和培训的工作应得到高度奖励。

111 **labour supply** 劳动力供给

- **D** It consists of people who are of working age and who are willing and able to work.
- 定 劳动力的供给包括了到达工作年龄愿意并且能够工作的人。

112 labour force participation /pɑː,tɪsɪˈpeɪʃn/ rate
劳动力参与率

- **D** the percentage of the working-age population that is working, rather than unemployed
- **定** 正在工作而不是失业状态的人口与适宜工作年龄人口的百分比

113 equilibrium /ˌiːkwɪˈlɪbriəm/ wage rate
均衡工资率

- **D** It is determined when the wage rate workers are willing to work for equals the wage rate that firms (employers) are prepared to pay.
- **定** 工人愿意为之工作的工资率等于公司（雇主）准备支付的工资率时的工资率。

114 employment /ɪmˈplɔɪmənt/ right
劳动者权利

- **D** the laws imposed to prevent discrimination against workers due to gender, race, religion and disability
- **定** 旨在防止由于性别、种族、宗教和残疾而歧视工人的法律

115 discrimination /dɪˌskrɪmɪˈneɪʃn/
n. 歧视

- **D** when a group of workers is treated unfavourably
- **定** 当一群工人受到不利对待时

116 primary /ˈpraɪməri/ sector
第一产业

- **D** production that makes direct use of nature sources
- **定** 直接利用自然资源进行生产（的行业）
- **B** agriculture, fishing, forestry, mining, quarrying and oil extraction
- **释** 农业、渔业、林业、采矿、采石和石油开采

117 secondary /ˈsekəndri/ sector
第二产业

- **D** manufacturing and construction sector and is concerned with production in areas of an economy
- **定** 制造业和建筑业，并与经济领域的生产相关

- **E** car production and the construction of airport runways
- **译** 汽车生产和机场跑道建设

118 **tertiary** /ˈtɜːʃəri/ **sector**   服务行业

- **D** It refers to service industries.
- **定** 指服务业。
- **E** teaching, medical and the legal services
- **释** 例如：教育业、医药业和法律业

119 **elasticity** /ˌiːlæˈstɪsəti/ **of demand for labour**
劳动力需求弹性

- **D** a measure of the responsiveness of demand for labour to a change in the wage rate
- **定** 衡量劳动力需求对工资率变化的反应程度。

120 **elasticity of supply for labour**
劳动力供给弹性

- **D** a measure of the responsiveness of supply for labour to a change in the wage rate
- **定** 衡量劳动力供应对工资率变化的反应程度。

121 **specialisation** /ˌspeʃəlaɪˈzeɪʃən/   n. 专业化

- **D** the concentration on particular tasks or products
- **定** 专注于特定任务或产品

122 **division** /dɪˈvɪʒn/ **of labour**   劳动分工

- **D** the separation of a production process into a series of tasks, with each one completed by a different worker or group of employees
- **定** 将生产过程分为一系列任务，每个任务由不同的工人或不同组员工完成。
- **D** It occurs when a worker becomes an expert in a particular profession or in a part of a production process.
- **释** 当工人成为特定行业或一部分生产过程的专家时，就会发生这种情况。

123 **bartering** /ˈbɑːtərɪŋ/   *n.* 以货易货

- **D** the act of swapping items in exchange for other items through a process of bargaining and negotiation
- **定** 通过讨价还价和谈判的方式交换物品以换取其他物品的行为。

124 **trade unions** /ˈjuːniənz/   工会

- **D** organisation that exists to protect the rights of workers
- **定** 以保护工人权利而存在的组织

125 **craft** /krɑːft/ **unions**   同业公会

- **E** These are the oldest type of labour unions, which were originally formed to organise workers according to their particular skills.
- **释** 这些是最早的工会类型，最初是由具有特定技艺的工人组织起来的。

126 **general unions**   总工会

- **E** These trade unions are usually prepared to accept anyone into membership regardless of the place they work, the nature of their work or their industrial qualifications.
- **释** 这些工会通常会接纳任何人，无论他们在什么地方工作，从事何种工作或具有何种行业资格。

127 **industrial** /ɪnˈdʌstriəl/ **unions**   行业公会

- **E** These trade unions represent all workers in their industry, irrespective of their skills or the type of work done.
- **释** 这些工会代表其行业中的所有工人，不论其技能或工作类型如何。

128 **white collar** /ˈkɒlə(r)/ **unions**   白领公会

- **E** These labour unions recruit professional, administrative and salaried workers and other non-manual workers.
- **释** 这些工会招募专业的、行政的和带薪的工人以及其他非体力劳动者。

129 **collective** /kəˈlektɪv/ **bargaining**   集体谈判

- 🇩 the process where trade unions act as a means of communication and negotiation between employers and employees
- 🇨 在集体谈判过程中，工会作为雇主与雇员之间沟通和谈判的过程

130 **real income**   实际收入

- 🇩 income adjusted for inflation
- 🇨 经通货膨胀调整的收入

131 **industrial actions**   产业行动；（罢工）劳工行动

- 🇩 disruptive activities, such as a strike or work to rule, that workers carry out to strengthen their bargaining position regarding demands for improved wage and working conditions, or to address other grievances
- 🇨 破坏性活动，例如罢工或合法怠工，工人们这样做是为了加强谈判地位，以达到改善薪酬和工作环境的目的或者解决其他令他们不满的问题。

132 **strike** /straɪk/   *n.* 罢工

- 🇩 a group of workers stopping work to put pressure on an employer to agree to their demand
- 🇨 一群工人停止工作，向雇主施加压力，以使雇主同意他们的要求。

133 **work-to-rule** /ˈwɜːk tu ruːl/   *n.* 合法怠工

- 🇩 It means that workers literally work to fulfil the minimum requirements of their jobs and will not do anything outside what is written in their contract of employment.
- 🇨 合法怠工意味着工人实际上是为了满足其工作的最低要求而工作，并且不会做雇用合同上未写明的任何事。

134 **go-slow** /ˈɡəʊ sləʊ/   *n.* 怠工

- 🄳 It occurs when workers decide to complete their work in a leisurely way and therefore productivity falls.
- 🄳 这种情况会出现在工人决定悠闲地完成工作时,从而导致生产率下降。

135 **sit-in** /ˈsɪtɪn/   *n.* 静坐罢工

- 🄳 Trade union members turn up to work and occupy the premises but do not undertake their normal work.
- 🄳 工会成员上班并占用办公场所,但不做平时会做的工作。

136 **industry** /ˈɪndəstri/   *n.* 行业

- 🄳 a group of firms producing the same product
- 🄳 生产相同产品的一群公司

137 **plant** /plɑːnt/   *n.* 工厂

- 🄳 a production unit or workplace such as a factory, farm, office or branch
- 🄳 生产单位或工作场所,例如工厂、农场、办公室或者政府部门

138 **firm** /fɜːm/   *n.* 公司

- 🄳 an organisation in which resources are combined to produce goods and services
- 🄳 整合资源以生产商品和服务的组织。

139 **sole** /səʊl/ **trader**   个体户

- 🄳 It is a business owned by a single person, also known as a sole proprietorship.
- 🄳 个人拥有的企业,也称为独资企业。

140 **unlimited** /ʌnˈlɪmɪtɪd/ **liability** /ˌlaɪəˈbɪləti/ 无限责任

- 🅓 This means that if the business goes into debt and makes a loss, the sole trader is personally liable for repaying the debts, even if this means personal belongings have to be sold to do so.
- 🅓 这意味着如果企业负债，蒙受损失，独资经营者个人有责任偿还债务，即便这意味着必须出售个人财产。

141 **limited** /ˈlɪmɪtɪd/ **liability** 有限责任

- 🅓 It means that in the event of the company going bankrupt they would not lose more than the amount they had invested in the company.
- 🅓 投资人的损失在企业破产的情况下不会超过他们对公司的投资额的一种公司性质。

142 **partnership** /ˈpɑːtnəʃɪp/ *n.* 合伙人制

- 🅓 a business organisation owned by more than one person
- 🅓 由两个或以上的人所拥有的商业组织

143 **private limited company** 个人有限责任公司

- 🅓 a business organisation that is able to raise permanent capital from the issue and sale of shares to private individuals
- 🅓 能够通过向私人发行和出售股票筹集永久资本的商业组织。

144 **public limited company** 公共有限责任公司

- 🅓 a business organisation that is able to raise permanent capital from the sale of shares to the general public through a stock exchange
- 🅓 能够通过证券交易所向公众出售股票来筹集永久资本的商业组织。

145 **memorandum** /ˌmeməˈrændəm/ **of association**
/əˌsəʊʃiˈeɪʃn/　　　　　　　　　　　　　　　　公司章程

- **D** a document that records the name, registered business address, amount of share capital and outline of the company's operations
- 定 记录公司名称、公司注册地址、股本金额和公司经营概况的文件。

146 **articles** /ˈɑːtɪklz/ **of association**　　组织章程

- **D** a lengthier document that contains information about shareholders' voting rights and the details and duties of the directors of the company
- 定 较具体的文件，其中包含有关股东的投票权以及公司董事的详细信息和职责的信息

147 **multinational** /ˌmʌltiˈnæʃnəl/ **corporation**
/ˌkɔːpəˈreɪʃn/　　　　　　　　　　　　　　　　跨国企业

- **D** an organisation that operates in two or more countries
- 定 在两个或多个国家运营的组织
- 回 multinational companies (MNCs)

148 **co-operatives** /kəʊˈɒpərətɪvz/　　*n.* 合作企业

- **D** business organisations that are owned and run by their members and have a common aim of creating value for their members in a socially responsible way
- 定 由成员所有和经营的商业组织，其共同目标是以对社会负责的方式为其成员创造价值。

149 **public corporation**　　　　　　　　　　公共企业

- **D** an organisation that provids goods and services for the general public
- 定 为公共提供商品和服务的组织

150 the quaternary /kwə'tɜːnərɪ/ sector 知识产业，第四产业

- **D** It covers service industries that are knowledge based.
- **定** 一种涵盖了以知识为基础的服务行业

151 internal /ɪn'tɜːnl/ growth 内部增长

- **D** an 'organic' increase in the scale of production in a firm through the employment of additional factors of production
- **定** 通过使用其他生产要素，企业的生产规模"有机"增长。
- **E** It is referred to as natural or organic growth.
- **释** 内部增长被称为自然或有机增长。

152 external /ɪk'stɜːnl/ growth 外部增长

- **D** an increase in the size of a firm through its takeover of, or merger with, another organisation
- **定** 通过收购或合并另一个组织来扩大公司规模。

153 horizontal /ˌhɒrɪ'zɒntl/ merger /'mɜːdʒə(r)/ 水平兼并

- **D** This occurs when two or more firms producing similar goods or services at the same stage of production combine to form a larger enterprise.
- **定** 两个或多个生产相似商品或服务的公司在同一生产阶段时合并组成一个较大的企业。

154 vertical /'vɜːtɪkl/ merger 垂直兼并

- **D** a merger between two or more firms at different stages of production of the same product, such as between a farm and a food processing company
- **定** 生产同一产品的不同阶段的，两个或多个公司之间的合并，例如农场和食品加工公司之间的合并。

155 conglomerate /kən'glɒmərət/ merger 混合兼并

- **D** the combining of two or more firms in different industries into a single enterprise
- **定** 将两个或多个不同行业的公司合并为一个企业。

156 rationalisation /ˌræʃnəlaɪ'zeɪʃn/ n. 合理化

- **D** eliminating unnecessary equipment and plant to make a firm more efficient
- **定** 消除不必要的设备和工厂以提高公司效率。

157 backward integration /ˌɪntɪ'greɪʃn/ 向后合并

- **D** a merger with a firm at an earlier stage of the supply chain such as a raw material supplier
- **定** 与供应链前端的公司合并,比如原材料供应商。

158 forward integration 向前合并

- **D** a merger with a firm at a later stage of the supply chain such as a retailer
- **定** 与供应链后端的公司合并,比如零售商。

159 diversification /daɪˌvɜːsɪfɪ'keɪʃn/ n. 多样化

- **D** producing a range of different products for different home and/or overseas markets to spread market risks
- **定** 为国内和(或)海外不同的市场生产一系列不同的产品,以此分散市场风险。

160 internal economies of scale 内部规模经济

- **D** cost savings that arise from within the business
- **定** 由企业本身的增长或规模扩大引起的成本节约。

161 external economies of scale 外部规模经济

- **D** lower long-run average cost arising from an expansion of an industry
- **定** 由企业所在的行业增长或地区发展引起的长期平均成本节约。

162 diseconomies of scale 规模不经济

- **D** Diseconomies of scale arise when a firm gets too large and average costs of production start to rise.
- **定** 当企业规模过大且平均生产成本开始上升时,就会出现规模不经济。

163 internal diseconomies of scale
内部规模不经济

- **D** higher long-run average cost arising from a firm growing too large
- **定** 由于公司规模过大,导致长期平均成本较高。

164 external diseconomies of scale
外部规模不经济

- **D** higher long-run average cost arising from an industry growing too large
- **定** 行业规模过大导致长期平均成本较高。

165 consumer spending 消费支出

- **D** the amount that individuals spend on goods and services
- **定** 个人在商品和服务上花费的金额。

166 bad debts 坏账

- **D** It occurs when people and businesses cannot repay a loan.
- **定** 当人们和企业无法偿还贷款时,就会发生坏账。

167 collateral /kəˈlætərəl/ n. 抵押品

- **D** It means security for a loan.
- **定** 抵押即贷款的担保。

168 **conspicuous** /kənˈspɪkjuəs/ **consumption**

炫耀性消费

- It occurs when people purchase highly expensive goods and services due to status or a desired image.
- 当人们由于地位或欲望的追求而购买非常昂贵的商品和服务而发生的炫耀性消费。

169 **dissaving** /dɪˈseɪvɪŋ/

n. 动用储蓄

- It occurs when people spend their savings.
- 人们花费他们的积蓄。

170 **cost** /kɒst/

n. 成本

- the payments made by firms in the production process
- 公司在生产过程中支付的金额。

171 **fixed cost**

固定成本

- the costs of production that have to be paid regardless of how much a firm produces or sells
- 无论企业生产或销售多少都必须支付的生产成本。

172 **variable** /ˈveəriəbl/ **cost**

变动成本

- the costs of production that change when the level of output changes
- 当产出水平变化时会发生变化的生产成本。

173 **total cost**

总成本

- the sum of all fixed and variable costs
- 所有固定成本和变动成本的总和

174 average cost 平均成本

- **D** total cost divided by total quantity
- 定 总成本除以总数量

175 revenue /ˈrevənjuː/ n. 营收

- **D** the money payable to a business from the sale of its products
- 定 销售一企业的产品应支付给该企业的款项。

176 profit maximisation /ˌmæksɪmaɪˈzeɪʃn/ 利润最大化

- **D** the goal of most private-sector firms
- 定 大多数私营企业的目标
- **E** Profits are maximised when the positive difference between a firm's sales revenues and its costs of production is at its greatest.
- 释 当公司的销售营收与生产成本之间的正差最大时，利润便会最大化。

177 profit /ˈprɒfɪt/ n. 利润

- **D** the positive difference between a firm's total revenues and its total costs of production
- 定 公司总营收与总生产成本之间是正差。

178 objectives /əbˈdʒektɪvz/ n. 目标

- **D** the goals or targets of an organisation, such as business survival, growth, higher market share and profit maximisation
- 定 组织的目标，例如企业生存、增长、更高的市场份额和利润最大化。

179 market structure /ˈstrʌktʃə(r)/ 市场结构

- **D** the key characteristics of a particular market
- 定 特定市场的重要特征
- **E** It includes number of firms, market power, entry and exit barrier and etc.
- 释 市场结构包括公司数量、市场支配力、进入和退出壁垒等。

180 perfect competition 完全竞争

- It describes a market where there is immense competition.
- 完全竞争描述了一个竞争激烈的市场。

181 price takers 价格接受者

- Price-takers are individuals or companies that must accept prevailing prices in a market, lacking the market share to influence market price on their own.
- 在市场中的每一个个人（买者或者卖者），他们所面对的价格都是由市场给定的。也就是经市场供需调整后的均衡价格，而不是由企业自行决定。

182 homogeneous /ˌhɒməˈdʒiːniəs/ product 同质产品

- This means that the products being sold are identical.
- 同质产品意味着出售的产品是完全相同的。

183 price makers 价格制定者

- Those who have significant power to influence the market supply and hence prices.
- 价格制定者指那些具有重大影响力从而影响市场供应并因此影响价格的人。

184 monopoly /məˈnɒpəli/ n. 垄断

- a market structure where one supplier dominates the market
- 由单一供应商主导市场的市场结构

185 cost-plus pricing 成本加成定价

- This involves working out the average cost of each unit of output and then adding a certain amount or certain percentage on top to earn profit.
- 成本加成定价包含计算出每个产出单位的平均成本，然后在该成本上增加一定数量或一定百分比以获取利润。

186　competition-based pricing　　竞争导向定价

- **E** This occurs when a firm sets its price according to the prices being charged by its rivals.
- **释** 企业根据其竞争对手收取的价格进行定价会发生竞争导向定价。

187　penetration /ˌpenɪˈtreɪʃn/ pricing　　渗透定价

- **E** This involves setting a low price in order to enter a new market.
- **释** 通过设定低价的方式来进入新市场。

188　loss leader pricing　　牺牲品定价

- **E** This happens when the price is set below the costs of production, thus making a loss in the short run.
- **释** 当价格被定为低于生产成本时会发生牺牲品定价,因此在短时间内有损失。

189　price skimming /skɪmɪŋ/　　撇脂定价法

- **E** This pricing policy involves a firm setting an initially high price in order to maximise profits.
- **释** 撇脂定价法与公司设定最初的高价格以使利润最大化有关。

190　promotional /prəˈməʊʃənl/ pricing　　促销定价

- **E** This commonly used pricing policy involves firms temporarily reducing their prices to attract more customers.
- **释** 促销定价是一种常用的定价政策,包含公司暂时降低价格以吸引更多客户。

191　barriers /ˈbæriəz/ to entry　　进入壁垒

- **D** the obstacles that prevent other firms from effectively entering the market
- **释** 防止其他公司有效进入市场的障碍

192 **financial economies of scale** 金融规模经济

- **D** It occurs as large firms are able to borrow money from banks more easily than small firms because they are perceived to be less risky to the financial institutions.
- **定** 相比小型企业,大型企业更容易从银行借到钱,因为金融机构认为它们的风险较小。

193 **managerial /ˌmænəˈdʒɪəriəl/ economies of scale** 管理规模经济

- **D** It occurs as large firms have the resources to employ specialists to undertake functions within the firm.
- **定** 大型公司有资源聘请专家来承担公司内部的职能。

194 **marketing economies of scale** 市场规模经济

- **D** It occurs as big firms tend to have a large advertising budget and therefore can spend large amounts of money on promoting their products.
- **定** 大公司倾向于投入大量广告预算,因此花费大量金钱来推广其产品。

195 **research and development economies of scale** 研发规模经济

- **D** It occurs as large firms may be able to fund research and development, and therefore can be innovative and create products that enable them to be leaders in their area of business.
- **定** 大公司可能有能力为研究和开发提供资金,因此可以进行创新并开发产品,使它们能够成为该商业领域的领导者。

196 **risk-bearing /rɪsk ˈbeərɪŋ/ economies of scale** 风险忍受规模经济

- **D** It occurs as large firms tend to produce a range of products and operate in many locations.
- **定** 大型企业倾向于生产一系列产品并在许多地方开展业务。

197 **takeover** /ˈteɪkəʊvə(r)/   *n.* 收购

- **D** A takeover occurs when a firm is taken over by another firm.
- **曰** 指的是一家公司被另一家公司接管。

198 **technical economies of scale**   科技规模经济

- **D** It occurs as large firms can afford to purchase expensive pieces of machinery and automated equipment for the manufacturing process.
- **曰** 大型企业有能力支付为生产而购买的昂贵机械化和自动化设备的金额。

199 **legal tender**   法定货币

- **D** a form of money that has to be accepted in settlement of debt
- **曰** 债务清算中必须被接受的一种货币形式。
- **同** money

200 **piece rate system**   计件工资率

- **D** a payment based on the productivity of workers
- **曰** 基于工人生产力的支付金额

201 **job security** /sɪˈkjʊərəti/   工作保障

- **D** the fact of your job being permanent, so that you will probably not lose it
- **曰** 一份工作是永久的,你不会失去工作。

202 **sales revenue** /ˈrevənjuː/ **maximisation** /ˌmæksɪmaɪˈzeɪʃn/   销售收入最大化

- **D** earning as much revenue as possible
- **曰** 赚取尽可能多的收入。

203 **pure monopoly**   完全垄断

- **D** a single firm that controls 100% of the supply of a product to a market
- **曰** 控制产品向市场百分之百供应的一家公司

204 **corporation** /ˌkɔːpəˈreɪʃn/ **tax** 企税，公司（所得）税

- a tax on profits of a company
- 公司利润税

205 **average variable cost** 平均变动成本

- total variable cost divided by output
- 总变动成本除以产出

206 **average fixed cost** 平均固定成本

- total fixed cost divided by output
- 总固定成本除以产出

207 **long run** 长期

- the time period when all factors of production can be changed and all cost are variable
- 在该时段内所有生产要素都可改变，所有成本都是多变的。

208 **price** /praɪs/ *n.* 价格

- the amount of money that has to be given to obtain a product
- 获得产品所必须支付的金额。

209 **total revenue** /ˈrevənjuː/ 总营收

- the total amount of money received from selling a product
- 从销售某产品中得到的总金额

210 **average revenue** 平均营收

- the total revenue divided by the quantity sold
- 总营收除以销售量

211 **profit satisficing** 利润满意

- sacrificing some profit to achieve other goals
- 牺牲一些利润以实现其他目标。

212 **competitive** /kəmˈpetɪtɪv/ **market**   竞争市场

- **D** a market with a number of firms that compete with each other
- **定** 由许多相互竞争的公司组成的市场

213 **normal profit**   正常利润

- **D** the minimum level of profit required to keep a firm in the industry in the long run
- **定** 使公司长期存活在行业中所需的最低利润水平。

214 **supernormal** /ˌsuːpəˈnɔːməl/ **profit**   超额利润

- **D** profit above that needed to keep a firm in the market in the long run
- **定** 高于使公司长期存活在市场中所需利润的部分。

215 **barriers** /ˈbæriəz/ **to exit**   退出壁垒

- **D** anything that makes it difficult for a firm to stop making the product
- **定** 任何使公司难以停止生产该产品的事物。

216 **scale of production**   生产规模

- **D** the size of production units and the methods of production used
- **定** 生产单位的规模和所使用的生产方法

217 **sunk** /sʌŋk/ **costs**   沉没成本

- **D** costs that cannot be recovered if the firm leaves the industry
- **定** 企业离开该行业时无法收回的成本。

第四节
Government and the Macroeconomy
政府和宏观经济

扫一扫
听本节音频

218 **local government** 　　　　　　　　　　　地方政府

- a government organisation with the authority to administer a range of policies within an area of the country
- 有权管理国家某个范围内的一系列政策的政府组织

219 **natural monopoly** 　　　　　　　　　　　自然垄断

- an industry where a single firm can produce at a lower average cost than two or more firms because of the existence of significant economies of scale
- 由于存在显著的规模经济，单个企业的平均生产成本可以低于两个或多个企业的行业。

220 **strategic** /strə'tiːdʒɪk/ **industries** 　　　战略行业

- industries that are important for the economic development and safety of the country
- 对国家的经济发展和安全至关重要的行业

221 **trade block** 　　　　　　　　　　　贸易区，贸易集团

- a regional group of countries that remove trade restrictions between countries
- 取消国家间贸易限制的区域性国家集团

222 **free international trade** 　　　　　　自由国际贸易

- the exchange of goods and services between countries without any restriction
- 国家间无限制地进行商品和服务的交换

223 economic growth 经济增长

D an increase in the output of an economy and in the long run, an increase in the economy's productive potential
定 经济产出增加，从长远来看，经济生产潜力增加。

224 actual economic growth 实际经济增长

D an increase in the output of an economy
定 经济产出增加

225 potential /pə'tenʃl/ economic growth 潜在经济增长

D an increase in an economy's productive capacity
定 经济生产能力的提高

226 aggregate /'æɡrɪɡət/ demand 总需求

D the total demand for goods and services in an economy
定 经济体中对商品和服务的总需求
E It is determined by consumer spending, investment, public expenditure and spending by overseas residents on exports.
释 总需求由消费者的支出、投资、公共支出以及海外居民在出口产品上的支出决定。

227 aggregate supply 总供给

D the total output or supply of all goods and services in an economy that all producers are willing and able to supply
定 经济体中所有生产者愿意并能够提供的所有商品和服务的总产出或总供给。

228 business cycle 商业周期

D It describes the fluctuations in the economic activity of a country overtime, thus creating a long-term trend of economic growth in the economy.
定 商业周期描述了一个国家长期经济活动的波动，从而创造了经济中经济增长的长期趋势。

229 full employment 完全就业

- **D** the level of employment when aggregate demand for labour equals to aggregate supply of labour
- **定** 劳动力总需求等于劳动力总供给时的就业人口

230 labour force 劳动力

- **D** the total supply of labour or economically active population in an economy
- **定** 经济体中劳动人口或从事经济活动人口的总供给。

231 labour market 劳动力市场

- **D** any set of arrangements that brings together all those people willing and able to supply their labour to organisations that want to hire labour
- **定** 将所有愿意并能够向希望雇佣劳动力的组织提供劳动力的人聚集、安排在一起。

232 labour diseconomies 劳动力不规模

- **D** rising unit costs resulting from shortages of labour or increasing disputes with trade unions as a firm grows beyond its optimum size
- **定** 随着公司扩大超出最适宜规模时,由于劳动力短缺或与工会的纠纷增加而导致的单位成本上升。

233 labour productivity 劳动生产力

- **D** the average output per worker per hour
- **定** 每个工人每小时的平均产出量

234 economically inactive 非从事经济活动的人口

- **D** those people who are not in the labour force
- **定** 那些非劳动力

235 **economically active** 从事经济活动的人口

- **D** being a member of the labour force, both the employed and the unemployed
- 定 劳动力的一员,无论是就业者还是失业者

236 **unemployment rate** 失业率

- **D** the percentage of the labour force who are willing and able to work but are without jobs
- 定 愿意并能够工作但目前没有工作的劳动力(占总劳动力)的百分比。

237 **price stability** 价格稳定

- **D** the price level in the economy not changing significantly over time
- 定 经济中的价格水平不会随时间的变化有很大波动。

238 **inflation** /ɪnˈfleɪʃn/ **rate** 通胀率

- **D** the percentage rise in the price level of goods and services over time
- 定 商品和服务的价格水平随时间的变化而上升的百分比。

239 **balance of payments** 国际收支

- **D** the record of a country's economic transactions with other countries
- 定 一国与其他国家的经济交易记录。

240 **redistribution** /ˌriːdɪstrɪˈbjuːʃn/ **of income** 收入再分配

- **D** the process of redistributing income from rich to poor
- 定 从富人到穷人的收入再分配的过程

241 **budget** /ˈbʌdʒɪt/   *n.* 预算

- **D** the relationship between government revenue and government spending
- **定** 政府营收与政府支出之间的关系

242 **budget deficit** /ˈdefɪsɪt/   预算赤字

- **D** It means the government spending is higher than government revenue.
- **定** 预算赤字意味着政府支出高于政府收入。

243 **budget surplus** /ˈsɜːpləs/   预算盈余

- **D** It means the government revenue is higher than government spending.
- **定** 预算盈余意味着政府收入高于政府支出。

244 **balanced budget**   平衡预算

- **D** It occurs when government spending and revenue are equal.
- **定** 政府支出与收入相等就是平衡预算

245 **national debt**   国债

- **D** the total amount the government has borrowed over time
- **定** 随着时间变化,政府的借款总额。

246 **direct tax**   直接税

- **D** a tax on a person's or firm's income and wealth
- **定** 对个人或公司的收入和财富的征税
- **E** It is called direct tax because the people of firms responsible for paying the tax have to bear the burden of the tax.
- **释** 之所以被称为直接税,是因为负责缴税的公司人员必须承担该税收。

247 **indirect tax** 间接税

- **D** a tax that is imposed on expenditure, it is indirect in that the tax is only paid when the product on which the tax is levied is purchased
- **定** 对花销、支出征收的税,是间接发生的,因为只有在购买了征收税的产品时才需缴税。

248 **progressive** /prə'gresɪv/ **tax** 累进税

- **D** a tax which takes a larger percentage of the income or wealth of the rich
- **定** 一种占据富人收入比例较大的税。

249 **proportional** /prə'pɔːʃənl/ **tax** 比例税

- **D** a tax which takes the same percentage of the income or wealth of all taxpayers
- **定** 一种占据所有纳税人收入相同比例的税。

250 **regressive** /rɪ'gresɪv/ **tax** 递减税

- **D** a tax which takes a larger percentage of the income or wealth of the poor
- **定** 一种占据穷人收入比例较大的税。

251 **income tax** 收入所得税

- **D** a tax on income that people receive from their employment and investment income
- **定** 向人们从就业和投资中获得的收入征税。

252 **taxable** /'tæksəbl/ **income** 应税收入

- **D** income above the free tax level
- **定** 高于个税起征点的部分

253 **corporation** /ˌkɔːpəˈreɪʃn/ **tax**
企税，公司（所得）税

- **D** a tax on the profits of firms
- **定** 对企业利润征的税

254 **capital** /ˈkæpɪtl/ **gain tax** 资本利得税，资本收益税

- **D** a tax on the profit made on assets when they are sold for a higher price than what they were bought for
- **定** 对以高于原本购买价格的价格出售资产所赚取的利润征的税。

255 **inheritance** /ɪnˈherɪtəns/ **tax** 遗产税

- **D** a tax on wealth above a certain amount which is passed on to other people, when a person dies
- **定** 当一人死亡时把一定财产转嫁给他人，超过一定数额时所征的税。

256 **sales tax** 营业税

- **D** a tax imposed when products are sold
- **定** 产品被销售后征收的税款。
- **E** Main examples are general sales tax and value added tax.
- **释** 营业税主要包括一般营业税和增值税。

257 **excise** /ˈeksaɪz/ **duties** 消费税

- **D** taxes charged on certain domestically produced goods
- **定** 对某些国产产品征收的税收
- **E** They are charged in addition to VAT.
- **释** 除增值税外，人们还需额外支付消费税。

258 **customs duties** 关税

- **D** taxes on imports and also called tariffs
- **定** 进口税，也称关税

259 license /ˈlaɪsns/ — *n.* 执照

- **D** a certificate needed to use a range of products
- **定** 使用一系列产品所需的东西

260 local taxes — 地方税

- **D** They are used to pay for local services such as education, fire service, libraries, roads and refuse collection.
- **定** 地方税用于支付地方服务，例如教育、消防、图书馆、道路和垃圾清运。
- **E** One kind of the tax is based on the property of local firms and the other is based largely on the value of household property.
- **释** 地方税的一种是基于本地企业的不动产价值征收，还有一种是基于家庭不动产价值征收。

261 stamp duty — 印花税

- **D** a progressive tax paid on the sale of commercial or residential property
- **定** 印花税是一种累进税，在出售商用房屋或个人住宅的凭证上征收。

262 carbon tax — 烟尘排放税；碳税

- **D** a tax imposed on vehicle manufacturers or firms that produce excessive carbon emissions
- **定** 对产生过量碳排放的汽车制造商或公司征收的税收。

263 tax avoidance /əˈvɔɪdəns/ — 避税

- **D** the legal act of not paying taxes
- **定** 合法的避免纳税行为。

264 tax evasion /ɪˈveɪʒn/ — 逃税

- **D** It refers to non-payment of taxes due, perhaps by a business under-declaring its level of profits illegally.
- **定** 逃税指未付的应缴税款，可能是由一家企业低报了其利润水平导致的不合法的行为。

265 **windfall** /ˈwɪndfɔːl/ **tax**   暴利税

- ⓓ a tax charged on individuals and firms that gain an unexpected one-off amount of money, such as a person winning the lottery or a firm gaining from a takeover bid
- 定 对获得一笔意外款项的个人和公司收取的税，例如赢得彩票的人或从收购条约中获得收益的公司。

266 **equity** /ˈekwəti/   *n.* 公平

- ⓓ This means the fairness in the sense that the amount of tax people and firms have to pay should be based on their ability to pay.
- 定 征税原则公平，即征税必须基于纳税个人和企业的实际纳税能力
- ⓔ canons of taxation
- 释 税收原则

267 **certainty** /ˈsɜːtnti/   *n.* 确定性

- ⓓ The timing and amount to be paid must be certain and open.
- 定 缴税的时间和金额必须明确并且公开。

268 **convenience** /kənˈviːniəns/   *n.* 便利性

- ⓓ a tax should be easy to pay
- 定 易于缴纳税收
- ⓔ canons of taxation
- 释 税收原则

269 **economy** /ɪˈkɒnəmi/   *n.* 经济性

- ⓓ the cost of collecting a tax should be considerably less than the revenue it generates
- 定 征税成本应大大低于税收本身。
- ⓔ canons of taxation
- 释 税收原则

270 **flexibility** /ˌfleksə'bɪləti/   *n.* 灵活性

- **D** It should be possible to change the tax if economic activities change or government aims change.
- **定** 如果经济活动发生变化或政府目标发生变化,应该有可能改变税收。

271 **efficiency** /ɪ'fɪʃnsi/   *n.* 有效性

- **D** A tax should improve the performance of markets or at least not significantly reduce the efficiency of markets.
- **定** 税收应改善市场绩效或至少不会显著降低市场效率。

272 **transparent** /træns'pærənt/   *adj.* 透明的

- **D** that tax payers should know exactly what they are paying.
- **定** 纳税人应明确知道他们支付的是什么。
- **E** canons of taxation
- **定** 税收原则

273 **tax base**   计税基数

- **D** the source of tax revenue; that is what is taxed.
- **定** 即应纳税的来源,建议"应纳税的基数"

274 **tax burden** /'bɜːdn/   税负

- **D** It relates to the amount of tax paid by people and firms.
- **定** 税负与人和企业所缴纳的税额有关。

275 **automatic** /ˌɔːtə'mætɪk/ **stabiliser** /'steɪbɪˌlaɪzə/
自动稳定器

- **D** forms of government expenditure and taxation that reduce fluctuations in economic activity, without any change in government policy
- **定** 在政府政策不改变的情况下,会随着经济周期自动变化的财政支出(失业救济金)或税收增长,起着抑制经济过热或者缓解经济紧缩的作用。

276 **inflation** /ɪnˈfleɪʃn/   *n.* 通胀

- ▢ the rise in the price level of goods and services over time
- ▢ 商品和服务的价格水平随时间上升。

277 **informal economy**   非正式经济

- ▢ that part of the economy that is not regulated, protected or taxed by the government
- ▢ 经济中不受政府管制、保护或征税的部分。

278 **flat tax**   统一税率

- ▢ A pure flat rate system would involve income tax; corporation tax and VAT being set at the same rate with no exceptions.
- ▢ 不论个人所得税、企业所得税和增值税都按照统一税率征收

279 **fiscal** /ˈfɪskl/ **policy**   财政政策

- ▢ decisions on government spending and taxation designed to influence aggregate demand
- ▢ 关于政府支出和税收的决定,旨在影响总需求。

280 **expansionary** /ɪkˈspænʃənri/ **fiscal policy**
扩张性财政政策

- ▢ a government policy that involves expanding public expenditure and/or cutting total taxation to boost aggregate demand during downturn in economic activity
- ▢ 扩张性财政政策是一种政府政策,包含扩大公共支出和/或削减总税收,以在经济活动下滑期间增加总需求。

281 **contractionary** /kənˈtrækʃənərɪ/ **fiscal policy**
收缩性财政政策

- ▢ a government macroeconomic policy that involves cutting public expenditure and/or increasing total taxation to reduce aggregate demand if an economy is overheating with the general level of prices rising rapidly
- ▢ 收缩性财政政策是一种政府宏观经济政策,包括在经济过热且

总体价格水平快速上涨的情况下，削减公共支出和/或增加总税收以减少总需求。

282 **administrative** /əd'mɪnɪstrətɪv/ **lags** 　　行政延迟

- 🇩 Time lags between recognising the need for fiscal policy intervention and actually implementing appropriate action, such as approving tax changes or alterations to the government budget.
- 🇨 在认识到需要采取财政政策干预到实际执行适当行动之间存在时间延迟，例如批准税收变更或政府预算变更。

283 **recognition** /ˌrekəg'nɪʃn/ **lag** 　　认定延迟

- 🇩 There is a time lag in recognising that government intervention is needed to affect the level of economic activity.
- 🇨 在认识到需要政府干预才能影响经济活动的水平之前，存在时间滞后。

284 **impact lag** 　　影响延迟

- 🇩 There is a time lag between implementing fiscal policy and seeing the actual effects on the economy.
- 🇨 实施财政政策与看到对经济的实际影响之间存在时间差。

285 **monetary** /'mʌnɪtri/ **policy** 　　货币政策

- 🇩 a government demand-side policy that involves changes in the interest rate or supply of money in an economy to manage the overall level of economic activity
- 🇨 货币政策是政府需求方政策，包含经济体中利率或货币供应的变化，以管理经济活动的整体水平。

286 **foreign exchange rate** 　　汇率

- 🇩 the equilibrium market price of one national currency in terms of another currency established through trade in currencies on the foreign exchange market
- 🇨 汇率是通过外汇市场上的货币交易建立的一种本国货币相对于另一种货币的均衡市场价格。

287 **expansionary** /ɪkˈspænʃənri/ **monetary policy** 扩张性货币政策

- **D** increases in the money supply and/or decrease the rate of interest designed to increase aggregate demand
- **定** 增加货币供应量和/或降低利率以增加总需求

288 **contractionary** /kənˈtrækʃənəri/ **monetary policy** 收缩性货币政策

- **D** the policy that cuts in the money supply and/or increase the rate of interest designed to reduce aggregate demand
- **定** 减少货币供应量和/或提高利率以减少总需求的政策

289 **supply-side policy** 供应面政策

- **D** measures designed to increase aggregate supply
- **定** 旨在增加总供应量的措施

290 **deregulation** /ˌdiːˌregjuˈleɪʃn/ *n.* 去规则化

- **D** the removal of rules and regulations that have been enforced by law in order to remove barriers to entry to markets and to reduce the costs of complying with the rules and regulations
- **定** 去除法律强制执行的规则和法规,以消除进入市场的壁垒并减少遵守规则和法规的成本。

291 **enterprise** /ˈentəˌpraɪz/ **zones** 经济开发区

- **D** These are areas with relatively high rates of unemployment where the government creates financial incentives for firms to relocate.
- **定** 经济开发区是失业率相对较高的地区,政府为企业搬迁提供了经济激励。

292 **labour market reform** 劳动力市场改革

- **D** It is designed to make labour market work more efficiently.
- **定** 劳动力市场改革旨在使劳动力市场更有效地运作。

ⓔ The intention is to increase the quality, quantity and flexibility of labour.
㊌ 劳动力市场改革的目的是提高人才的质量、数量和灵活性。

293 gross /ɡrəʊs/ domestic /dəˈmestɪk/ product (GDP) 国民生产总值

ⓓ total goods and services produced in an economy for a given time period
㊋ 一定时间段内经济体生产的商品和服务的总量
ⓔ This output can be measured according to the output, income and expenditure methods.
㊌ 国民生产总值可根据生产法、收入法和支出法进行衡量。

294 circular /ˈsɜːkjələ(r)/ flow of income 所得循环

ⓓ the movement of expenditure, income and output around the economy
㊋ 经济中支出、收入和产出的流动循环。

295 value added 增值

ⓓ the difference between the sales revenue received and the cost of raw materials used
㊋ 收到的销售收入与所用的原材料成本之间的差额。

296 transfer payment 转移支付

ⓓ payment made by a government to individuals, usually through a social welfare programme, including unemployment benefits, disability allowances and old-age pensions
㊋ 政府通常通过社会福利项目向个人支付的款项,包括失业救济金、伤残津贴和养老金。
ⓔ They are 'transfers' because they do not involve payment for goods or services and are paid to people who are not engaged in productive activities from tax revenues paid by people and businesses that are economically active.
㊌ 转移支付是不涉及商品或服务的支付,而是将从事经济活动的人和企业的纳税收入支付给未从事生产活动的人。

297 **nominal** /ˈnɒmɪnl/ **GDP**　　　　名义国民生产总值

- ⓓ the total market or monetary value of the GDP of an economy
- 定 经济体的国民生产总值的总市场或货币价值
- ⓔ This is also referred to as money GDP or GDP at current prices.
- 释 名义国民生产总值也被称为货币 GDP 或以当前价格计算的 GDP。

298 **real GDP**　　　　实际国民生产总值

- ⓓ GDP at constant prices and so adjusted for inflation
- 定 实际国民生产总值是具有不变购买力的货币单位衡量的国民生产总值，根据通货膨胀进行调整。

299 **subsistence** /səbˈsɪstəns/ **agriculture** /ˈæɡrɪkʌltʃə(r)/　　　　自给农业

- ⓓ the output of agricultural goods for farmers' personal use
- 定 农民自用的农产品产量

300 **recession** /rɪˈseʃn/　　　　*n.* 经济衰退 / 萧条

- ⓓ a reduction in real GDP over a period of six months or more
- 定 六个月或更长时间内的实际国民生产总值下降

301 **international monetary fund (IMF)**　　　　国际货币基金组织

- ⓓ an international organisation which promotes international cooperation and helps countries with balance of payments problems
- 定 促进国际合作并帮助国际收支平衡问题国家的国际组织

302 **indexation** /ˌɪndekˈseɪʃn/　　　　*n.* 指数化

- ⓓ the automatic adjustment of a monetary variable, such as wages, taxes, welfare or pension benefits, by the increase in the consumer or retail prices index, so that its value rises at the same rate as inflation

🇬 指数化是指通过消费者或零售物价指数的增长对货币变量（例如工资、税收、福利或养老金福利）进行自动调整，从而使其价值增长到与通货膨胀率相同。

303 **sustainable** /sə'steɪnəbl/ **economic growth**
可持续性经济发展

- 🇩 growth in real output that is achieved without depleting natural resources or harming the natural environment
- 🇬 可持续性经济发展是指在不消耗自然资源或不破坏自然环境的情况下实现的实际产出增长。

304 **employment** /ɪmˈplɔɪmənt/ *n.* 就业人口

- 🇩 the amount of labour force who are involved in a productive activity for which a payment is received
- 🇬 从事某一生产活动并收到报酬的劳动力数量。

305 **unemployment** /ˌʌnɪmˈplɔɪmənt/ *n.* 失业人数

- 🇩 the amount of labour force without a job while willing and able to work
- 🇬 失业人数是指目前没有工作的、但愿意且有能力工作的劳动力数量。

306 **flexible labour force** 灵活劳动力

- 🇩 A labour force is one which adjusts quickly and smoothly to changes in market conditions.
- 🇬 灵活劳动力是指能够迅速、顺畅地适应市场条件变化的劳动力。

307 **labour market participation** /paːˌtɪsɪˈpeɪʃn/ **rate** 劳动力参与率

- 🇩 the proportion of the working-age population who are in the labour force
- 🇬 劳动力（包括就业人口和失业人口）占劳动年龄人口的比率

308 claimant /ˈkleɪmənt/ count 请领失业补助

- **D** a measure of unemployment which counts as unemployed those in receipt of unemployment benefits
- **定** 请领失业补助是衡量失业人数的方法,将领取失业救济金的人视为失业人员。

309 labour force survey measure 劳动人口调查

- **D** a measure of unemployment which counts as unemployed people who identify as such in a survey
- **定** 劳动人口调查是衡量失业人数的方法,将调查中确定为失业的人视为失业人员。

310 frictional /ˈfrɪkʃənəl/ unemployment 摩擦性失业

- **D** an economic situation in which people find themselves voluntarily out of work usually for short periods of time as they move between jobs
- **定** 摩擦性失业是指人们在转换工作时通常会在很短的时间内自愿失业的经济状况。

311 structural /ˈstrʌktʃərəl/ unemployment 结构性失业

- **D** It refers to joblessness among workers because their skills are out of date and no longer wanted due to changes in demand patterns or technologies that have resulted in the decline of some established industries in an economy.
- **定** 结构性失业指的是工人中的失业,一是因为技术过时失业,二是由于需求模式或技术的变化导致经济中某些成熟行业的衰落,工人不再被需要。

312 cyclical /ˈsɪklɪkəl/ unemployment 周期性失业

- **D** joblessness caused by deficient demand during an economic downturn or recession
- **定** 周期性失业是经济下滑或衰退期间需求不足导致的失业。

313 **search unemployment** 求职性失业

- **D** unemployment arising from workers who have lost their jobs looking for a job they are willing to accept
- **定** 求职性失业是指发生在已失业的工人身上，他们正寻找愿意接受的工作。

314 **casual** /ˈkæʒuəl/ **unemployment** 临时性失业

- **D** the inevitable time delay when a worker transits from one job to another due to the expiration of previous job contract
- **定** 由于先前的工作合同到期，工人从一项工作过渡到另一项工作时不可避免的时间延迟。

315 **seasonal** /ˈsiːzənl/ **unemployment** 季节性失业

- **D** unemployment caused by a fall in demand at particular times of the year
- **定** 季节性失业是指在一年中特定时间内，因需求下降而导致的失业。

316 **regional** /ˈriːdʒənl/ **unemployment** 地区性失业

- **D** unemployment that is disproportionately concentrated in a particular region in an economy
- **定** 经济体中某一特定区域失业过多集中的情况。

317 **technological unemployment** 科技性失业

- **D** unemployment caused by worker being replaced by capital equipment
- **定** 科技性失业是指工人被资本设备取代而导致的失业。

318 **voluntary** /ˈvɒləntri/ **unemployment** 自愿性失业

- **D** joblessness resulting from people choosing not to continue in paid employment
- **定** 自愿性失业是指人们选择不继续带薪工作而导致的失业。

319 **deflation** /ˌdiːˈfleɪʃn/   *n.* 通货紧缩

- **D** a sustained fall in the prices of goods and services
- **定** 商品和服务价格的持续下跌

320 **disinflation** /dɪsɪnˈfleɪʃ(ə)n/   *n.* 通胀率下降

- **D** a fall in the rate of inflation
- **定** 通货膨胀率的下滑

321 **customer price index (CPI)**   消费物价指数

- **D** a measure of inflation based on changes in the average price of a basket of goods and services purchased by a 'typical' household and which expresses these average prices as an index number series
- **定** 根据"典型"家庭购买的一篮子商品和服务的平均价格变化来衡量通货膨胀的指标,并将这些平均价格表示为指数序列。

322 **retail prices index (RPI)**   零售物价指数

- **D** It is an index which measures changes in the price of a number of goods and services in an economy over a period of time, which includes a number of items that are not included in the consumer price index, such as the costs of housing.
- **定** 零售物价指数是衡量在一段时间内某个经济体中多种商品和服务价格变化的指数,同时包括一些未包含在消费物价指数中的项目,例如住房成本。

323 **cost-push inflation** /ɪnˈfleɪʃn/   成本推动型通胀

- **D** persistently rising general price levels caused by increasing production costs
- **定** 由于生产成本增加,总价格水平持续上涨。

324 **demand-pull inflation**   需求拉动通胀

- **D** a persistent increase in the general level of prices resulting from a continued excess of demand over supply
- **定** 由于需求持续超过供应,总体价格水平持续上涨。

325 **wage-price spiral** /ˈspaɪrəl/ 工资价格螺旋上升

- It is an economic situation in which workers demand higher wages to compensate them for the impact of rising inflation on the real value of their earnings and in so doing force producers to pass on increased wage costs to consumers in higher prices, resulting in even higher wage demands, and so on.
- 工资价格螺旋上升是一种特定的经济形势，此时工人要求更高的工资以补偿通货膨胀对收入实际价值的影响，从而迫使生产者以更高的价格将增加的工资成本转嫁给消费者，进而又导致更高的工资需求如此循环往复。

326 **hyperinflation** /ˌhaɪpərɪnˈfleɪʃn/ *n.* 恶性通胀

- an inflation rate that is very high and out of control, as a result of which confidence in a currency can be lost because its real value is eroded very quickly
- 极高的通货膨胀率，并且处于失控状态，因为货币实际价值很快被削弱，导致人们对货币丧失信心。

327 **monetary inflation** 货币通胀

- rises in the price level caused by an excessive growth of the money supply
- 货币通胀是指货币供应量过度增长导致价格水平上升。

328 **monetarists** /ˈmʌnɪtərɪsts/ *n.* 货币主义学派

- a group of economists who think that inflation is caused by the money supply growing more rapidly than output
- 货币主义学派是指那些认为通货膨胀是由货币供应的增长快于经济实际产出的增长而导致的经济学家。

329 **menu costs** 菜单成本

- costs involved in having to change prices as a result of inflation
- 菜单成本是由于通货膨胀而不得不改变价格所涉及的成本。

330 **shoe-leather** /ʃuː ˈleðə(r)/ **costs** 鞋底成本

D costs involved in moving money around to gain high interest rates or when consumers spend time and money trying to find the best prices

定 鞋底成本是转移资金以获取高利率或消费者花费时间和金钱试图找到最佳价格时所涉及的成本。

331 **base year** 基准年

D It refers to the starting year when calculating a price index.

定 基准年是指计算价格指数时的起始年份。

332 **imported inflation** 进口通胀

D It is triggered by higher import prices, forcing up costs of production and thus causing domestic inflation.

定 进口通胀是指由较高的进口价格引发的，迫使生产成本上升，因此导致国内通货膨胀。

第五节
Economic Development 经济发展

333 **human development index** 人类发展指数

D a statistical measure complied with different development indicators by the United Nations to measure and contrast economic development in different countries

定 联合国根据不同发展指标汇编的统计度量，用以衡量和对比不同国家的经济发展。

334 **genuine** /ˈdʒenjuɪn/ **progress indicator** /ˈɪndɪkeɪtə(r)/ **(GPI)** 真实发展指数

D a measure of living standards which takes into account a variety of indicators including income, leisure time, distribution of income and environmental standards

定 一种衡量生活水平的指标，将各种指标考虑在内，包括收入、休闲时间、收入分配和环境标准。

335 **living standards** 生活水平

D They are referred to as developed economies or more economically developed countries.

定 生活水平在发达经济体或经济更发达的国家被提及。

336 **real GDP per capita** /ˈkæpɪtə/ 实际人均国内生产总值

D It is the gross domestic product of a country divided by the population size.

定 一个国家国内生产总值除以人口规模。

B They are measured according to GDP per capita, the cost of living and material wealth.

释 根据人均国民生产总值、生活成本和物质财富来衡量的。

337 material wealth 物质财富

- This indicator looks at ownership of consumer durable goods by the average person, such as cars, jewellery, televisions and mobile phones.
- 物质财富指标着眼于普通人对耐用消费品的所有权,例如汽车、珠宝、电视和手机。

338 government expenditure /ɪkˈspendɪtʃə(r)/ 政府支出

- the total value of a government's consumption and investment spending and transfer payments, such as unemployment benefits and state pension schemes
- 政府的消费投资支出以及转移支付的总价值,例如失业救济金和国家养老金计划。

339 purchasing /ˈpɜːtʃəsɪŋ/ power parity /ˈpærəti/ 购买力平价法

- an exchange rate based on the ratio of the price of a basket of products in different countries
- 基于不同国家一篮子产品的价格比率的汇率

340 gender inequality index (GII) 性别不平等指数

- a measure of gender inequalities in terms of reproductive health, empowerment and labour market participating
- 性别不平等指数是衡量在生殖健康、授权和劳动力市场参与方面的性别不平等的指标。

341 happy life expectancy /ɪkˈspektənsi/ index (HLEI) 幸福预期寿命指数

- an index obtained by life expectancy multiplied by a happiness index
- 预期寿命乘以幸福指数的指数

342 gross /ɡrəʊs/ national happiness
国民幸福指数

- 🇩 a measure of living standards which includes a wide number of indicators including income, psychological wellbeing, education and ecological diversity
- 🇨 衡量生活水平的指标，其中包括收入、心理健康、教育和生态多样性等众多指标。

343 absolute /ˈæbsəluːt/ poverty /ˈpɒvəti/
绝对贫穷

- 🇩 an economic condition of lacking both money and basic necessities needed to successfully live, such as food, water, education, health care and shelter
- 🇨 在绝对贫穷经济状况下，缺乏金钱和生存所需的基本必需品，例如食物、水、教育、健康保障和住房。

344 relative poverty
相对贫穷

- 🇩 an economic condition of having fewer resources than others in the same society, usually measured by the extent to which a person's or household's financial resources fall below the average income level of others in their economy
- 🇨 处在相对贫穷经济条件的人，其资源少于同一社会中的其他人，通常以个人或家庭的财务资源低于其经济体中他人平均收入水平的多少来衡量。

345 vicious /ˈvɪʃəs/ circle of poverty
贫困恶性循环理论

- 🇩 a situation where people become trapped in poverty and are likely to have worse than average education and healthcare
- 🇨 人们陷入贫困的情况，可能享受到低于平均教育和平均医疗的服务。

346 **multidimensional** /ˌmʌltɪdaɪˈmenʃənəl/
poverty index
多维贫穷指数

- **D** a measure of poverty based on deprivations in education, health and standard of living
- 定 衡量基于教育、健康和生活质量匮乏的贫穷程度

347 **emigration** /ˌemɪˈɡreɪʃn/
n. 移民出境

- **D** the act of leaving the country to live in another country
- 定 离开本国移居到另一国家的行为

348 **birth rate**
出生率

- **D** the number of births per 1,000 population in a year
- 定 一年内平均每千人中的出生数量

349 **death rate**
死亡率

- **D** the number of deaths per 1,000 population in a year
- 定 一年内平均每千人中的死亡数量

350 **immigration** /ˌɪmɪˈɡreɪʃn/
n. 移民入境

- **D** the introduction of people from overseas into the population of a country
- 定 将来自海外的人引进一个国家的人口

351 **net immigration**
净移民

- **D** more people coming to live in the country than people leaving the country to live elsewhere
- 定 净移民是指进入该国居住的人数多于离开该国居住在其他地方的人数。

352 **infant** /ˈɪnfənt/ **mortality** /mɔːˈtæləti/ **rate** 婴儿死亡率

- **D** the number of deaths per 1,000 live births in a year
- **定** 一年内每千名婴儿出生后死亡的数量

353 **net migration** /maɪˈɡreɪʃn/ 净移民

- **D** the difference between immigration and emigration
- **定** 移民入境人口和移民出境人口的差值

354 **population pyramid** /ˈpɪrəmɪd/ 人口金字塔

- **D** a graph that shows the distribution of males and females in various age groups in a population
- **定** 人口金字塔是显示人口中各个年龄段的男性和女性分布的图表。

355 **population structure** 人口结构

- **D** It is a component of the environment for the members of the population.
- **定** 人口结构是整个人口环境的组成部分。

356 **overpopulation** /ˌəʊvəˌpɒpjuˈleɪʃn/ *n.* 人口过剩

- **D** an economic condition in which there are too many people and too few resources
- **定** 人口过剩是指人口数量过多但资源过少的经济状况。

357 **working population** 劳动人口

- **D** the economically active population or labour force in an economy
- **定** 经济体中从事经济活动的人口数量或劳动力

358 **dependent** /dɪˈpendənt/ **population** 依赖人口

- **D** that part of a population that is economically inactive (not in paid employment) and therefore relies on others to produce the goods and services it consumes

D 依赖人口是没有经济活动能力（非有偿就业）的一部分人口，依赖他人生产其消费的商品和服务。

359 dependency ratio 抚养比率

D a measure that contrasts the number of people in the dependent population of a country with the working population in the same country

定 抚养比率将一个国家的依赖人口数量与该国家的工作人口数量进行比较的指标。

360 natural rate of population growth 人口自然增长率

D population resulting solely from the difference between the birth rate and death rate, i.e. excluding net migration

定 人口自然增长率是指仅由出生率和死亡率之差计算出的人口数量，即不包括净移民。

361 adult literacy /ˈlɪtərəsi/ rate 成人识字率

D a measure of the number of people of working age as a proportion of the total population in a country who are able to read and write

定 成人识字率是衡量一个国家中具有读写能力的、处于工作适宜年龄的人数占总（工作年龄）人口的比例。

362 gender imbalance 性别不平衡

D an excess of males or females in a population, usually caused by factors other than nature, such as sex-selection bias, wars and male-dominated inward economic migration

定 人口中男性或女性过多，通常是由自然以外的其他因素引起的，例如性别选择偏见、战争和男性占大多数的经济移民入籍者。

363 **economically active population** 从事经济活动的人口

- **D** those people in a population willing and able to participate in productive activity and are therefore either in paid employment or actively seeking employment
- 定 那些愿意且能够参加生产活动的人,因此不是有偿就业,就是在积极寻求工作的过程中。
- 同 working population

364 **optimum** /ˈɒptɪməm/ **population** 最优化人口

- **D** It refers to the number of people which, when combined with the other resources of land, capital and existing technical knowledge, gives the maximum output of goods and services per head of the population.
- 定 在最优化人口数量下,土地、资本和现有技术知识等其他资源结合起来能使人均商品和服务的产出最大化。

365 **overcrowding** /ˌəʊvəˈkraʊdɪŋ/ *n.* 过度拥挤

- **D** the traffic congestion caused by the increases in population which may put pressure on housing and social capital
- 定 人口增加造成的交通拥堵,可能给住房和社会资本带来压力。

366 **internal migration** 国内迁徙

- **D** Workers tend to migrate from rural to urban areas in search of better jobs and higher income.
- 定 工人倾向于从农村迁移至城市地区,以寻求更好的工作和更高的收入。

367 **economic development** 经济发展

- **D** an improvement in economic welfare
- 定 经济福利的改善
- **E** It includes improving living standards, reducing poverty, expanding the range of economic and social choices, and

increasing freedom and self-esteem.

🈯 经济发展包含改善生活质量，减少贫困，扩大经济和社会选择范围以及增加自由和自尊。

368 **unbalanced** /ˌʌnˈbælənst/ **economies**　经济失衡

🇩 Certain markets may be under-developed such as the financial sectors

🈯 某些市场可能不发达，例如金融业。

369 **foreign aid**　外部援助

🇩 The transfer of fund or goods and services to developing countries, it has the potential to increase development, but it can create economic and political dependency.

🈯 向发展中国家提供资金或商品和服务，可能会促进发展，但也可能会造成经济和政治依赖。

370 **the World Bank**　世界银行

🇩 an international organisation which provides long term loans on favourable terms, to promote development

🈯 世界银行是以优惠条件提供长期贷款来促进发展的国际组织。

371 **the IMF (international moneytary fund)**
国际货币基金组织

🇩 an international organisation that promotes international trade and global financial stability

🈯 国际货币基金组织是促进国际贸易和全球金融稳定的国际组织。

372 **gross national income per capita**
人均国民总收入

🇩 This calculates the total expenditure in the economy (gross domestic product) plus net income from assets abroad, divided by the population size.

🈯 由经济总支出（国内生产总值）加国外资产的净收入，再除以人口数量。

373 low-and middle-income countries

中低收入国家

- **D** They are often referred to as developing economies or less economically developed countries.
- 定 中低收入国家通常被称为发展中经济体或经济发展水平较弱的国家。

374 high-income countries

高收入国家

- **D** They are often referred to as developed economies or more economically developed countries.
- 定 高收入国家通常被称为发达经济体或经济更发达的国家。

375 literacy /ˈlɪtərəsi/ rate

识字率

- **D** Literacy rate measures the proportion of the population aged 15 and above who can read and write.
- 定 识字率衡量的是 15 岁及以上可读写的人口占总人口的比例。

376 life expectancy /ɪkˈspektənsi/

预期寿命

- **D** Life expectancy measures the number of years that the average person in a country is anticipated to live for, based on statistical trends.
- 定 预期寿命是根据统计趋势来衡量一个国家的平均预期寿命。

377 infrastructure /ˈɪnfrəstrʌktʃə(r)/

n. 基础设施

- **D** It refers to the system of transportation and the communication networks necessary for the efficient functioning of an economy, such as buildings, mass transportation, roads, water systems, JCT systems including the Internet, airports and power supplies.
- 定 基础设施是指经济体有效运行所必需的运输系统和通信网络，例如建筑物、公共交通、道路、供水系统以及包括互联网、机场和电力供应的 JCT 系统。

378 **demographics** /ˌdeməˈgræfɪks/   *n.* 人口学

- **D** the study of population distribution and trends
- **定** 人口分布与趋势研究
- **E** such demographics include differences in the composition of gender, age distribution and the dependency ratio
- **释** 人口学包括性别组成差异、年龄结构差异和抚养比率差异。

379 **age distribution** /ˌdɪstrɪˈbjuːʃn/   年龄分布

- **D** This refers to the number of people within different age groups in the population.
- **定** 年龄结构是指人口中不同年龄阶段的人口数量。

380 **population growth**   人口增长

- **D** It refers to the rate of change in the size of a country's population.
- **定** 人口增长是指一个国家人口规模的变化率。

第六节
International Trade and Globalisation
国际贸易和全球化

扫一扫
听本节音频

381 **tariff** /ˈtærɪf/   *n.* 关税

- Ⓓ a tax on imports
- 🖲 进口税
- 🔳 customs duties

382 **exports** /ˈekspɔːts/   *n.* 出口

- Ⓓ goods and/or services that are produced domestically in one country and sold to other countries
- 🖲 出口是指在国内生产并出售给其他国家的商品和 / 或服务。

383 **imports** /ˈɪmpɔːts/   *n.* 进口

- Ⓓ goods and/or services that are produced in foreign countries and consumed by people in the domestic economy
- 🖲 进口是指在国外生产并由国内的人消费的商品和 / 或服务。

384 **free trade**   自由贸易

- Ⓓ International trade can take place without any forms of protection (barriers to trade).
- 🖲 国际贸易可以在没有任何形式的保护下（贸易壁垒）进行。

385 **globalisation** /ˌɡləʊbəlaɪˈzeɪʃn/   *n.* 全球化

- Ⓓ the process by which the world is becoming increasingly interconnected through trade and other links
- 🖲 全球化是世界通过贸易和其他纽带越来越紧密联系的过程。

386 **trade protection** 贸易保护

- **D** the use of trade barriers to restrain foreign trade, thereby limiting overseas competition
- **定** 贸易保护是指利用贸易壁垒限制对外贸易,从而限制海外竞争。

387 **quota** /ˈkwəʊtə/ *n.* 配额

- **D** a limit placed on imports or exports
- **定** 限制进口或出口的数量
- **E** An import quota sets a quantitative limit on the sale of foreign goods into a country.
- **释** 进口配额设定了向国家销售外国商品的数量限制。

388 **embargo** /ɪmˈbɑːgəʊ/ *n.* 禁运

- **D** a ban on imports or exports
- **定** 禁止进口或出口

389 **exchange control** 外汇管制

- **D** a limit on the amount of foreign currency that can be obtained
- **定** 对于可以获取的外币数量的限制

390 **voluntary** /ˈvɒləntri/ **export restraints** /rɪˈstreɪnts/ **(VERS)** 自愿出口限制

- **D** agreements with other governments to restrict their exports to the country
- **定** 自愿出口限制是指与其他政府达成的协议,目的是限制其他国家对该国的出口数量。

391 **infant industries** /ˈɪndəstriz/ 新兴产业

- **D** new industries with relatively low output and high cost
- **定** 产量低、成本高的新产业

392 **declining** /dɪˈklaɪnɪŋ/ **industries** 衰落产业

- **D** old industries which are going out of business
- **定** 即将退出市场的旧产业

393 **strategic** /strəˈtiːdʒɪk/ **industries** 战略产业

- **D** industries that are considered important for the survival or development of the country
- **定** 对国家的生存或发展至关重要的行业

394 **dumping** /ˈdʌmpɪŋ/ *n.* 倾销

- **D** selling products in a foreign market at a price below the cost of production
- **定** 倾销是指以低于生产成本的价格在国外市场销售产品。
- **E** the act of selling exports at artificially low prices. Below those charged by domestic firms, and often less than the costs of production.
- **释** 倾销是以人为的低价出售出口产品的行为，低于国内企业提供的售价并往往低于生产成本。

395 **foreign exchange rate** 外汇汇率

- **D** the price of one currency in terms of another currency or currencies
- **定** 一种货币相对于另一种货币的价格

396 **fixed** /fɪkst/ **exchange rate** 固定汇率

- **D** an exchange rate whose value is set at a particular level in terms of another currency or currencies
- **定** 固定汇率是以另一种或多种货币为基准，将汇率值设置在特定水平的汇率。

397 **devaluation** /ˌdiːˌvæljuˈeɪʃn/ *n.* 贬值

- **D** a fall in the value of a fixed exchange rate
- **定** 固定汇率贬值

398 revaluation /ˌriːvæljuˈeɪʃn/ — *n.* 重估

- **D** a rise in the value of a fixed exchange rate
- **定** 固定汇率的价值上升

399 floating /ˈfləʊtɪŋ/ exchange rate — 浮动汇率

- **D** an exchange rate which can change frequently as it is determined by market forces
- **定** 浮动汇率是由市场力量决定的可频繁变化的汇率。

400 appreciation /əˌpriːʃiˈeɪʃn/ — *n.* 升值

- **D** a rise in the value of a floating exchange rate
- **定** 浮动汇率的价值上升

401 depreciation /dɪˌpriːʃiˈeɪʃn/ — *n.* 贬值

- **D** a fall in the value of a floating exchange rate
- **定** 浮动汇率贬值

402 foreign direct investment (FDI) — 外国直接投资

- **D** setting up production units or buying existing production units in another country
- **定** 外国直接投资是指在另一个国家建立生产单位或购买现有生产单位。

403 hot money flows — 热钱流动

- **D** the movement of money around the world to take advantage of differences in interest rates and exchange rates
- **定** 热钱流动是指利用利率和汇率差异在世界范围内转移货币。

404 visible trade balance — 可见贸易差额

- **D** the value of exported goods and the value of imported goods
- **定** 出口商品的价值和进口商品的价值
- **E** The visible trade balance is a record of the export and import of physical goods. It is also known as the trade in goods balance

释 可见贸易差额是实物商品进出口的记录，也被称为货物贸易差额。

405 visible /'vɪzəbl/ exports   有形出口

- **例** goods that are sold to foreign customers, with money flowing into the domestic economy
- **释** 有形出口是指出售给国外客户的商品，导致资金流入国内经济。

406 visible /'vɪzəbl/ imports   有形进口

- **例** goods bought by domestic customers from foreign sellers, with money flowing out of the domestic economy
- **释** 有形进口是指国内客户从国外销售商购买商品，导致资金从国内经济中流出。

407 invisible /ɪn'vɪzəbl/ trade balance
无形贸易收支差额

- **定** a record of the export and import of services (intangible products)
- **释** 服务（无形产品）的进出口记录

408 trade in goods deficit /'defɪsɪt/   货物贸易逆差

- **定** expenditure on imported goods exceeding revenue from exported goods
- **释** 货物贸易逆差是指进口商品的支出超过出口商品的营收。

409 trade in goods surplus /'sɜːpləs/   货物贸易顺差

- **定** revenue, from exported goods exceeding expenditure on imports
- **释** 货物贸易顺差是指出口商品的营收超过进口商品的支出。

410 trade in services   服务贸易

- **定** the value of exported services and the value of imported services
- **释** 出口服务的价值和进口服务的价值

411 **trade in service surplus** 服务贸易顺差

- **D** revenue from exported services exceeding expenditure on imported services
- **定** 服务贸易顺差是指出口服务的收入超过进口服务的支出。

412 **primary** /ˈpraɪməri/ **income** 主要收入

- **D** income earned by people working in different countries and investment income which comes into and goes out of the country
- **定** 初级收入是在不同国家工作的人所赚取的收入以及流入和流出该国的投资收入。

413 **secondary** /ˈsekəndri/ **income** 次要收益

- **D** transfers between residents and non-residents of money, goods or services, not in return for anything else
- **定** 次要收益是指居民与非居民间的金钱转移和商品或服务的转移,不以其他任何东西作为回报。

414 **current account** 经常账目

- **D** Within the balance of payments, current account records the trade in goods, trade in services, investment income and current transfers.
- **定** 在国际收支中,经常账目是货物贸易、服务贸易、投资收入和经常转移的纽带。

415 **balance of payments** 贸易收支差额

- **D** a financial record of a country's transactions with the rest of the world for a given time period, usually over one year
- **定** 在一定时间段内(通常为一年),一国与世界其他地区进行交易的财政记录。

416 **net income flows and transfers** 净收入流动和转移
/'trænsfɜː(r)z/

- 定 a record of a country's net income earned from capital flows
- 定 一个国家从资本流动中获得的净收入记录

417 **trade balance** 贸易收支

- 定 the difference between a country's total export earnings and its total import expenditure
- 定 一个国家的出口总收入与其进口总支出的差额

418 **exchange rate** 汇率

- 定 the price of one currency measured in terms of other currencies
- 定 以其他货币衡量一种货币的价格

419 **international** /ˌɪntəˈnæʃnəl/ **trade** 国际贸易

- 定 the exchange of goods and services beyond national borders
- 定 跨越国界的商品和服务的交换

420 **wage** /weɪdʒ/ *n.* 工资

- 定 the return for labour services, paid hourly or weekly. Payment depends on the amount of time worked
- 定 按小时或周支付的劳务报酬，取决于工作时间
- 同 salary

421 **comparative** /kəmˈpærətɪv/ **advantage** 比较优势

- 定 the situation where one country has a lower opportunity cost in the production of a good than another country
- 定 一个国家生产某个商品的机会成本低于另一国家的情况

422 **specialisation** /ˌspeʃəlaɪˈzeɪʃn/ *n.* 专业化

- 定 It occurs when individuals, firms, regions or countries concentrate on the production of a particular good or service.
- 定 个人、企业、地区或国家专注于某一特定商品或服务的生产。

423 **regional specialisation** 地区专业化

- **D** It occurs when certain areas concentrate on the production of certain goods or services.
- 定 某些地区专注于某些商品或服务的生产。
- **E** For example, Hollywood, in Los Angeles, is famous for its motion pictures industry.
- 释 比如位于洛杉矶,因其电影业而闻名的好莱坞。

424 **international** /ˌɪntəˈnæʃnəl/ **specialisation** 国际专业化

- **D** It occurs when certain countries concentrate on the production of certain goods or services due to cost advantages - perhaps arising from an abundance of resources.
- 定 国际专业化是指某些国家由于成本优势(可能源于资源丰富)而专注于某些商品或服务的生产的情况。

425 **economies of scale** 规模经济

- **D** It means the firms can enjoy cost-saving benefits from large-scale operations.
- 定 规模经济是指公司可以从规模化的运营中享受成本节约的好处。

426 **over specialisation** 过度专业化

- **D** It occurs when an individual, firm, region or country concentrates too much on producing a very limited number of goods and services.
- 定 个人、公司、地区或国家过分专注于生产种类十分有限的商品和服务。
- **E** This will cause structural and regional unemployment.
- 释 过度专业化将导致结构性和区域性失业。

427 **high labour turnover** /ˈtɜːnəʊvə(r)/ 高员工更换率

- **D** It occurs if lots of workers choose to leave their jobs in search of more challenging and less boring ones.
- 定 当许多工人选择离职去寻找更有挑战性的、更有趣的工作时,这种情况就会发生。

428 **visible** /ˈvɪzəbl/ **trade balance** 有形贸易差额

- 🄓 A record of the export and import of physical goods, which is also known as the balance of trade in goods.
- 🄓 实体货物进出口记录,也称为货物贸易差额。

429 **current transfer** /ˈtrænsfɜː/ *n.* 国际支付

- 🄓 They are money flows from one country to another, or a gift of money from one government to another.
- 🄓 国际支付是从一个国家流向另一个国家的资金,或者是把资金作为礼物从一个政府流向另一个政府。

430 **speculation** /ˌspekjuˈleɪʃn/ *n.* 投机

- 🄓 It means the foreign exchange traders and investment companies move money around the world to take advantage of higher interest rates and variations in exchange rates to earn a profit.
- 🄓 投机是外汇交易员和投资公司在世界各地转移资金,目的是利用较高的利率和汇率变动来谋利。

431 **barriers** /ˈbæriəz/ **to trade** 贸易壁垒

- 🄓 They are obstructions to free trade, imposed by a government to safeguard national interests by reducing the competitiveness of foreign firms.
- 🄓 政府为维护国家利益而实施的自由贸易壁垒,以降低外国公司的竞争力。

432 **administrative** /ədˈmɪnɪstrətɪv/ **barriers** 行政阻碍

- 🄓 Countries often use bureaucratic rules and regulations as a form of protection.
- 🄓 国家常使用官僚规章制度来作为一种保护形式。
- 🄔 It includes strict rules regarding food safety, environmental standards and product quality.
- 🄔 行政阻碍包括有关食品安全、环境标准和产品质量的严格规定。

第二章 A-Level AS 阶段高频专业词汇

第一节
Basic Economic Ideas and Resource Allocation 基础经济概念和资源分配

扫一扫
听本节音频

433 production /prəˈdʌkʃn/   *n.* 生产；产品

- Ⓓ the process of creating goods and services in an economy
- Ⓒ 在经济体中创造商品和服务的过程

434 ceteris /ˈsitərɪs/ **paribus** /ˈpærɪbəs/   其他条件均同

- Ⓓ other things remain equal
- Ⓒ 其他情况均相同

435 economic law   经济法则

- Ⓓ an economic theory put forward by economists, such as the laws of demand and supply
- Ⓒ 由经济学家提出的经济理论，例如供求定律

436 microeconomics /ˌmaɪkrəʊiːkəˈnɒmɪks/   *n.* 微观经济

- Ⓓ the study of the behaviour of relatively small economic units, such as particular individuals, households or firms
- Ⓒ 研究相对较小的经济单位（例如特定的个人，家庭或公司）的行为

437 **macroeconomics** /ˌmækrəʊˌiːkəˈnɒmɪks/
/ˌmækrəʊˌekəˈnɒmɪks/ *n.* 宏观经济

- Ⓓ the study of economics at the national and international level
- 🈳 针对国家和国际层面的经济学研究

438 **margin** /ˈmaːdʒɪn/ *n.* 边际

- Ⓓ the difference between two amounts
- 🈳 两数之差

439 **short run** 短期

- Ⓓ time period when at least one factor of production is fixed
- 🈳 至少一个生产要素固定不变的时间段

440 **long run** 长期

- Ⓓ time period when all factors of production are variable
- 🈳 全部生产要素可变的时间段

441 **very long run** 极长期

- Ⓓ time period when technical progress is no longer assumed to be constant, as is the case in the short run and the long run, and the conditions of supply in an industry can be affected
- 🈳 技术进步不再被认为是恒定的时间段（短期和长期情况都如此），并且行业的供应条件受到影响

442 **positive statement** 实证表述

- Ⓓ objective and based on facts that can be tested as true or false
- 🈳 客观的，并基于可以被证实为真或假的事实

443 **normative statement** 规范表述

- Ⓓ a statement which is subjective and based on an opinion or a value judgement
- 🈳 基于主观意见或价值判断的主观陈述

444 **value judgement** 价值判断

- **D** an opinion which reflects a particular point of view
- **定** 反映某种特定观点的主观意见

445 **specialisation** /ˌspeʃəlaɪˈzeɪʃn/ *n.* 专业化

- **D** a situation where individuals and firms, regions and nations concentrate on producing some goods and services rather than others
- **定** 指个人和公司,地区和国家专注于生产某些商品和服务而不是其他产品的情况

446 **division** /dɪˈvɪʒn/ **of labour** 劳动力分工

- **D** the way in which production is divided into a sequence of specific tasks which enables workers to specialise in a particular type of job
- **定** 一种将生产过程分成一系列特定任务的方式,使工人能专注于特定类型的工作

447 **economic structure** 经济结构

- **D** the way in which an economy is organised in terms of sectors
- **定** 各个部门组成一个经济体的方式

448 **command or planned economy** 指令或计划经济

- **D** one where resource allocation decisions are taken by a central office
- **定** 一个由中央机构决定资源分配的经济

449 **reallocation** /ˌriːˌæləˈkeɪʃn/ **of resources** /rɪˈsɔːsɪz/ 资源再分配

- **D** where resources are deliberately moved from one product to another
- **定** 有目的性地将一种产品的资源转移到另一种产品上

450 **capital** /ˈkæpɪtl/ **consumption** /kənˈsʌmpʃn/
资本消耗（折旧）

- **D** the capital required to replace what is worn out
- **定** 更换旧物所需的资金

451 **developing economy**
发展中经济体

- **D** one in which there is not a high income per head
- **定** 人均收入不高的经济体

452 **near money**
近似货币

- **D** non-cash assets that can be quickly turned into cash
- **定** 可迅速兑现的非现金资产

453 **legal** /ˈliːgl/ **tender** /ˈtendə(r)/
法定货币

- **D** any form of payment which is legally recognised to settle a debt
- **定** 受到法律认可用于清偿债务的任何付款方式

454 **bank deposit** /dɪˈpɒzɪt/
银行存款

- **D** deposit of money in accounts in financial institutions, many of which in a modern economy are in electronic form
- **定** 存入金融机构账户的存款，在现代经济中许多存款以电子形式存在

455 **liquidity** /lɪˈkwɪdəti/
n. 流动性

- **D** the extent to which there is an adequate supply of assets that can be turned into cash
- **定** 能够转变为现金的资产数量的多少

456 **liabilities** /ˌlaɪəˈbɪlətɪz/
n. 负债

- **D** debt obligations
- **定** 债务义务

457 **private** /ˈpraɪvət/ **goods** 私人物品

- **D** ones consumed by someone and not available to anyone else
- **定** 被某人购买且无法被其他人使用

458 **excludability** /ɪkˌskluːdəˈbɪlɪtɪ/ *n.* 排他性

- **D** where it is possible to exclude one from consumption
- **定** 通过定价等手段使某人被排除在某商品的消费者之外

459 **rivalry** /ˈraɪvlri/ *n.* 竞争性

- **D** where consumption by one person reduces availability for others
- **定** 一个人的消费会减少他人的实用性

460 **non-excludable** /ɪksˈklʊdəbl/ *adj.* 非排他性的

- **D** It is not possible to exclude someone from using the good.
- **定** 不可能排除某人使用商品。

461 **non-rival** /nɒn ˈraɪvl/ *adj.* 非竞争性的

- **D** Its consumption by one person does not reduce consumption by someone else.
- **定** 他人的消费不会因一个人的消费而减少。

462 **quasi-public** /ˈkweɪzaɪ ˈpʌblɪk/ **goods** 准公共物品

- **D** ones that have some but not all of the characteristics of public goods
- **定** 具有公共物品的某些但非全部特征的商品

463 **information failure** 信息失灵

- **D** a situation where people do not have full or complete information
- **定** 人们拥有不完整的信息

464 **moral hazard** /ˈhæzəd/ 道德风险

- **D** the tendency for people who are sued or otherwise protected to take greater risks
- **定** 被起诉者或受到庇护者易冒更大的风险

465 **adverse** /ˈædvɜːs/ **selection** 逆向选择

- **E** One type of information failure. An example in insurance market is that adverse selection results in someone who is unsuitable for obtaining insurance.
- **释** 一种信息不对称。举个保险市场的例子,逆向选择会导致某人不适合投保。

第二节

The Price System and the Microeconomy
价格体系和微观经济

扫一扫
听本节音频

466 **notional** /ˈnəʊʃənl/ **demand**   名义需求

- Ⓓ This demand is speculative and not always backed up by the ability to pay.
- 㝬 名义需求具有风险性，而且不总有支付能力。

467 **effective** /ɪˈfektɪv/ **demand**   有效需求

- Ⓓ demand that is supported by the ability to pay
- 㝬 具有能力支付的需求

468 **demand** /dɪˈmɑːnd/ **curve**   需求曲线

- Ⓓ It represents the relationship between the quantity demanded and price of a product.
- 㝬 需求曲线表示需求量与产品价格之间的关系。

469 **demand schedule** /ˈʃedjuːl/   需求表

- Ⓓ a table giving the quantities sold of a product at different prices and enables a demand curve to be drawn from the information in the schedule
- 㝬 一张给出以不同价格出售的产品数量的表格，并且人们能够根据表中的信息绘制需求曲线

470 **derived** /dɪˈraɪvd/ **demand**   派生需求

- Ⓓ demand for the components of a product or for workers caused by demand for the final product
- 㝬 对最终产品的需求引起对产品组件或对工人的需求

471 **joint** /dʒɔɪnt/ **demand** 连带需求

- **D** when two goods are consumed together
- **定** 当两种商品一起销售

472 **supply curve** 供给曲线

- **D** It represents the relationship between the quantity supplied and the price of the product.
- **定** 供给曲线表示供应的数量与产品价格之间的关系。

473 **elasticity** /ˌiːlæˈstɪsəti/ *n.* 弹性

- **D** a numerical measure of responsiveness of one variable following a change in another variable, ceteris paribus
- **定** 当其他条件相同时，用数字衡量一个变量在另一个变量发生改变后做出相应变化的程度

474 **elastic** /ɪˈlæstɪk/ *adj.* 有弹性的

- **D** where the relative change in demand or supply is greater than the change in price
- **定** 需求或供应的相对变化大于价格的变化

475 **inelastic** /ˌɪnɪˈlæstɪk/ *adj.* 无弹性的

- **D** where the relative change in demand or supply is less than the change in price
- **定** 需求或供应的相对变化小于价格的变化

476 **perfectly inelastic** 完全无弹性的

- **D** where a change in price has no effect on the quantity demanded
- **定** 价格变化对需求量无影响

477 **perfectly elastic** /ɪˈlæstɪk/ 完全弹性的

- **D** where all that is produced is sold at a given price
- **定** 所有生产的产品都以给定价格出售

478 **income elasticity** /ˌiːlæˈstɪsəti/ **of demand (YED)** 需求收入弹性

- **D** a numerical measure of the responsiveness of the quantity demanded following a change in income
- **定** 对收入变化后需求量反应性的数值测量

479 **cross elasticity of demand** 需求的交叉弹性

- **D** a numerical measure of the responsiveness of the quantity demanded for one product following a change in the price of another related product
- **定** 当另一相关产品的价格变化后，一种产品的需求量反应性的数值测量

480 **disequilibrium** /ˌdɪsiːkwɪˈlɪbriəm/ *n.* 非平衡点

- **D** a situation where there is an imbalance between demand and supply in a market
- **定** 市场供求不平衡的情况

481 **equilibrium** /ˌiːkwɪˈlɪbriəm/ **price** 均衡价格

- **D** the price where demand and supply are equal, where the market clears
- **定** 市场出清，需求量与供给量相等时的价格

482 **equilibrium quantity** /ˈkwɒntəti/ 均衡数量

- **D** the amount that is traded at the equilibrium price
- **定** 在均衡价格时的交易量

483 **change in demand** 需求变化

- **D** There is a shift in the demand curve due to a change in factors other than the price of the product.
- **定** 由于需求曲线除产品价格以外的因素变化而改变。

484 specific tax 从量税

- **D** an indirect tax that is fixed per unit purchased
- **定** 一种间接税，每单位消费的税收固定

485 ad valorem /væˈlɔːrəm/ tax 从价税

- **D** a tax that is charged as a given percentage of the price
- **定** 按价格的一定百分比收取的税款

486 joint /dʒɔɪnt/ supply 连带供给

- **D** a situation where the process of producing one product leads to the production of another product
- **定** 一种产品生产的过程引发另一种产品生产的情况

487 transmission /trænsˈmɪʃn/ of preferences /ˈprefrənsɪz/ 偏好转移

- **D** the automatic way in which the market allows the preferences of consumers to be known to producers
- **定** 市场允许生产者了解消费者偏好的自动方式

488 price mechanism /ˈmekənɪzəm/ 价格机制

- **D** the operation of changes in price in a market to act as signals to producers to allocate resources according to changes in consumer demand
- **定** 生产者将市场价格变化作为消费者需求变化的信号来分配资源的操作

489 consumer surplus 消费者剩余

- **D** the difference between the value a consumer places on units consumed and the payment needed to actually purchase that product
- **定** 消费者认为消费一定数量的商品应付的价格与实际购买该产品所需的价格之间的差额
- **E** the triangle between the price line and the demand curve
- **释** 与价格线和需求曲线构成的三角关系

producer surplus 生产者剩余

- **D** the difference between the price a producer is willing to accept and what is actually paid
- 定 生产者愿意接受的价格与实际支付的价格之间的差额
- **E** the triangle between the price line and the supply curve
- 释 与价格线和供应曲线构成的三角关系

第三节
Government Microeconomic Intervention 政府的微观经济干预

扫一扫
听本节音频

491 **regulation** /ˌreɡjuˈleɪʃn/   *n.* 管理

- **D** various means by which government seeks to control production and consumption
- **定** 政府寻求控制生产和消费的各种手段

492 **maximum** /ˈmæksɪməm/ **price**   最高价格

- **D** a price that is fixed; the market price must not exceed this price
- **定** 市场价格不得超过的一个固定价格

493 **minimum** /ˈmɪnɪməm/ **price**   最低价格

- **D** a price that is fixed; the market price must not go below this price
- **定** 市场价格不得低于的一个固定价格

494 **canons** /ˈkænənz/ **of taxation**   征税准则

- **D** Adam Smith's criteria for a 'good' tax
- **定** 亚当·史密斯征收"好"税的标准
- **E** equitable, economic, transparent and convenient
- **释** 公平、节约、透明和便利

495 **incidence** /ˈɪnsɪdəns/   *n.* 影响程度

- **D** the extent to which the tax burden is borne by the producer or the consumer or both
- **定** 生产者或消费者其一，或两者承担税的程度

496 flat-rate tax 单一税率制

- **D** a tax with a constant marginal rate
- **定** 边际比率恒定的税

497 average rate of taxation 平均税率

- **D** It refers to the average percentage of total income which is paid in taxes.
- **定** 平均税率指纳税额占总收入的平均百分比。
- **E** This form of taxation can also be referred to as the average propensity to pay tax.
- **释** 这种征税形式也可以称为平均纳税倾向。

498 marginal /ˈmɑːdʒɪnl/ rates of taxation 边际税率

- **D** It refers to the proportion of an increase in income which is taken in tax.
- **定** 边际税率指收入增量中税费所占的份额。

第四节
The Macroeconomy 宏观经济

扫一扫
听本节音频

499 **macroeconomy** /ˈmækrəʊɪˈkɒnəmi/ *n.* 宏观经济

- **D** the economy as a whole
- **定** 整体经济

500 **aggregate** /ˈæɡrɪɡət/ **demand (AD)** 总需求

- **D** the total spending on an economy's goods and services at a given price level in a given time period
- **定** 在一定时间段内,在一定价格水平下经济商品和服务的总支出

501 **aggregate supply (AS)** 总供给

- **D** the total quantity of goods and services produced in an economy (real GDP) over a particular time period at different price levels
- **定** 特定时间段内经济体生产不同价格水平的商品和服务的总量(实际国内生产总值)

502 **long-run aggregate supply** 长期总供给

- **D** the total output of a country supplied in the period when prices of factors of production have fully adjusted
- **定** 在生产要素的价格完全调整后一个国家的总供给

503 **Keynesians** /ˈkeɪnziənz/ *n.* 凯恩斯理论

- **D** the theory of the economist John Maynard Keynes who maintain that government intervention is needed to achieve full employment
- **定** 经济学家约翰·梅纳德·凯恩斯的追随者们认为,需要政府干预才能实现充分就业。

504 new classical economists 新古典经济学家

- **D** economists who think that the LRAS curve is vertical and that the economy will move towards full employment without government intervention
- **定** 新古典经济学家认为长期总供给曲线（LRAS 曲线）是垂直的，并认为经济体会在没有政府干预的情况下实现充分就业。

505 macroeconomic equilibrium 宏观经济均衡

- **D** the output and price level achieved where AD equals AS
- **定** 当总需求（AD）和总供给（AS）相等时达到的产出和价格水平

506 inflation /ɪnˈfleɪʃn/ n. 通货膨胀

- **D** a sustained increase in an economy's price level
- **定** 经济体的价格水平持续上涨

507 creeping /ˈkriːpɪŋ/ inflation 爬行式通货膨胀

- **D** a low rate of inflation
- **定** 通货膨胀率低

508 accelerating /əkˈseləreɪtɪŋ/ inflation 迅速发展的通货膨胀

- **D** a situation where the rate of inflation is rising quickly, and is beginning to become a serious problem in an economy
- **定** 通货膨胀率迅速上升并开始成为经济中的严重问题的情况
- **E** (the inflation rate is) about 5% to 25%
- **释** （通货膨胀率）大约在 5% 至 25% 之间

509 household expenditure /ɪkˈspendɪtʃə(r)/ 住户开支

- **D** A survey is taken on a regular basis (usually every month) to record changes in the prices of a selection of goods and services that constitutes a representative basket.
- **定** 定期（通常每月）进行一次调查，以记录构成具有代表性的一篮子商品和服务的价格变化。

510 **sampling** /ˈsɑːmplɪŋ/   *n.* 抽样

- 🇩 the use of a representative sample of goods and services consumed in an economy to indicate changes in the cost of living
- 🇨 使用经济体中用于消费的代表性商品和服务样本来表明生活成本的变化

511 **weights** /weɪts/   *n.* 比重

- 🇩 The items in a representative sample of goods and services consumed in an economy will not all be of the same importance. Weights are given to each of the items to reflect the relative importance of the different components in the basket, so a price index involves a weighted average.
- 🇨 一个经济体中用于消费的代表性商品和服务样本中的项目并非一样重要。每个项目都被赋予了权重，反映一篮子中不同组件的相对重要性，因此价格指数包含加权平均值。

512 **money values**   货币价值

- 🇩 values at the prices operating at the time
- 🇨 以当时的价格计算的价值

513 **real values**   实际价值

- 🇩 values adjusted for inflation
- 🇨 经通货膨胀调整的价值

514 **anticipated** /ænˈtɪsɪpeɪtɪd/ **inflation** 预期通货膨胀

- 🇩 the expected future rate of inflation in an economy
- 🇨 经济体预计未来的通货膨胀率

515 **unanticipated** /ˌʌnænˈtɪsɪpeɪtɪd/ **inflation**
不可预期的通货膨胀

- 🇩 the actual rate of inflation in an economy minus the anticipated rate of inflation
- 🇨 经济体的实际通货膨胀率减去预期通货膨胀率

516 **fiscal** /ˈfɪskl/ **drag**   财政拖累

- **D** the income of people and firms being pushed into higher tax brackets as a result of inflation (reduce real income)
- **定** 通货膨胀导致人员和公司的税务收入上升（实际收入减少）

517 **inflationary** /ɪnˈfleɪʃənri/ **noise**   通货膨胀噪音

- **D** confusion over relative prices caused by inflation
- **定** 通货膨胀引起的相对价格混乱

第五节
International Trade 国际贸易

518　**financial** /faɪˈnænʃl/ **account**　　金融账户

- ⓓ within the balance of payments, a record of the transfer of financial assets between the country and the rest of the world
- ⓔ 在国际收支中记录该国与世界其他地区之间金融资产转移的账户

519　**net investment income**　　净投资收入

- ⓓ the net income that relates to investments
- ⓔ 与投资相关的净收入

520　**current transfers**　　经常转移

- ⓓ one-sided transaction transfers, in which there is no terms of exchange between the two parties
- ⓔ 双方之间没有交换条件的单面交易转移

521　**net errors** /ˈerə(r)z/ **and omissions** /əˈmɪʃnz/　　净差错和遗漏

- ⓓ figures included to ensure the balance of payments balances
- ⓔ 确保国际收支平衡的数字

522　**deficit** /ˈdefɪsɪt/　　*n.* 赤字

- ⓓ a negative balance when expenditure exceeds income
- ⓔ 负余额，支出超过收入

523　**surplus** /ˈsɜːpləs/　　*n.* 盈余

- ⓓ a positive balance when income exceeds expenditure
- ⓔ 正余额，收入超过支出

524 **external** /ɪkˈstɜːnl/ **balance** 外部平衡

- ⓓ the balance between receipts and payments in relation to international transactions between one country and other countries in the world
- ⓔ 一国与世界其他国家之间与国际交易相关的收支平衡

525 **marginal** /ˈmɑːdʒɪnl/ **propensity** /prəˈpensəti/ **to import** 边际进口倾向

- ⓓ the proportion of an increase in income that is spent on imported products
- ⓔ 收入增量中用于进口产品的份额

526 **foreign exchange** 外汇

- ⓓ the foreign currency that is used in other countries as a medium of exchange
- ⓔ 在其他国家用作交换媒介的外币

527 **nominal** /ˈnɒmɪnl/ **exchange rate** 名义汇率

- ⓓ an exchange rate that is expressed in money terms without taking into account the possible effects of inflation
- ⓔ 不考虑通货膨胀可能产生的影响，用货币表示的汇率

528 **real exchange rate** 实际汇率

- ⓓ the exchange rate that takes into account the effects of inflation in different countries
- ⓔ 考虑不同国家通货膨胀影响的汇率

529 **trade weighted** /ˈweɪtɪd/ **exchange rate** 贸易加权汇率

- ⓓ the price of one currency against a basket of currencies
- ⓔ 一种货币针对一篮子货币的价格

530 real effective /ɪˈfektɪv/ exchange rate   实际有效汇率

- a currency's value in terms of its real purchasing power
- 货币的实际购买力价值

531 floating /ˈfləʊtɪŋ/ exchange rate   浮动汇率

- an exchange rate that is determined by the foreign exchange market forces of demand and supply of currency
- 由外汇市场对货币的供给与需求的市场力量决定的汇率

532 fixed /fɪkst/ exchange rate   固定汇率

- an exchange rate set by the government and maintained by the central bank
- 政府设定并由中央银行维持的汇率

533 hot money flows   热钱流动

- flows of money moved around the world to take advantage of changes in interest rates and exchange rates
- 资金在世界各地流动,利用利率和汇率的变化来获利

534 managed /ˈmænɪdʒd/ float /fləʊt/   由政府操纵的汇率浮动

- where the exchange rate is influenced by state intervention
- 汇率受国家干预影响

535 depreciation /dɪˌpriːʃiˈeɪʃn/   n. 贬值

- a decrease in the international price of a currency caused by market forces
- 市场力量导致的货币国际价格下跌
- devaluation

536 **devaluation** /ˌdiːˌvæljuˈeɪʃn/   *n.* 货币贬值

- **D** a decision by the government to lower the international price of the currency
- **定** 政府决定降低该货币的国际价格
- **同** depreciation

537 **Marshall-Lerner condition**   马歇尔勒纳条件

- **D** the requirement that for a fall in the exchange rate to be successful in reducing a current account deficit; The sum of the price elasticities of demand for exports and imports must be greater than 1.
- **定** 为了使汇率下降能够成功减少经常账户的赤字，出口和进口需求的价格弹性之和必须大于 1。

538 **J-curve effect**   J 曲线效应

- **D** a fall in the exchange rate causing an increase in a current account deficit before it reduces it due to the time it takes for demand to respond
- **定** 由于响应需要一定时间，汇率下降在造成经常账户赤字减少前，会先导致其增加

539 **appreciation** /əˌpriːʃiˈeɪʃn/   *n.* 增值

- **D** an increase in the international price of a currency caused by market forces
- **定** 市场力量导致的货币国际价格上涨

540 **revaluation** /ˌriːvæljuˈeɪʃn/   *n.* 货币增值

- **D** a decision by the government to raise the international price of its currency
- **定** 政府决定提高其货币的国际价格
- **同** appreciation

541 **terms of trade** 进出口交换比率

- **D** a numerical measure of the relationship between export and import prices
- **定** 用数字测量进出口价格之间的关系

542 **absolute** /ˈæbsəluːt/ **advantage** 绝对优势

- **D** It is used in the context of international trade, a situation where, for a given set of resources, one country can produce more of a particular product than another country.
- **定** 绝对利益是在国际贸易中使用的。在这种情况下,对于给定的一组资源,一个国家生产某种特定产品的数量可以比另一个国家更多。

543 **comparative** /kəmˈpærətɪv/ **advantage** 比较优势

- **D** It is used in the context of international trade, a situation where a country can produce a product at a lower opportunity cost than another country.
- **定** 比较优势用于国际贸易中,一国能够以比另一国更低的机会成本生产某一产品的情况。

544 **bilateral** /ˌbaɪˈlætərəl/ **trade** 双边贸易

- **D** where trade takes place between two countries
- **定** 两国间进行贸易

545 **multilateral** /ˌmʌltiˈlætərəl/ **trade** 多边贸易

- **D** a more realistic situation than bilateral trade, where trade takes place between a number of countries
- **定** 多边贸易比双边贸易更接近现实的情况,即多个国家之间进行贸易。

546 globalisation /ˌɡləʊbəlaɪˈzeɪʃn/   *n.* 全球化

D the process whereby there is an increasing world market in goods and services, making an increase in multilateral trade more likely

定 全球化是世界商品和服务市场不断增长的过程，使多边贸易更可能增加。

547 free trade   自由贸易

D international trade not restricted by tariffs and other protectionist measures

定 国际贸易，不受关税和其他贸易保护主义措施的限制

548 trading possibility /ˌpɒsəˈbɪləti/ curve   贸易可能曲线

D a diagram showing the effects of a country specialising and trading

定 一幅曲线图，显示一个国家专营和贸易的影响

549 trade bloc /blɒk/   贸易集团

D a regional group of countries that have entered into trade agreements

定 已签订贸易协定的区域国家集团

550 free trade area   自由贸易区

D a trade bloc where member governments agree to remove trade restrictions among themselves

定 一类贸易集团，其中成员国政府同意取消他们之间的贸易限制

551 customs /ˈkʌstəmz/ union   关税联盟

D a trade bloc where there is free trade between member countries and a common external tariff on imports from non-members

定 一类贸易集团，其中成员国之间存在自由贸易，对非成员国的进口产品征收共同的对外关税

552 **monetary** /ˈmʌnɪtri/ **union** 货币联盟

- **D** a group of countries which decide to bring their economies closer together through the adoption of a single currency
- **定** 决定通过采用单一货币来拉近经济联系的一组国家

553 **economic union** 经济联盟

- **D** a group of countries which agree to integrate their economies as much as possible through various rules, laws, policies and regulations
- **定** 同意通过各种规则、法律、政策和法规尽可能整合经济的一组国家

554 **trade creation** 贸易创造

- **D** where high-cost domestic production is replaced by more efficiently produced imports from within the customs union
- **定** 关税同盟内部的进口生产更有效，替代国内高成本的生产

555 **trade diversion** /daɪˈvɜːʃn/ 贸易转移

- **D** where trade with a low-cost country outside a customs union is influenced by higher-cost products supplied from within
- **定** 与关税同盟外部的低成本国家的贸易受到同盟内部供应的较高成本产品的影响

556 **world trade organisations** 世界贸易组织

- **D** an organisation set in 1995 to promote free trade in the world through the reduction of trade barriers
- **定** 成立于 1995 年，旨在通过减少贸易壁垒来促进世界自由贸易的组织

557 **protectionism** /prəˈtekʃənɪzəm/ *n.* 贸易保护主义

- **D** protecting domestic producers from foreign competition
- **定** 保护国内生产商免受国外竞争

558 **tariff** /ˈtærɪf/   *n.* 关税

- Ⓓ a tax imposed on imports or exports
- 定 对进口或出口（产品）征收的税

559 **quota** /ˈkwəʊtə/   *n.* 定额

- Ⓓ a limit on imports or exports
- 定 对进口或出口的数量限制

560 **exchange control**   外汇管制

- Ⓓ restrictions on the purchases of foreign currency
- 定 对购买外币的限制

561 **embargo** /ɪmˈbɑːgəʊ/   *n.* 禁止贸易令

- Ⓓ a ban on imports and/or exports
- 定 禁止进口和/或出口

562 **voluntary** /ˈvɒləntri/ **export restraint** /rɪˈstreɪnt/   自愿出口限制

- Ⓓ an agreement by an exporting country to restrict the amount of a product that it sells to the importing country
- 定 出口国同意限制其销售给进口国的产品数量的协议

563 **sunset** /ˈsʌnset/ **industries** /ˈɪndəstriz/   夕阳产业

- Ⓓ industries that have passed their peak and are now in decline, with no realistic hope of recovery
- 定 已过顶峰时期但如今走下坡的产业，没有实际复苏的希望。

564 **dumping** /ˈdʌmpɪŋ/   *n.* 倾销

- Ⓓ selling products in a foreign market at a price below their cost of production
- 定 以低于生产成本的价格在国外市场销售产品。

第六节
Government Macroeconomic Intervention
政府的宏观经济干预

扫一扫
听本节音频

565 **discretionary** /dɪˈskreʃənəri/ **fiscal policy**
权衡性财政政策

- ⓓ deliberate changes in government spending and taxation
- ⓓ 故意改变政府支出和税收

566 **quantitative** /ˈkwɒntɪtətɪv/ **easing**   量化宽松

- ⓓ the process whereby the government of a country deliberately buys bonds and bills in order to increase the money supply in a country
- ⓓ 国家政府故意购买债券和票据以增加国家的货币供应量的过程

567 **open market operations**   公开市场操作

- ⓓ the process of a government buying or selling bonds in order to influence the money supply in an economy
- ⓓ 政府买卖债券以影响经济体中的货币供应的过程

568 **cyclical** /ˈsɪklɪkəl/ **budget deficit** /ˈdefɪsɪt/
周期性赤字

- ⓓ a budget deficit caused by changes in economic activity
- ⓓ 经济活动变化导致的预算赤字

569 **structural** /ˈstrʌktʃərəl/ **budget deficit** /ˈdefɪsɪt/
结构性赤字

- ⓓ a budget deficit caused by an imbalance between government spending and taxation
- ⓓ 由政府支出和税收之间的不平衡而引起的预算赤字

570 interest rate 利率

- Ⓓ the price of borrowing money and the reward for saving
- 㚈 借钱的价格和储蓄的奖励

571 supply side policy 供给面政策

- Ⓓ measures designed to increase aggregate supply
- 㚈 旨在增加总供应量的措施

572 expenditure /ɪk'spendɪtʃə(r)/ switching /swɪtʃɪŋ/ policy 支出转换政策

- Ⓓ policy measures designed to encourage people to switch from buying foreign-produced products to buying domestically produced products
- 㚈 一种政策措施,旨在鼓励人们从购买国外生产的产品转向购买国内生产的产品

573 expenditure dampening /'dæmpənɪŋ/ policy 支出削减政策

- Ⓓ policy measures designed to reduce imports and increase exports by reducing demand
- 㚈 一种政策措施,旨在通过降低需求来减少进口和增加出口
- 回 expenditure reducing policy

第三章 A-Level A2 阶段高频专业词汇

第一节 Basic Economic Ideas and Resource Allocation 基础经济概念和资源分配

扫一扫 听本节音频

574 **economic efficiency** 经济效率

- **D** It is achieved when scarce resources are used in the most efficient way to produce maximum output
- **定** 经济效率指以最有效的方式利用稀缺资源得到最大产出。

575 **average costs** 平均成本

- **D** the total cost of employing all the factor inputs divided by the number of units produces
- **定** 所有要素投入的总成本除以总产量

576 **productive** /prəˈdʌktɪv/ **efficiency** 生产效率

- **D** It is achieved when a firm is producing with the least-cost method.
- **定** 生产效率最高时,企业以最低成本开展生产。
- **E** At productive efficiency that marginal cost equals to average costs and the point is on the PPC.
- **样** 生产效率达到最高点时,边际成本等于平均成本,该点位于生产可能性曲线(PPC)上。

577 **allocative** /əˈlɒkətɪv/ **efficiency** 分配效率

- **D** Firms are producing those goods and services most wanted by consumers.
- **定** 分配效率最高时,企业生产消费者最需要的商品和服务。
- **E** At allocative efficiency, price is equal to marginal cost.
- **释** 分配效率达到最高时,价格等于边际成本。

578 **dynamic** /daɪˈnæmɪk/ **efficiency** 动态效率

- **D** the greater efficiency that can result from improvement in technical or productive efficiency over a period of time
- **定** 通过一段时间内技术或生产效率的提高带来更高的效率

579 **Pareto** /paˈreːtoː/ **optimality** /ˌɒptɪˈmælɪtɪ/ 帕累托最优

- **D** a situation where it is impossible to make someone better off without making someone else worse off
- **定** 帕累托最优时,如果不让某个人境况恶化,就不可能再让另外某个人境况更好。

580 **externality** /ˌekstɜːˈnæləti/ *n.* 外部效应

- **D** an effect where the actions of producers or consumers lead to side effects on third parties who are not involved in the action
- **定** 生产者或消费者的行为对不参与该行为的第三方产生副作用
- **E** sometimes referred to as spillover effects
- **释** 有时也称为溢出效应

581 **negative** /ˈnegətɪv/ **externality** 负外部效应

- **D** an effect where the side effects have a negative impact and inflict costs to third parties
- **定** 当副作用对第三方产生消极影响,导致第三方成本升高的效应

582 **positive externality** /ˌekstɜː'næləti/ 正外部效应

- **D** an effect where the side effects have a positive impact and provide benefits to third parties
- **定** 当副作用对第三方产生积极影响，为第三方带来收益的效应

583 **external** /ɪk'stɜːnl/ **benefits** 外部效益

- **D** benefits that are received by third parties not involved in the action
- **定** 未参与该行为的第三方所获得的收益

584 **cost–benefit analysis (CBA)** 成本效益分析

- **D** a method for assessing the desirability of a project taking into account the costs and benefits involved
- **定** 在考虑项目成本和收益的情况下，评估项目是否可取的方法

585 **shadow price** 影子价格

- **D** a price that is applied where there is no recognised market price available
- **定** 暂无公认市场价格时采用的价格

第二节 The Price System and the Microeconomy 价格体系和微观经济

扫一扫
听本节音频

586 **utility** /juːˈtɪləti/   *n.* 效用

- Ⓓ the satisfaction received from consumption
- 㝢 从消费中获得的满意度

587 **marginal** /ˈmɑːdʒɪnl/ **utility**   边际效用

- Ⓓ the utility derived from the consumption of one more unit of the good or service
- 㝢 消费者在每增加一个单位消费品的时候产生的效用

588 **diminishing** /dɪˈmɪnɪʃɪŋ/ **marginal utility**   边际效用递减

- Ⓓ the fall in marginal utility as consumption increases
- 㝢 边际效用随消费的增加而下降

589 **behaviour economics** /ˌiːkəˈnɒmɪks/   行为经济学

- Ⓓ an approach to decision making which argues that the behaviour of individuals is often based on ideas that do not correspond to the traditional view of rational economic behaviour
- 㝢 一种决策方法，认为个人的行为通常是基于某种思想的，而这种思想与理性经济行为的传统观点相悖

590 **equi-marginal** /ˌiːkwə ˈmɑːdʒɪnl/ **principle**   等边际法则

- Ⓓ A consumer will maximise total satisfaction by equating the utility or satisfaction per unit of money spent on the marginal unit of each product consumed.

- 当消费者的消费满足感达到最大化时，会使消费的每种产品的边际单位上花费的每单位货币的效用或满意度相等。

591 budget line　　　　　　　　　　　　预算线

- a line that shows all the possible combinations of two products that a consumer would be able to purchase with fixed prices and a given income
- 预算线显示了在价格固定、收入恒定的情况下，消费者有能力购买的两种产品的所有可能组合。

592 price effect　　　　　　　　　　　　价格效应

- the effect on the consumption of a product which occurs as a result of a price change
- 价格变动对某一产品消费的影响

593 substitution /ˌsʌbstɪ'tjuːʃən/ effect　　替代效应

- the effect where following a price change, a consumer will substitute the cheaper product for the one that is now relatively more expensive
- 在价格变动之后，消费者将用较便宜的产品代替现在相对较贵的产品。

594 income effect　　　　　　　　　　　收入效应

- the effect where following a price change, a consumer has higher real income and will purchase more of this product
- 价格降低时，消费者的实际收入变高，将购买更多该产品。

595 indifference /ɪn'dɪfrəns/ curve　　　　无差异曲线

- This shows the different combinations of two goods that give a consumer equal satisfaction.
- 该曲线显示的是两种商品给消费者带来相同满意度的不同组合方式。

596 **marginal** /ˈmɑːdʒɪnl/ **rate of substitution** /ˌsʌbstɪˈtjuːʃən/   边际替代率

- the rate at which a consumer is willing to substitute one good for another
- 消费者愿意用一种商品替代另一种商品的比率

597 **isoquant** /ˈaɪsəʊkwænt/   *n.* 等产量曲线

- a curve showing a particular level of output
- 显示特定产出水平的曲线

598 **total product**   总产量

- total output produced by the factors of production
- 生产要素所带来的总产出

599 **production function**   生产函数

- This shows the maximum possible output from a given set of factor inputs.
- 该函数显示的是要素投入恒定时，可能达到的最大产出。

600 **average product**   平均产量

- the output per unit of the variable factor
- 每单位可变要素的产出

601 **marginal product**   边际产量

- the change in output arising from the use of one more unit of a factor of production
- 因增投一个生产要素而引起的产出变化

602 **diminishing** /dɪˈmɪnɪʃɪŋ/ **returns**   收益递减

- an additional unit of input leading to a fall in the marginal product
- 增加一个单位投入时导致边际产量下降

603 **firm** /fɜːm/   *n.* 企业

- **D** any business that adopts factors of production in order to produce goods and services
- **定** 投入生产要素以生产商品和服务的任何商业体

604 **fixed** /fɪkst/ **costs**   固定成本

- **D** those costs that are independent of output in the short run
- **定** 短期内与产出量无关的成本

605 **variable** /ˈveəriəbl/ **costs**   变动成本

- **D** costs that arise from the use of variable inputs, and that vary or change as output increases or decreases (hence they are 'variable')
- **定** 使用可变投入所产生的成本,以及随着产出增加或减少而变化或改变的成本(因此它们是"变动的")
- **E** An example of a variable cost is wages, or the payment for labour resources.
- **样** 变动成本的一个例子是工资或给劳动力资源的酬劳。

606 **increasing returns to scale**   规模收益递增

- **D** It refers to the situation where the output of a firm increases more than the proportional change in all its inputs; given a percentage increase in all inputs, output increases by a larger percentage.
- **定** 规模收益递增指的是某一企业产出的增长速度超过其生产规模的扩大速度的状态,即产出的增长比例高于投入生产要素的增长比例。

607 **decreasing returns to scale**   规模收益递减

- **D** It refers to the situation where the output of a firm increases less than the proportional change in all its inputs; given a percentage increase in all inputs, output increases by a smaller percentage.

定 规模收益递减指的是某一企业产出的增长速度低于其生产规模的扩大速度的状态,即产出的增长比例低于生产规模的增长比例。

608 returns to scale 规模报酬

D the relationship between the level of output produced by a firm and the quantity of inputs required to produce that output
定 企业的产出与实现该产出所需的投入量之间的关系

609 economies of scale 规模经济

D decreases in the average costs of production when a firm increases its output by varying all its inputs in the long run
定 长期改变企业的所有投入来增加产出,此时平均生产成本下降。
E Economies of scale explains the downward-sloping portion of the long-run average total cost curve: as a firm increases its size, the costs per unit of output fall.
释 规模经济对应的是长期平均总成本曲线向下倾斜的部分:随着企业规模的增加,单位产出的成本下降。

610 diseconomies /ˌdɪsɪ'kɒnəmɪz/ of scale
规模不经济

D increases in the average costs of production when a firm increases its output by varying all its inputs in the long run
定 长期改变企业的所有投入来增加产出,此时平均生产成本上升。
E Diseconomies of scale are responsible for the upward-sloping part of the long-run average total cost curve: as a firm increases its size, costs per unit of output increase.
释 规模不经济对应的是长期平均总成本曲线向上倾斜的部分:随着企业规模的增加,单位产出的成本上升。

611 internal /ɪn'tɜ:nl/ economies of scale
内部规模经济

D the advantage of a firm growing in size in the form of a reduction in the average cost of production
定 以降低平均生产成本的形式扩大规模的企业优势

612　**financial** /faɪˈnænʃl/ **economies**　金融经济体

- a reduction in average cost as a result of a larger firm being able to negotiate more favourable borrowing terms on a loan
- 由于一家较大的企业能够协商获得更优惠的借贷条件而实现平均成本降低。

613　**technical economies**　技术经济体

- a reduction in average cost as a result of the application of advanced technology in a firm, which brings about a greater degree of efficiency
- 由于在企业中应用先进技术，从而带来更高的效率，使得平均成本降低。

614　**risk-bearing economies**　风险负担经济体

- By diversifying into different markets, the overall pattern of demand is more predictable and so a firm can save on costs.
- 通过多元化进入不同的市场，整体需求模式更加可预测，企业通过这种方式来节省成本。

615　**minimum** /ˈmɪnɪməm/ **efficient** /ɪˈfɪʃnt/ **scale**
最小有效规模

- the lowest level of output where average cost is at the minimum
- 平均成本最低时的最低产出水平

616　**marginal** /ˈmɑːdʒɪnl/ **revenue** /ˈrevənjuː/
边际收入

- the additional revenue arising from the sale of an additional unit of output
- 多出售一单位产出所产生的额外收入

617 abnormal /æbˈnɔːml/ profit /ˈprɒfɪt/ 非正常利润

- **D** It refers to positive economic profit, arising when total revenue is greater than total economic costs.
- **定** 非正常利润指的是当总收入大于总经济成本时所产生的正向经济利润。

618 small and medium enterprises /ˈentəˌpraɪzɪz/ (SMEs) 中小型企业

- **D** firms with fewer than 250 employees; small firms have fewer than 50 employees.
- **定** 雇员少于 250 人的企业；小企业的雇员少于 50 名。

619 multinational /ˌmʌltiˈnæʃnəl/ corporations /ˌkɔːpəˈreɪʃnz/ (MNCs) 跨国企业

- **D** firms that operate in different countries
- **定** 在不同国家或地区运营的企业

620 perfect competition 完全竞争

- **D** an ideal market structure that has many buyers and sellers, identical or homogeneous products, and no barriers to entry
- **定** 理想的市场结构需要有许多买卖双方，产品相同或同质，没有市场准入门槛。

621 monopolistic /məˌnɒpəˈlɪstɪk/ competition 垄断性竞争

- **D** a market structure where there are many firms, differentiated products and few barriers to entry
- **定** 在该市场结构中，有许多企业和差异化产品，市场准入门槛较低

622 **oligopoly** /ˌɒlɪˈgɒpəli/   *n.* 寡头垄断

- **D** one of the four market structures, with the following characteristics: small number of large firms in the industry; firms have significant control over price; firms are interdependent; products may be differentiated or homogeneous; there are high barriers to entry
- **C** 四个市场结构之一,具有以下特征:行业中的大企业数量很少;企业对价格有强势控制力;企业是相互依存的;产品可能有差异,也可能同质;准入门槛很高

623 **imperfect** /ɪmˈpɜːfɪkt/ **competition**   不完全的竞争

- **D** any market structure except for perfect competition
- **C** 除了完全竞争之外的任何市场结构

624 **limit pricing**   限制性定价

- **D** Firms deliberately lower prices and abandon a policy of profit maximisation to stop new firms from entering a market.
- **C** 企业故意降低价格并放弃利润最大化政策以阻止新企业进入市场。

625 **integration** /ˌɪntɪˈgreɪʃn/   *n.* 整合

- **D** the process whereby two or more firms come together through a takeover, merger or acquisition
- **C** 两个或多个企业通过接管、合并或收购而在一起的过程

626 **merger** /ˈmɜːdʒə(r)/   *n.* 合并

- **D** where two or more firms come together under one management
- **C** 两个或多个企业集合归同一个管理层管理。

627 **vertical** /ˈvɜːtɪkl/ **integration**   垂直整合

- **D** a situation where a firm joins with another firm at an earlier stage of the production process (backward vertical integration) or a later stage of the production process (forward vertical integration)

定 和生产过程的上一步进行的合并称为后向垂直整合，和生产过程的下一步进行合并称为前向垂直整合。
同 vertical merger

628 horizontal /ˌhɒrɪˈzɒntl/ integration 横向整合

- D a situation where a firm grows through a merger or acquisition of another firm in the same industry
- 定 通过合并或收购同一行业的另一家企业来实现企业成长。
- 同 horizontal merger

629 conglomerate /kənˈglɒmərət/ integration 跨行业联合

- D a merger between firms which are operating in completely different markets rather than in different stages of the same market
- 定 在完全不同的市场（而不是在同一市场的不同阶段）运营的企业之间的合并
- 同 conglomerate merger

630 price agreement 价格协定

- D an agreement where firms in an oligopolistic market agree to fix prices between themselves
- 定 寡头市场中的企业协定一个固定的价格

631 price leadership 价格领袖

- D a type of tacit (or informal) collusion among oligopolistic firms, where a dominant firm in the industry (which may be the largest, or the one with lowest costs) sets a price and also initiates any price changes; The remaining firms in the industry become price-takers, accepting the price that has been established by the leader.
- 定 寡头企业之间的一种默契（或非正式）勾结，该行业中一家主导的企业（可能是规模最大的或成本最低的企业）设定价格，任何价格变动也由其发起；行业中其余的企业成为价格接受者，接受该领袖确定的价格。

- **E** Under price leadership, price changes tend to be infrequent, and are undertaken by the leader only when major demand or cost changes occur.
- **释** 在价格领袖的带领下,很少发生价格变动,并且仅在主要需求或成本发生变化时由价格领袖执行。

632 **cartel** /kɑːˈtel/   *n.* 垄断联盟

- **D** It is a formal agreement between firms in an industry to undertake concerted actions to limit competition; it is formed in connection with collusive oligopoly. It may involve fixing the quantity to be produced by each firm, or fixing the price at which output can be sold, and other actions.
- **释** 垄断联盟是行业内企业之间采取一致行动限制竞争的正式协议,与寡头勾结垄断相关。该协议可能包括固定每个企业可以生产的数量,或固定产品可以出售的价格等措施。
- **E** The objective is to increase the monopoly power of the firms in the cartel. Cartels are illegal in many countries.
- **释** 垄断联盟的目的是增强联盟中企业的垄断能力。垄断联盟在许多国家都是非法的。

633 **x-inefficiency** /eks ˌɪnɪˈfɪʃənsi/   *n.* X-非效率

- **D** It is achieved where the typical costs are above those experienced in a more competitive market.
- **释** 在这种情况下,典型成本高于其他竞争激烈的市场中的成本。

634 **contestable** /ˈkɒntestəbl/ **market**   可竞争市场

- **D** any market structure where there is a threat that potential entrants are free and able to enter this market
- **释** 在这种市场结构中,存在潜在企业自由进入市场的威胁。

635 **sunk** /sʌŋk/ **costs**   沉没成本

- **D** costs which were paid when a firm entered a market and are non-reversable when it leaves
- **释** 企业进入市场时支付的费用,且离开该市场时此费用无法回收。

636 **economies of scope** /skəʊp/ 范围经济

- **D** Reduction in average total costs is made possible by a firm increasing the different goods it produces.
- **定** 通过增加企业生产商品的种类，可以降低平均总成本。

637 **sales maximisation** /ˌmæksɪmaɪˈzeɪʃn/ 销售量最大化

- **D** a firm's objective to maximise the volume of sales
- **定** 企业实现最大销售量的目标

638 **satisficing** /ˈsætɪsˌfaɪsɪŋ/ *n.* 满意结果

- **D** a firm's objective to make a reasonable level of profit
- **定** 企业赚取合理利润水平的目标

639 **game theory** 博弈论

- **D** a mathematical technique analysing the behaviour of decision-makers who are dependent on each other, and who use strategic behaviour as they try to anticipate the behaviour of their rivals.
- **定** 这是一种分析决策者行为的数学技巧，这些决策者相互依赖，在试图预测竞争对手的行为时使用战略行为。
- **E** Game theory is used to explain competing firms exhibit behaviour whereby the actions of one will impact on all other firms in the oligopoly market.
- **释** 博弈论被用来解释在寡头垄断市场中竞争企业相互依存，因此一个企业的行为会影响到所有其他企业。

640 **principal-agent** /ˈprɪnsəpl ˈeɪdʒənt/ **problem** 委托代理问题

- **D** the problem that can occur as a result of the different objective of an owner and a manager
- **定** 由于所有者和管理者的目标不同而发生的问题

641 **prisoner's dilemma** /dɪˈlemə/   囚徒困境

- **D** a situation where two prisoners must decide whether to confess, without knowing whether the other will confess or not
- **定** 两名囚徒在不知道对方是否认罪的前提下必须决定是否认罪的情况。

642 **kinked** /kɪŋkt/ **demand curve**   拐折的需求曲线

- **D** a means of analysing the behaviour of firms in oligopoly where there is no collusion
- **定** 分析没有勾结的寡头垄断企业行为的一种方法

第三节
Government Microeconomic Intervention
政府的微观经济干预

扫一扫
听本节音频

643 **deadweight** /ˌdedˈweɪt/ **loss** 无谓损失

- Ⓓ the welfare loss when due to market failure, desirable consumption and production does not take place
- 定 由于市场失灵而无法进行理想的消费和生产时所产生的福利损失

644 **prohibition** /ˌprəʊɪˈbɪʃn/ *n.* 禁止

- Ⓓ the banning of a certain product in an economy
- 定 在经济体中禁止某种产品

645 **regulations** /ˌregjuˈleɪʃnz/ *n.* 规章制度

- Ⓓ a wide range of legal and other requirements that come from governments and other organisations
- 定 政府和其他组织的各种法律和其他要求

646 **pollution permit** /ˈpɜːmɪt/ 排放许可

- Ⓓ a form of license given by governments that allows a firm to pollute up to a certain level
- 定 政府颁发的一种许可形式,该许可允许企业有一定程度的污染。

647 **property** /ˈprɒpəti/ **rights** 产权

- Ⓓ where owners have a right to decide how their assets may be used
- 定 所有者决定如何使用其资产的权利

648 **information failure** /ˈfeɪljə(r)/   信息失灵

- **D** where people lack of the full information that would allow them to make the best decisions about consumptions.
- **释** 当信息失灵发生时,人们由于缺乏完整的信息,无法做出有关消费的最佳决策。

649 **nudge** /nʌdʒ/ **theory**   微调理论

- **D** an attempt by a government to alter the economic behaviour of people in particular way
- **释** 政府尝试以某种特定的方式使人们的经济行为发生改变。

650 **Lorenz curve**   洛伦茨曲线

- **D** a curve illustrating the degree of equality (or inequality) of income distribution in an economy; It plots the cumulative percentage of income received by cumulative shares of the population.
- **释** 洛伦茨曲线是描绘经济中收入分配的均等(或不平等)程度的曲线,描绘了人口累计份额所获得的收入累计百分比。
- **E** Perfect income equality would be represented by a straight line. The closer the Lorenz curve is to the straight line, the greater the equality in income distribution.
- **释** 在收入完全平等的情况下,该曲线将是一条直线。洛伦兹曲线越接近直线,收入分配就越平等。

651 **Gini coefficient** /ˌkəʊɪˈfɪʃnt/   基尼系数

- **D** a summary measure of the information contained in the Lorenz curve of an economy, defined as the area between the diagonal and the Lorenz curve, divided by the entire area under the diagonal.
- **释** 对经济体中洛伦兹曲线所含信息的概括度量,定义为:对角线和洛伦兹曲线之间的面积除以对角线下方的整体面积。
- **E** The Gini coefficient has a value between 0 and 1; the larger the Gini coefficient, and the closer it is to 1, the greater is the income inequality.
- **释** 基尼系数的值在 0 到 1 之间;基尼系数越大,越接近 1,则收入不平等现象越严重。

652 **means-tested benefits** 资产测查补助

- **D** benefits that are paid only to those whose incomes fall below a certain level
- **定** 仅向收入低于特定水平的人员提供的福利

653 **poverty** /ˈpɒvəti/ **trap** /træp/ 贫穷陷阱

- **D** It arises when low incomes result in low (or zero) savings, permitting only low (or zero) investments in physical, human and natural capital, and therefore low productivity of labour and of land, which in turn gives rise to low, if any, growth in income (sometimes growth may be negative), and hence low incomes once again.
- **定** 贫穷陷阱指的是低收入导致低（或零）储蓄，在物质、人力和自然资本上只能进行低（或零）投资，从而导致劳动和土地生产力低下，这又会进一步导致低（如果有的话）收入增长（有时增长可能为负），因此收入依然停留在较低水平。
- **E** A poverty trap may occur in a family, a community, a part of an economy, or in an economy as a whole. An important feature of the poverty trap is that poverty is transmitted from generation to generation.
- **释** 贫困陷阱可能发生在家庭、社区、经济体的一部分或整个经济体中。贫困陷阱的一个重要特征是贫困世代相传。

654 **universal** /ˌjuːnɪˈvɜːsl/ **benefits** 统一利好

- **D** benefits that are available to all irrespective of income or wealth
- **定** 不论其收入或财富高低，所有人均可获得的利益。

655 **negative** /ˈnegətɪv/ **income tax** 负所得税

- **D** a unified tax and benefits system where people are taxed or receive benefits according to a single set of rules
- **定** 负所得税是一套统一的税收和福利系统，根据某套规则，人们可能会被征税，也可能会获得利益。

656 **intergenerational** /ˌɪntərˌdʒenəˈreɪʃənl/ **equity**
代际公平

- Ⓓ the responsibility that government has to provide for a more equitable future distribution of income and wealth
- 定 政府为使未来收入和财富的分配更加公平而必须承担起的责任

657 **derived** /dɪˈraɪvd/ **demand**
引致需求

- Ⓓ where the demand for a good or service depends upon the use that can be made from it
- 定 引致需求是对某商品或服务的需求,取决于它的用途。

658 **marginal** /ˈmɑːdʒɪnl/ **physical production**
边际物质产品

- Ⓓ the amount of extra output that is produced if a firm increases its output by using an additional unit of labour
- 定 当企业通过增加一单位劳动来提高产出时所产生的额外产出。

659 **marginal revenue** /ˈrevənjuː/ **product**
边际收益产量

- Ⓓ the addition to total revenue as a result of employing one more worker
- 定 由于多雇用一名工人而增加的总收入

660 **transfer earnings** /ˈɜːnɪŋz/
转移收入

- Ⓓ the amount that is earned by a factor of production in its best alternative use
- 定 生产要素在其最佳替代用途中所赚取的金额

661 **economic rent**
经济租金

- Ⓓ a payment made to a factor of production above what is necessary to keep it in its current use
- 定 支付给生产要素的款项,高于使其保持当前使用所必需的数额。

662 **monopsony** /məˈnɒpsəni/   *n.* 买方垄断

- **D** where there is a single buyer in a market
- **定** 市场上只有一个买家。

663 **government failure**   政府失灵

- **D** where government intervention to correct market failure causes further inefficiencies
- **定** 政府干预纠正市场失灵，却导致进一步低效率的情况。

664 **pecuniary** /pɪˈkjuːniəri/ **advantage**   金钱利益

- **D** the advantage of employment that are in the form of financial rewards or benefit
- **定** 以经济奖励或福利的形式提供的就业优势

665 **non-pecuniary** /nɒn pɪˈkjuːniəri/ **advantage**
    非金钱利益

- **D** the advantage of employment, other than the money is gained, such as the job satisfaction gained from a particular form of employment
- **定** 除获得金钱之外的就业优势，例如从特定形式的就业中获得的工作满意度。

666 **net advantage**   净利益

- **D** the overall advantage of employment, taking into account both the pecuniary and the non-pecuniary advantage
- **定** 同时兼顾金钱和非金钱优势的就业总体优势

667 **trade union** /ˈjuːniən/   工会

- **D** an organisation of workers which involved in collective bargaining with employers to achieve certain objectives
- **定** 一个与雇主进行集体谈判以实现某些目标的工人组织

668 **collective** /kəˈlektɪv/ **bargaining** /ˈbɑːɡənɪŋ/
集体谈判

- **D** the process of negotiation between trade union representatives of the workers and their employers on such issues as remunerations (payment) and working conditions
- **定** 工会的工人代表与雇主在薪酬（支付）和工作条件等问题上的谈判过程

669 **closed shops**
唯工会会员雇佣制

- **D** a requirement that all employees in a specific workplace belong to a particular trade union
- **定** 在特定工作场所中，所有雇员都属于特定工会的要求。

第四节
The Macroeconomy 宏观经济

670 sustainable /sə'steɪnəbl/ development
可持续发展

- **D** development which meets the needs of the present without compromising the ability of future generations to meet their own needs
- **定** 在不损害子孙后代满足其自身需求的能力的前提下，满足当前需求的发展。

671 output gap
产出缺口

- **D** a gap between actual and potential output
- **定** 实际产出与潜在产出之间的差距

672 negative output gap
负产出缺口

- **D** a situation where actual output is below potential output
- **定** 实际产出低于潜在产出的情况

673 positive output gap
正产出缺口

- **D** a situation where actual output is above potential output
- **定** 实际产出高于潜在产出的情况

674 trade cycle
贸易周期

- **D** fluctuations in economic activity over a period of years
- **定** 几年内经济活动的波动

675 national income 国民收入

- **D** the total income of an economy, often used interchangeably with the value of aggregate output, particularly in the context of macroeconomic models
- **定** 一个经济体的总收入,通常可以换算成总产出的价值,尤其是在宏观经济模型的背景下。

676 gross national income (GNI) 国民总收入

- **D** the total output produced by a country's citizens wherever they produce it
- **定** 一国公民在任何地方生产的总产出

677 money GDP 货币 GDP

- **D** total output measured in current prices
- **定** 以当前价格计量的总产出

678 GDP deflator /dɪˈfleɪtə/ 国内生产总值平减指数

- **D** a ratio of price indices used in national income statistics to remove the effect of price changes, so that the figures can be seen as representing real changes in output
- **定** 国民收入统计中使用的价格指数比率,旨在消除价格变化的影响,因此这些数字可代表产出的实际变化。

679 shadow economy 影子经济

- **D** the output of goods and services not included in official national income figures
- **定** 未列入官方国民收入数字的商品和服务的产出

680 purchasing power parity /ˈpærəti/ (PPP) 购买力平价

- **D** special exchange rates between currencies that make the buying power of each currency equal to each other
- **定** 使得每种货币的购买力相等的特殊汇率

681 measurable /ˈmeʒərəbl/ economic welfare /ˈwelfeə(r)/ (MEW)
经济福利尺度

- **D** a composite measure of living standards that adjusts GDP for factors that reduce living standards and factors that improve living standards
- **定** 经济福利尺度是生活水平的综合衡量指标，根据降低和提高生活水平的因素来调整 GDP。

682 human development index (HDI)
人类发展指数

- **D** a composite indicator of development which includes indicators that measure three dimensions of development: income per capita, levels of health and educational attainment
- **定** 人类发展指数是发展的综合指标，其中包括衡量发展三个方面的指标：人均收入、健康水平和教育程度。
- **E** It is considered to be a better indicator of development than single indicators such as GNI per capita.
- **释** 人类发展指数被认为是比人均国民总收入等单一指标更好的发展指标。

683 multidimensional /ˌmʌltɪdaɪˈmenʃənəl/ poverty index (MPI)
多维贫困指数

- **D** a composite measure of deprivation in terms of the proportion of households that lack the requirements for a reasonable standard of living
- **定** 多维贫困指数是衡量贫困的综合指标，衡量缺乏合理生活水平要求的家庭的比例。

684 Kuznets curve
库兹涅茨曲线

- **D** a curve that shows the relationship between economic growth and income inequality
- **定** 描绘经济增长与收入不平等之间关系的曲线

685 **developed economies** 发达经济体

- **D** economies with a high GDP per head
- **定** 人均 GDP 高的经济体

686 **developing economy** 发展中经济体

- **D** an economy with a low GDP per head
- **定** 人均 GDP 低的经济体

687 **poverty cycles** 贫困周期

- **D** the links between, for example, low income, low savings, low investment and low productivity
- **定** 例如，低收入、低储蓄、低投资和低生产率之间的关系

688 **development traps** 发展陷阱

- **D** restrictions on the growth of developing economies that arise from low levels of savings and investment
- **定** 低储蓄和低投资水平对发展中经济体发展的限制

689 **emerging** /iˈmɜːdʒɪŋ/ **economies** 新兴经济体

- **D** economies with a rapid growth rate and that provide good investment opportunities
- **定** 经济快速增长并提供良好投资机会的经济体

690 **World Bank** 世界银行

- **D** a development assistance organisation, composed of 185 member countries which are its joint owners, that extends long-term credit (loans) to developing country governments for the purpose of promoting economic development and structural change
- **定** 一个发展援助组织，由 185 个成员国构成且共同拥有，它向发展中国家政府提供长期信贷（贷款），旨在促进经济发展和结构改革。

691 **quaternary** /kwəˈtɜːnərɪ/ **sector** 第四产业

- **D** industries involved in providing knowledge-based services
- **定** 提供知识服务的行业

692 **Malthusian theory** 马尔萨斯理论

- **D** the view that population grows in geometric progression whereas the quantity of food grows in arithmetic progression
- **定** "人口呈几何式增长，而食物数量以算术式增长"的观点

693 **Prebisch-Singer Hypothesis** /haɪˈpɒθəsɪs/ 辛格假说

- **D** a theory that suggests that the terms of trade tend to move against developing economies so that developing economies have to export more to gain a given quantity of imports
- **定** 辛格假说表明贸易条件只有倾向于对发展中经济体不利，才能让发展中经济体必须出口更多来获得一定数量的进口。

694 **participation** /pɑːˌtɪsɪˈpeɪʃn/ **rate** 参与率

- **D** the proportion of the population which is either in employment or officially registered as unemployed
- **定** 正在就业或已正式登记失业的人口所占的比例

695 **natural rate of unemployment** /ˌʌnɪmˈplɔɪmənt/ 自然失业率

- **D** the rate of unemployment that exists when the aggregate demand for labour equals the aggregate supply of labour at current wage rate and price level
- **定** 在当前的工资和价格水平下，劳动总需求和劳动总供给相同时所存在的失业率。

696 **labour force survey** 劳动力调查

- **D** a measure of unemployment based on a survey that identifies people who are actively seeking a job
- **定** 基于一项调查的失业衡量标准，该调查旨在确认正在积极寻求工作的人。

697 **multiplier** /ˈmʌltɪplaɪə(r)/   *n.* 乘数

- a numerical estimate of a change in injection in relation to the final change in national income
- 最终国民收入的变化相对于最初注入资金变化的数值估计。

698 **multiplier effect**   乘数效应

- the final impact on aggregate demand being greater than the initial change in injection
- 对总需求的最终影响大于初始注入资金的变化。

699 **open economy**   开放经济

- an economy that is involved in trade with other economies
- 与其他经济体进行交易的经济体

700 **closed economy**   封闭经济

- an economy that does not trade with other economies
- 不与其他经济体进行交易的经济体

701 **marginal** /ˈmɑːdʒɪnl/ **propensity** /prəˈpensəti/ **to save**   边际储蓄倾向

- the fraction of additional income that is saved; the larger the MPS, the smaller the Keynesian multiplier.
- 额外收入的储蓄比例；边际储蓄倾向越大，凯恩斯乘数就越小。

702 **marginal rate of taxation**   边际税率

- the fraction of additional income that is paid as taxes; the larger the MPT, the smaller the Keynesian multiplier.
- 额外收入的纳税比例；边际税率倾向越大，凯恩斯乘数就越小。

703 **marginal propensity** /prə'pensəti/ **to import**
边际进口倾向

- **D** the fraction of additional income spent on imports; the larger the MPM, the smaller the Keynesian multiplier.
- **定** 用于进口的额外收入的比例；边际进口倾向越大，凯恩斯乘数就越小。

704 **aggregate** /'ægrɪɡət/ **expenditure** /ɪk'spendɪtʃə(r)/
支出合计

- **D** the total amount spent in the economy at different levels of income
- **定** 在不同的收入水平下的经济总支出

705 **average propensity to consume**
平均消费倾向

- **D** the proportion of income that is consumed
- **定** 收入用于消费的的比例

706 **marginal propensity to consume**
边际消费倾向

- **D** the proportion of extra income that is spent; the larger the MPC, the greater the Keynesian multiplier.
- **定** 额外收入的消费比例；边际消费倾向越大，凯恩斯乘数就越大。

707 **consumption** /kən'sʌmpʃn/ **function** 消费函数

- **D** the relationship between income and consumption
- **定** 收入与消费之间的关系

708 **saving function**
储蓄函数

- **D** the relationship between income and saving
- **定** 收入与储蓄之间的关系

709 **government spending** 政府开支

- **D** spending undertaken by the government, as part of its fiscal policy or as part of an effort to meet particular economic and social objectives
- **定** 政府的支出，可能是财政政策的一部分，也可能是为实现特定的经济和社会目标所做的努力。
- **同** government expenditure

710 **net exports** 净出口

- **D** exports minus imports
- **定** 出口减去进口的差值

711 **injection** /ɪnˈdʒekʃn/ *n.* 注入

- **D** In the circular flow of income model, it refers to the entry into income flow of funds corresponding to investment, government spending or exports.
- **定** 在收入循环流动模型中，注入是指进入与投资、政府支出或出口相对应的资金收入流。

712 **withdrawal** /wɪðˈdrɔːəl/ *n.* 漏出

- **D** In the circular flow of income model, it refers to the leakage from the income flow of funds corresponding to savings, taxes or imports.
- **定** 在收入循环流动模型中，漏出是指从与储蓄、税收或进口相对应的资金收入流中流失。

713 **paradox** /ˈpærədɒks/ **of thrift** /θrɪft/ 节约悖论

- **D** where the fact of people saving more results in a fall in saving due to lower spending and income
- **定** 当人们储蓄更多时会导致支出和收入的减少，使得储蓄反而降低。

714 **inflationary** /ɪnˈfleɪʃənri/ **gap** 通货膨胀缺口

- 🅳 the excess of aggregate expenditure over potential output (equivalent to a positive output gap)
- 🅲 总支出超过潜在产出的差额（相当于正产出缺口）。

715 **deflationary** /ˌdiːˈfleɪʃənri/ **gap** 通货紧缩缺口

- 🅳 a shortage of aggregate expenditure so that potential output is not reached (equivalent to a negative output gap)
- 🅲 总支出不足，导致无法实现潜在产出（相当于负产出缺口）。

716 **autonomous** /ɔːˈtɒnəməs/ **investment** 自主投资

- 🅳 investment that is made independent of income
- 🅲 与收入无关的投资

717 **induced investment** 引致投资

- 🅳 investment that is made in response to changes in income
- 🅲 由于收入变化而相应进行的投资

718 **accelerator** /əkˈseləreɪtə(r)/ **theory** 加速原理

- 🅳 a model that suggests investment depends on the rate of change in income
- 🅲 该模型显示投资依赖收入的变化率。

719 **capital-output ratio** /ˈreɪʃiəʊ/ 资本产出率

- 🅳 a measure of the amount of capital used to produce a given amount, or value, of output
- 🅲 用来衡量获得特定数量或价值产出的资本

720 **quantity** /ˈkwɒntəti/ **theory of money** 货币数量论

- 🅳 the theory that links inflation in an economy to changes in the money supply
- 🅲 将经济中的通货膨胀与货币供应量变化联系起来的理论。

721 Fisher Equation /ɪˈkweɪʒn/ — 费雪方程式

- **D** the statement that MV = PY...; M represents some measure of the money supply; V, the velocity of this monetary measure; P, the price level; Y the Real GDP.
- **E** 表达式为 MV = PY……，M 为货币数量，V 为货币流通速度，P 为价格水平，Y 为实际 GDP。

722 narrow money — 狭义货币

- **D** money that can be spent directly
- **E** 可以直接花掉的钱

723 broad money — 广义货币

- **D** money used for spending and saving
- **E** 用于支出和储蓄的钱

724 credit multiplier /ˈmʌltɪplaɪə(r)/ — 信用乘数

- **D** the process by which banks can make more loans than deposits available
- **E** 通过这个过程，银行可以提供的贷款多于可用存款。

725 liquidity /lɪˈkwɪdəti/ ratio — 流动资产比率

- **D** the proportion of a bank's assets held in liquid form
- **E** 流动资产占银行总资产的比例

726 government securities /sɪˈkjʊərətɪs/ — 政府债券

- **D** bills and bonds issued by the government to raise money
- **E** 政府发行的，用于筹集资金的票据和债券。

727 quantitative /ˈkwɒntɪtətɪv/ easing — 量化宽松

- **D** a central bank buying government bonds from the private sector to increase the money supply
- **E** 中央银行从私营部门购买政府债券以增加货币供应量。

728 **transmission** /trænsˈmɪʃn/ **mechanism** /ˈmekənɪzəm/
传导机制

- **D** the theoretical process which connects changes in the stock of money in an economy to changes in the level of income and output
- **定** 将经济中货币存量的变化与收入和产出水平的变化联系起来的理论过程。

729 **total currency** /ˈkʌrənsi/ **flow**　货币总流量

- **D** the currency plus capital plus financial balances of the balance of payments
- **定** 现有货币、资本与国际收支的财务余额的总额

730 **liquidity** /lɪˈkwɪdəti/ **preference** /ˈprefrəns/
流动偏好

- **D** a Keynesian concept that explains why people demand money
- **定** 这是凯恩斯主义的一个概念，解释了人们为什么需要资金。

731 **transactions** /trænˈzækʃnz/ **motive**　交易动机

- **D** the desire to hold money for the day-to-day buying of goods and services
- **定** 持有货币用于日常购买商品和服务的需求

732 **precautionary** /prɪˈkɔːʃənəri/ **motive**　预防动机

- **D** a reason for holding money for unexpected or unforeseen events
- **定** 持有资金的理由是为了应对意外或不可预见的事件发生。

733 **active balances**　活动性余额

- **D** the amount of money held by households or firms for possible future use
- **定** 持有资金的理由是家庭或企业将来可能会使用。

734 **speculative** /ˈspekjələtɪv/ **motive** 投机动机

- **D** a reason for holding money with a view to make future gains from buying financial assets
- **定** 持有资金的理由是购买金融资产以期获得未来收益。

735 **idle** /ˈaɪdl/ **balances** 闲置余额

- **D** the amount of money held temporarily as the returns from holding financial assets are too low
- **定** 由于持有金融资产的收益太低而暂时持有的资金额。

736 **liquidity** /lɪˈkwɪdəti/ **trap** 流动性陷阱

- **D** a situation where interest rates cannot be reduced any more in order to stimulate an upturn in economy activity
- **定** 为了要刺激经济活动而无法再降低利率的情况。

737 **dependence** /dɪˈpendəns/ *n.* 依赖

- **D** a situation where the economic development of a developing economy is hindered by its relationships with developed economies
- **定** 与发达经济体的关系阻碍发展中经济体发展的情况。

738 **virtuous** /ˈvɜːtʃuəs/ **cycle** 良性循环

- **D** the links between, for example, an increase in investment, increase in productivity, increase in income and increase in saving
- **定** 例如，追加投资、提高生产率、增加收入和追加储蓄之间的关系。

第五节　Government Macroeconomic Intervention 政府的宏观经济干预

扫一扫 听本节音频

739　inflation /ɪnˈfleɪʃn/ target　通胀目标

- **D** a type of monetary policy carried out by some central banks that focuses on achieving a particular inflation target, rather than focusing on the goals of low and stable rate of inflation and low unemployment
- **定** 一些中央银行实施的一种货币政策，旨在实现特定的通胀目标，而不是着眼于低而稳定的通胀率或者低失业率。

740　Phillips Curve　菲利普斯曲线

- **D** a curve that shows the relationship between the unemployment rate and the inflation rate over a period of time
- **定** 菲利普斯曲线描绘的是一段时间内失业率和通胀率之间的关系。

741　expectations-augmented /ˌekspekˈteɪʃnz ɔːgˈmentɪd/ Phillips curve　期望增大菲利普斯曲线

- **D** a diagram that shows that while there may be a trade-off between unemployment and inflation in the short run, there is no trade-off in the long run
- **定** 期望增大菲利普斯曲线显示的是，尽管短期内失业与通货膨胀之间可能存在权衡取舍，但长期而言不存在。

742　Tinbergen's /ˈtɪnˌbɜːgənz/ Rule　丁伯根法则

- **D** For every policy aim there must be at least one policy measure.
- **定** 每个政策目标都必须至少有一项政策措施。

743 **government macroeconomic** /ˌmækrəʊˌiːkəˈnɒmɪk/ **failure**　　政府宏观经济失灵

- Ⓓ government intervention reducing rather than increasing economic performance
- 定 政府干预未能改善经济形势,反而使其恶化的情况。

744 **counter-cyclically** /ˈkaʊntə(r) sɪklɪkəli/
adv. 反周期地

- Ⓓ going against the fluctuations in economic activity
- 定 与经济活动的波动背道而驰

745 **Laffer curve**　　拉菲曲线

- Ⓓ a curve showing tax revenue rising at first as the tax rate is increasing and then falling beyond a certain rate
- 定 拉菲曲线描绘的是税收首先随着税率的增加而增加,然后超过一定税率又开始下降。

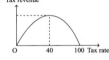

A

abnormal profit 非正常利润 243
absolute advantage 绝对优势 228
absolute poverty 绝对贫穷 190
accelerating inflation 迅速发展的通货膨胀 221
accelerator theory 加速原理 263
acceptability 可接受性 144
active balances 活动性余额 265
actual economic growth 实际经济增长 168
ad valorem tax 从价税 216
administrative barriers 行政阻碍 206
administrative lags 行政延迟 178
adult literacy rate 成人识字率 193
adverse selection 逆向选择 212
age distribution 年龄分布 197
aggregate demand (AD) 总需求 220
aggregate demand 总需求 168
aggregate expenditure 支出合计 261
aggregate supply (AS) 总供给 220
aggregate supply 总供给 168
allocative efficiency 分配效率 235
allocative efficiency 配置效率 140
anticipated inflation 预期通货膨胀 222
appreciation 升值 201
appreciation 增值 227
articles of association 组织章程 155
automatic stabiliser 自动稳定器 176
autonomous investment 自主投资 263
average cost 平均成本 160
average costs 平均成本 234
average fixed cost 平均固定成本 165

average product 平均产量 239
average propensity to consume 家庭消费比例 145
average propensity to consume 平均消费倾向 261
average propensity to save 家庭储蓄占比 146
average rate of taxation 平均税率 219
average revenue 平均营收 165
average variable cost 平均变动成本 165

B

backward integration 向后合并 157
bad debts 坏账 158
balance of payments 国际收支 170
balance of payments 贸易收支差额 203
balanced budget 平衡预算 171
bank deposit 银行存款 210
barriers to entry 进入壁垒 162
barriers to exit 退出壁垒 166
barriers to trade 贸易壁垒 206
bartering 以货易货 151
base year 基准年 187
behaviour economics 行为经济学 237
bilateral trade 双边贸易 228
birth rate 出生率 191
bonus 奖金 148
broad money 广义货币 264
budget deficit 预算赤字 171
budget line 预算线 238
budget surplus 预算盈余 171
budget 预算 171
business cycle 商业周期 168

C

canons of taxation 征税准则 218
capital consumption 资本消耗（折旧） 210
capital gain tax 资本利得税，资本收益税 173
capital 资本品 132

capital-intensive 资本密集型的 135
capital-output ratio 资本产出率 263
carbon tax 烟尘排放税；碳税 174
cartel 垄断联盟 246
casual unemployment 临时性失业 184
central bank 中央银行 145
certainty 确定性 175
ceteris paribus 其他条件均同 207
chain of production 生产链 131
change in demand 需求变化 215
choice 选择 131
circular flow of income 所得循环 180
claimant count 请领失业补助 183
closed economy 封闭经济 260
closed shops 唯工会会员雇佣制 254
collateral 抵押品 158
collective bargaining 集体谈判 152
collective bargaining 集体谈判 254
command or planned economy 指令或计划经济 209
commission 佣金 148
comparative advantage 比较优势 228
comparative advantage 比较优势 204
competition-based pricing 竞争导向定价 162
competitive market 竞争市场 166
complements 互补品 136
conglomerate integration 跨行业联合 245
conglomerate merger 混合兼并 157
conspicuous consumption 炫耀性消费 159
consumer spending 消费支出 158
consumer surplus 消费者剩余 216
consumption function 消费函数 261
consumption 消费 146
contestable market 可竞争市场 246
contraction in demand 需求缩减 136
contraction in supply 供给缩减 137
contractionary fiscal policy 收缩性财政政策 177
contractionary monetary policy 收缩性货币政策 179

contractual saving 合约储蓄 146
convenience 便利性 175
co-operatives 合作企业 155
corporation tax 企税 165
corporation tax 企税，公司（所得）税 173
cost 成本 159
cost–benefit analysis (CBA) 成本效益分析 236
cost-plus pricing 成本加成定价 161
cost-push inflation 成本推动型通胀 185
counter-cyclically 反周期地 268
craft unions 同业公会 151
credit multiplier 信用乘数 264
creeping inflation 爬行式通货膨胀 221
cross elasticity of demand 需求的交叉弹性 215
current account 经常账目 203
current transfer 国际支付 206
current transfers 经常转移 224
customer price index (CPI) 消费物价指数 185
customs duties 关税 173
customs union 关税联盟 229
cyclical budget deficit 周期性赤字 232
cyclical unemployment 周期性失业 183

D

deadweight loss 无谓损失 249
death rate 死亡率 191
declining industries 衰落产业 200
decreasing returns to scale 规模收益递减 240
deficit 赤字 224
deflation 通货紧缩 185
deflationary gap 通货紧缩缺口 263
demand curve 需求曲线 213
demand for labour 劳动力需求 147
demand schedule 需求表 213
demand 需求 135
demand-pull inflation 需求拉动通胀 185
demerit goods 无益品 142

demographics 人口学 197
dependence 依赖 266
dependency ratio 抚养比率 193
dependent population 依赖人口 192
depreciation 贬值 201
depreciation 贬值 226
depreciation 折旧 133
deregulation 去规则化 179
derived demand 派生需求 213
derived demand 引致需求 252
devaluation 贬值 200
devaluation 货币贬值 227
developed economies 发达经济体 258
developing economy 发展中经济体 210
developing economy 发展中经济体 258
development traps 发展陷阱 258
diminishing marginal utility 边际效用递减 237
diminishing returns 收益递减 239
direct tax 直接税 171
direct taxes 直接税 138
discretionary fiscal policy 权衡性财政政策 232
discrimination 歧视 149
diseconomies of scale 规模不经济 158
diseconomies of scale 规模不经济 241
disequilibrium 非平衡点 138
disequilibrium 非平衡点 215
disinflation 通胀率下降 185
disposable income 可支配收入 145
dissaving 动用储蓄 159
diversification 多样化 157
division of labour 劳动分工 150
division of labour 劳动力分工 209
dumping 倾销 200
dumping 倾销 231
durability 耐久性 144
dynamic efficiency 动态效率 141
dynamic efficiency 动态效率 235

E

earnings 收入 147
economic agent 经济人 134
economic development 经济发展 194
economic efficiency 经济效率 234
economic good 经济商品 130
economic growth 经济增长 168
economic law 经济法则 207
economic rent 经济租金 252
economic structure 经济结构 209
economic system 经济体制 134
economic union 经济联盟 230
economically active population 从事经济活动的人口 194
economically active 从事经济活动的人口 170
economically inactive 非从事经济活动的人口 169
economies of scale 规模经济 205
economies of scale 规模经济 241
economies of scope 范围经济 247
economy 经济性 175
effective demand 有效需求 213
efficiency 有效性 176
elastic 有弹性的 214
elasticity of demand for labour 劳动力需求弹性 150
elasticity of supply for labour 劳动力供给弹性 150
elasticity 弹性 214
embargo 禁运 199
embargo 禁止贸易令 231
emerging economies 新兴经济体 258
emigration 移民出境 191
employment right 劳动者权利 149
employment 就业人口 182
enterprise zones 经济开发区 179
entrepreneur 企业家 132
equilibrium price 均衡价格 215
equilibrium quantity 均衡数量 215
equilibrium wage rate 均衡工资率 149

equilibrium 平衡点 136
equi-marginal principle 等边际法则 237
equity 公平 175
excess demand 需求过剩 137
excess supply 供给过剩 138
exchange control 外汇管制 199
exchange control 外汇管制 231
exchange rate 汇率 204
excise duties 消费税 173
excludability 排他性 211
expansionary fiscal policy 扩张性财政政策 177
expansionary monetary policy 扩张性货币政策 179
expectations-augmented Phillips curve 期望增大菲利普斯曲线 267
expenditure dampening policy 支出削减政策 233
expenditure switching policy 支出转换政策 233
exports 出口 198
extension in demand 需求增长 136
extension in supply 供给增长 137
external balance 外部平衡 225
external benefits 外部利益 141
external benefits 外部效益 236
external costs 外部成本 142
external diseconomies of scale 外部规模不经济 158
external economies of scale 外部规模经济 158
external growth 外部增长 156
externality 外部效应 235

F

factor mobility 生产要素流动性 132
factors of production 生产要素 131
financial account 金融账户 224
financial economies of scale 金融规模经济 163
financial economies 金融经济体 242
firm 公司 153
firm 企业 240

fiscal drag 财政拖累 223
fiscal policy 财政政策 177
Fisher Equation 费雪方程式 264
fixed cost 固定成本 159
fixed costs 固定成本 240
fixed exchange rate 固定汇率 200
fixed exchange rate 固定汇率 226
flat tax 统一税率 177
flat-rate tax 单一税率制 219
flexibility 灵活性 176
flexible labour force 灵活劳动力 182
floating exchange rate 浮动汇率 201
floating exchange rate 浮动汇率 226
foreign aid 外部援助 195
foreign direct investment (FDI) 外国直接投资 201
foreign exchange rate 汇率 178
foreign exchange rate 外汇汇率 200
foreign exchange 外汇 225
forward integration 向前合并 157
free good 免费商品 130
free international trade 自由国际贸易 167
free rider 搭便车 140
free trade area 自由贸易区 229
free trade 自由贸易 198
free trade 自由贸易 229
frictional unemployment 摩擦性失业 183
full employment 完全就业 169
functions of money 货币的职能 144
fundamental economic problem 基本经济问题 131

G

game theory 博弈论 247
GDP deflator 国内生产总值平减指数 256
gender imbalance 性别不平衡 193
gender inequality index (GII) 性别不平等指数 189
general unions 总工会 151

genuine progress indicator (GPI) 真实发展指数 188
geographic mobility 地域流动性 133
Gini coefficient 基尼系数 250
globalisation 全球化 198
globalisation 全球化 229
go-slow 怠工 153
government expenditure 政府支出 189
government failure 政府失灵 253
government macroeconomic failure 政府宏观经济失灵 268
government securities 政府债券 264
government spending 政府开支 262
gross domestic product (GDP) 国民生产总值 180
gross national happiness 国民幸福指数 190
gross national income (GNI) 国民总收入 256
gross national income per capita 人均国民总收入 195

H

happy life expectancy index (HLEI) 幸福预期寿命指数 189
high labour turnover 高员工更换率 205
high-income countries 高收入国家 196
homogeneous product 同质产品 161
horizontal integration 横向整合 245
horizontal merger 水平兼并 156
hot money flows 热钱流动 201
hot money flows 热钱流动 226
household expenditure 住户开支 221
human development index (HDI) 人类发展指数 257
human development index 人类发展指数 188
hyperinflation 恶性通胀 186

I

idle balances 闲置余额 266
immigration 移民入境 191
impact lag 影响延迟 178
imperfect competition 不完全的竞争 244
imported inflation 进口通胀 187

imports 进口 198
incidence 影响程度 218
income effect 收入效应 238
income elasticity of demand (YED) 需求收入弹性 215
income tax 收入所得税 172
increasing returns to scale 规模收益递增 240
indexation 指数化 181
indifference curve 无差异曲线 238
indirect tax 间接税 172
indirect taxes 间接税 138
induced investment 引致投资 263
industrial actions 产业行动；(罢工)劳工行动 152
industrial unions 行业公会 151
industry 行业 153
inelastic 无弹性的 214
infant industries 新兴产业 199
infant mortality rate 婴儿死亡率 192
inferior goods 劣等商品 137
inflation rate 通胀率 170
inflation target 通胀目标 267
inflation 通货膨胀 221
inflation 通胀 177
inflationary gap 通货膨胀缺口 263
inflationary noise 通货膨胀噪音 223
informal economy 非正式经济 177
information failure 信息失灵 211
information failure 信息失灵 250
infrastructure 基础设施 196
inheritance tax 遗产税 173
injection 注入 262
integration 整合 244
interest rate 利率 233
intergenerational equity 代际公平 252
internal diseconomies of scale 内部规模不经济 158
internal economies of scale 内部规模经济 157
internal economies of scale 内部规模经济 241
internal growth 内部增长 156

internal migration 国内迁徙 194
international monetary fund (IMF) 国际货币基金组织 181
international specialisation 国际专业化 205
international trade 国际贸易 204
investment 投资 133
invisible trade balance 无形贸易收支差额 202
isoquant 等产量曲线 239

J

J-curve effect J 曲线效应 227
job security 工作保障 164
joint demand 连带需求 214
joint supply 连带供给 216

K

Keynesians 凯恩斯理论 220
kinked demand curve 拐折的需求曲线 248
Kuznets curve 库兹涅茨曲线 257

L

labour diseconomies 劳动力不规模 169
labour force participation rate 劳动力参与率 149
labour force survey measure 劳动人口调查 183
labour force survey 劳动力调查 259
labour force 劳动力 132
labour force 劳动力 169
labour market participation rate 劳动力参与率 182
labour market reform 劳动力市场改革 179
labour market 劳动力市场 169
labour productivity 劳动生产力 169
labour productivity 劳动生产率 133
labour supply 劳动力供给 148
labour 劳动力 132
labour-intensive 劳动密集型的 135
Laffer curve 拉菲曲线 268
land 陆地，大地，地带，土地；自然资源 132

legal tender 法定货币 164
legal tender 法定货币 210
liabilities 负债 210
license 执照 174
life expectancy 预期寿命 196
limit pricing 限制性定价 244
limited liability 有限责任 154
liquidity preference 流动偏好 265
liquidity ratio 流动资产比率 264
liquidity trap 流动性陷阱 266
liquidity 流动性 210
literacy rate 识字率 196
living standards 生活水平 188
local government 地方政府 167
local taxes 地方税 174
long run 长期 165
long run 长期 208
long-run aggregate supply 长期总供给 220
Lorenz curve 洛伦茨曲线 250
loss leader pricing 牺牲品定价 162
low-and middle-income countries 中低收入国家 196

M

macroeconomic equilibrium 宏观经济均衡 221
macroeconomics 宏观经济 208
macroeconomy 宏观经济 220
Malthusian theory 马尔萨斯理论 259
managed float 由政府操纵的汇率浮动 226
managerial economies of scale 管理规模经济 163
margin 边际 208
marginal physical production 边际物质产品 252
marginal product 边际产量 239
marginal propensity to consume 边际消费倾向 261
marginal propensity to import 边际进口倾向 225
marginal propensity to import 边际进口倾向 261
marginal propensity to save 边际储蓄倾向 260

marginal rate of substitution 边际替代率 239
marginal rate of taxation 边际税率 260
marginal rates of taxation 边际税率 219
marginal revenue product 边际收益产量 252
marginal revenue 边际收入 242
marginal utility 边际效用 237
market demand 市场需求 136
market economy 市场经济 134
market failure 市场失灵 140
market mechanism 市场机制 135
market structure 市场结构 160
market supply 市场供给 137
market 市场 134
marketing economies of scale 市场规模经济 163
Marshall-Lerner condition 马歇尔勒纳条件 227
material wealth 物质财富 189
maximum price 最高价格 218
means-tested benefits 资产测查补助 251
measurable economic welfare (MEW) 经济福利尺度 257
memorandum of association 公司章程 155
menu costs 菜单成本 186
merger 合并 244
merit goods 有益品 142
microeconomics 微观经济 207
minimum efficient scale 最小有效规模 242
minimum price 最低价格 218
mixed economy 混合经济 135
monetarists 货币主义学派 186
monetary inflation 货币通胀 186
monetary policy 货币政策 178
monetary union 货币联盟 230
money GDP 货币 GDP 256
money values 货币价值 222
money 货币 144
monopolistic competition 垄断性竞争 243
monopoly 垄断 143
monopoly 垄断 161

monopsony 买方垄断 253
moral hazard 道德风险 212
mortgage 抵押贷款 146
multidimensional poverty index (MPI) 多维贫困指数 257
multidimensional poverty index 多维贫穷指数 191
multilateral trade 多边贸易 228
multinational companies (MNCs) 跨国企业 143
multinational corporation 跨国企业 155
multinational corporations (MNCs) 跨国企业 243
multiplier effect 乘数效应 260
multiplier 乘数 260

N

narrow money 狭义货币 264
national debt 国债 171
national income 国民收入 256
national minimum wage 国家最低工资 148
nationalisation 国有化 140
natural monopoly 自然垄断 167
natural rate of population growth 人口自然增长率 193
natural rate of unemployment 自然失业率 259
near money 近似货币 210
needs 需求 130
negative externality 负外部效应 235
negative income tax 负所得税 251
negative output gap 负产出缺口 255
net advantage 净利益 253
net errors and omissions 净差错和遗漏 224
net exports 净出口 262
net immigration 净移民 191
net income flows and transfers 净收入流动和转移 204
net investment income 净投资收入 224
net investment 净投资 133
net migration 净移民 192
new classical economists 新古典经济学家 221
nominal exchange rate 名义汇率 225

nominal GDP 名义国民生产总值 181
non-excludable 非排他性的 211
non-pecuniary advantage 非金钱利益 253
non-rival 非竞争性的 211
normal goods 正常商品 136
normal profit 正常利润 166
normative statement 规范表述 208
notional demand 名义需求 213
nudge theory 微调理论 250

O

objectives 目标 160
occupational mobility 职业流动性 133
oligopoly 寡头垄断 244
open economy 开放经济 260
open market operations 公开市场操作 232
opportunity cost 机会成本 132
optimum population 最优化人口 194
output gap 产出缺口 255
over specialisation 过度专业化 205
overcrowding 过度拥挤 194
overpopulation 人口过剩 192
overtime pay 加班费 148

P

paradox of thrift 节约悖论 262
Pareto optimality 帕累托最优 235
participation rate 参与率 259
partnership 合伙人制 154
pecuniary advantage 金钱利益 253
penetration pricing 渗透定价 162
perfect competition 完全竞争 161
perfect competition 完全竞争 243
perfectly elastic 完全弹性的 214
perfectly inelastic 完全无弹性的 214
Phillips Curve 菲利普斯曲线 267

piece rate system 计件工资率 164
planned economy 计划经济 135
plant 工厂 153
pollution permit 排放许可 249
population growth 人口增长 197
population pyramid 人口金字塔 192
population structure 人口结构 192
positive externality 正外部效应 236
positive output gap 正产出缺口 255
positive statement 实证表述 208
potential economic growth 潜在经济增长 168
poverty cycles 贫困周期 258
poverty trap 贫穷陷阱 251
Prebisch-Singer Hypothesis 辛格假说 259
precautionary motive 预防动机 265
price agreement 价格协定 245
price discrimination 价格歧视 139
price effect 价格效应 238
price elasticity of demand (PED) 需求的价格弹性 139
price elasticity of supply (PES) 供给的价格弹性 139
price fixing 限定价格 143
price leadership 价格领袖 245
price makers 价格制定者 161
price mechanism 价格机制 216
price skimming 撇脂定价法 162
price stability 价格稳定 170
price takers 价格接受者 161
price 价格 165
primary income 主要收入 203
primary sector 第一产业 149
principal-agent problem 委托代理问题 247
prisoner's dilemma 囚徒困境 248
private benefits 私人利益 141
private costs 私人成本 142
private good 私人物品 143
private goods 私人物品 211
private limited company 个人有限责任公司 154

private sector 私营部门 139
privatisation 私有化 140
producer surplus 生产者剩余 217
production function 生产函数 239
production possibility curve 生产可能性曲线 133
production 生产；产品 207
productive efficiency 生产效率 234
productively efficient 生产效率的 141
profit maximisation 利润最大化 160
profit satisficing 利润满意 165
profit 利润 160
profit-related pay 以利润为基础的收入 147
progressive tax 累进税 172
prohibition 禁止 249
promotional pricing 促销定价 162
property rights 产权 249
proportional tax 比例税 172
protectionism 贸易保护主义 230
public corporation 公共企业 155
public good 公共物品 143
public limited company 公共有限责任公司 154
public sector 国营部门；公共部门 140
purchasing power parity (PPP) 购买力平价 256
purchasing power parity 购买力平价法 189
pure monopoly 完全垄断 164

Q

quantitative easing 量化宽松 232
quantitative easing 量化宽松 264
quantity theory of money 货币数量论 263
quasi-public goods 准公共物品 211
quaternary sector 第四产业 259
quota 定额 231
quota 配额 199

R

rate of interest 利息 145
ration 配给 143
rationalisation 合理化 157
real effective exchange rate 实际有效汇率 226
real exchange rate 实际汇率 225
real GDP per capita 实际人均国内生产总值 188
real GDP 实际国民生产总值 181
real income 实际收入 152
real values 实际价值 222
reallocation of resources 资源再分配 209
recession 经济衰退 / 萧条 181
recognition lag 认定延迟 178
redistribution of income 收入再分配 170
regional specialisation 地区专业化 205
regional unemployment 地区性失业 184
regressive tax 递减税 172
regulation 管理 218
regulations 规章制度 249
relative poverty 相对贫穷 190
research and development economies of scale 研发规模经济 163
resource 资源 130
retail prices index (RPI) 零售物价指数 185
returns to scale 规模报酬 241
revaluation 货币增值 227
revaluation 重估 201
revenue 营收 160
risk-bearing economies of scale 风险忍受规模经济 163
risk-bearing economies 风险负担经济体 242
rivalry 竞争性 211

S

salary 工资 147
sales maximisation 销售量最大化 247
sales revenue maximisation 销售收入最大化 164

sales tax 营业税 173
sampling 抽样 222
satisficing 满意结果 247
saving function 储蓄函数 261
saving ratio 储蓄占比 146
saving 储蓄 145
scale of production 生产规模 166
scarcity 稀缺性 131
search unemployment 求职性失业 184
seasonal unemployment 季节性失业 184
secondary income 次要收益 203
secondary sector 第二产业 149
self-sufficient 自给自足的 144
shadow economy 影子经济 256
shadow price 影子价格 236
share options 认股权 147
shoe-leather costs 鞋底成本 187
short run 短期 208
sit-in 静坐罢工 153
small and medium enterprises (SMEs) 中小型企业 243
social benefits 社会利益 141
social costs 社会成本 141
socially optimum output 社会最优产量 142
sole trader 个体户 153
specialisation 专业化 150
specialisation 专业化 204
specialisation 专业化 209
specific tax 从量税 216
speculation 投机 206
speculative motive 投机动机 266
stamp duty 印花税 174
strategic industries 战略产业 200
strategic industries 战略行业 167
strike 罢工 152
structural budget deficit 结构性赤字 232
structural unemployment 结构性失业 183
subsidy 补贴 138

subsistence agriculture 自给农业 181
substitutes 替代品 136
substitution effect 替代效应 238
sunk costs 沉没成本 166
sunk costs 沉没成本 246
sunset industries 夕阳产业 231
supernormal profit 超额利润 166
supply curve 供给曲线 214
supply side policy 供给面政策 233
supply 供给 137
supply-side policy 供应面政策 179
surplus 盈余 224
sustainable development 可持续发展 255
sustainable economic growth 可持续性经济发展 182

T

takeover 收购 164
target savers 目标储蓄者 146
tariff 关税 198
tariff 关税 231
tax avoidance 避税 174
tax base 计税基数 176
tax burden 税负 176
tax evasion 逃税 174
taxable income 应税收入 172
taxes 税收 138
technical economies of scale 科技规模经济 164
technical economies 技术经济体 242
technological unemployment 科技性失业 184
terms of trade 进出口交换比率 228
tertiary sector 服务行业 150
the IMF (international moneytary fund) 国际货币基金组织 195
the quaternary sector 知识产业，第四产业 156
the World Bank 世界银行 195
third party 第三方 141
Tinbergen's Rule 丁伯根法则 267

total cost 总成本 159
total currency flow 货币总流量 265
total product 总产量 239
total revenue 总营收 165
trade balance 贸易收支 204
trade bloc 贸易集团 229
trade block 贸易区，贸易集团 167
trade creation 贸易创造 230
trade cycle 贸易周期 255
trade diversion 贸易转移 230
trade in goods deficit 货物贸易逆差 202
trade in goods surplus 货物贸易顺差 202
trade in service surplus 服务贸易顺差 203
trade in services 服务贸易 202
trade protection 贸易保护 199
trade union 工会 253
trade unions 工会 151
trade weighted exchange rate 贸易加权汇率 225
trading possibility curve 贸易可能曲线 229
transactions motive 交易动机 265
transfer earnings 转移收入 252
transfer payment 转移支付 180
transmission mechanism 传导机制 265
transmission of preferences 偏好转移 216
transparent 透明的 176

U

unanticipated inflation 不可预期的通货膨胀 222
unbalanced economies 经济失衡 195
unemployment rate 失业率 170
unemployment 失业人数 182
unitary price elasticity 单位需求（或供应）价格弹性 139
universal benefits 统一利好 251
unlimited liability 无限责任 154
utility 效用 237

V

value added 增值 180
value judgement 价值判断 209
variable cost 变动成本 159
variable costs 变动成本 240
vertical integration 垂直整合 244
vertical merger 垂直兼并 156
very long run 极长期 208
vicious circle of poverty 贫困恶性循环理论 190
virtuous cycle 良性循环 266
visible exports 有形出口 202
visible imports 有形进口 202
visible trade balance 可见贸易差额 201
visible trade balance 有形贸易差额 206
voluntary export restraint 自愿出口限制 231
voluntary export restraints (VERS) 自愿出口限制 199
voluntary unemployment 自愿性失业 184

W

wage differential 薪资差异 148
wage rate 工资率 147
wage 工资 204
wage-price spiral 工资价格螺旋上升 186
wants 欲望 131
wealth 财富 145
weights 比重 222
white collar unions 白领公会 151
windfall tax 暴利税 175
withdrawal 漏出 262
working population 劳动人口 192
work-to-rule 合法怠工 152
World Bank 世界银行 258
world trade organisations 世界贸易组织 230

X

x-inefficiency X-非效率 246